John Winter
7820 Santa Rosa Rd
Buelton , 93427

800-251-4000

The Genesis Connection

The Genesis Connection

by
John L. Wiester

THOMAS NELSON PUBLISHERS
Nashville • Camden • New York

Published in Nashville, Tennessee, by Thomas Nelson, Inc. and distributed in Canada by Lawson Falle, Ltd., Cambridge, Ontario.

Printed in the United States of America.

Bible text in this publication is from the New American Standard Bible, © The Lockman Foundation 1960, 1962, 1963, 1968, 1971, 1972, 1973, 1975, and is used by permission.

Original drawings by Kay Weber.

Library of Congress Cataloging in Publication Data

Wiester, John L.
  The Genesis connection.

  1. Creation. 2. Cosmogony. 3. Bible and science.
I. Title.
BS651.W427   1983   231.7'65   83-13409
ISBN 0-8407-5296-2

To our children—my children and yours—who are searching for faith in a world of rapid technological advancements. May their understanding of what both Scripture and science are saying about our origins on this Earth give them a solid foundation upon which to build an abiding faith in our Creator.

CONTENTS

Introduction: The Search for Truth / 11
1 The Creation of the Universe / 17
2 Before the Beginning / 27
3 The Beginning / 37
4 The First Atmosphere and Water / 47
5 The First Land / 61
6 The Seeds of Life / 77
7 Light for the Earth / 97
8 Life in the Sea and in the Air / 117
9 Life on the Land / 135
10 Primates—The Monkey Puzzle / 157
11 The Emergence of Man / 177
12 Ages and Days / 191
13 The Genesis Connection / 201
14 His Way, His Time / 211
Appendix / 219
Notes / 229
Glossary / 233
Sources and Suggested Readings / 243
Index / 251

ACKNOWLEDGMENTS

It simply is not possible to thank all those whose scientific expertise, constructive criticism, and prayers have made this book possible. In a very real sense this is not my book. So many providential acts of information, insight, and timely help have arrived when needed that my faith in the power of prayer has grown immeasurably. I only hope that I have been a faithful communicator of His creation to you, the readers of this book.

The idea for *The Genesis Connection* was conceived by my pastor, Jeff Cotter, and me during a series of Bible study lectures on Genesis. At the time Jeff was presenting these lectures, I was engaged in a personal quest for truth. Do we owe our existence to creative acts of God or to random chance? A new way of looking at the scientific history of our origins became necessary in attempting to answer this question. I am most grateful to Jeff for contributing fresh insight to this crucial question.

A unique combination of circumstances made it possible for me to meet with Dr. Preston Cloud, a recognized authority on the combination of scientific disciplines covered in this book. While preferring not to engage in religious discussion, Dr. Cloud did aid in the scientific presentation of the first five chapters, and that meant a great deal to me. Dr. Fred Bush, an expert in ancient Hebrew at Fuller Theological Seminary, Pasadena, California, was similarly helpful in verifying that the interpretations of biblical language I was presenting were within the realm of the ancient Hebrew texts. Dr. William White's insightful review of both scriptural interpretation and scientific evidence has been stimulating and helpful.

My deepest thanks are due to those who have spent long hours of typing and editing on the manuscript. Thanks to Martha Gregg, Marylin Elam, Chloe Tyler, Shirley Toll, and Barbara Groessl. Thanks to Kay Weber and Don Prys for their inspired scientific illustrations. And most of all I am deeply grateful to Pastor Jeffrey Cotter, Pastor Gerald Lambert, and the entire congregation of the Santa Ynez Valley Presbyterian Church for their encouragement and prayers. That support has made this book a work of joy and fulfillment.

The editing assistance of Etta Wilson and Larry Stone at Thomas Nelson together with help at home from Cindy Piper, Maggie Le Pley, Harry Hollins, my wife Georgia, and daughters Allison and Joni is beyond measure.

Last of all, I wish to thank Peter Gillquist, the senior editor at Thomas Nelson. What a miracle to find, upon submitting the manuscript to Thomas Nelson in Nashville, Tennessee, that he lives and works only forty minutes from my cattle ranch in California. Praise the Lord for you, Peter, and for your guidance.

INTRODUCTION:
THE SEARCH FOR TRUTH

This book is intended to present the big picture—the major events in the history of the Cosmos, the planet Earth, and life upon it. It presents the latest scientific evidence as to how the Universe came into being and how the Earth came to possess its waters and its lands. It studies how life started and traces the fossil record of major life forms in the seas, in the air, and on the land. It deals extensively with the controversial origins of mankind. It is intended to enable the reader to compare the major events in cosmic, geologic, and biologic history with the biblical account of creation. Its major focus is on the vast panorama of history from the beginning of time to the advent of human life.

To be honest, I have written in a personal quest for truth. I am a recent convert to Christianity, having been led to Christ through the prayers and example of my faithful and loving wife. My conversion did not come easily. I was a materialist at heart and a practicing hedonist. My ego was fed by success in school, in business, and by attractive women. Who needed God? He might be necessary for others, but not for me.

I was an agnostic in religious matters. My scientific and worldly education had left me with an anti-religious bias. I regarded the Bible as an interesting collection of myths and legends with no real basis in history.

But I began to read. I was astonished to find that the claims of the New Testament rested on historical fact, not on myth or legend. The witness of the twelve apostles was particularly impressive to me. Twelve men simply do not expose themselves to daily ridicule, vilification, and death because of a myth.

On Friday of the crucifixion they were disillusioned men, they were cringing cowards. When they became convinced of the resurrection they turned into courageous giants among men. The real miracle was not their sudden change in character. It was their constant witness in the face of years of persecution and ridicule. One by one, most all of the apostles met a violent death. They could have been spared if only they had changed their testimony. They did not change it. They held to their witness through stoning, boiling in oil, and the agony of crucifixion. Their followers did the same.

This kind of witness is evidence of the highest order in any court. It convinced me of the truth of the New Testament. I read C. S. Lewis's *Mere Christianity* and John Stott's *Basic Christianity*. I began to read the Bible with new eyes. I prayed and asked Jesus Christ to come into my life. He came! I was baptized and received into the Christian church by my good friend and pastor, Jeff Cotter. My whole life was transformed. I was now full of the love and joy of knowing Jesus Christ.

But what of the Old Testament? I had never read it. It didn't seem relevant. I had become a Christian without reading it and had not felt the need to be convinced of its truth. But history has always fascinated me.

A friend suggested I read Werner Keller's *The Bible as History*. What a stimulating book! How fascinating to roam the ancient world with Abraham, Moses, David, and Solomon; to search for the lost cities of Sodom and Gomorrah. And the flood! To find that archeologists had discovered that a devastating flood of gigantic proportions occurred six thousand years ago was truly exciting.

I have personally experienced two major floods on my ranch on the Santa Ynez River in California. I have had to flee with my child in my arms in the early hours of the morning while muddy water poured into our home. I have rescued baby calves from the rising waters. I could feel the power of Noah's flood as it destroyed the known world in that ancient time.

Is the period of Noah's flood as far back as we can go in verifiable biblical history? I am a geologist by training and have taught historical geology in the laboratory at Stanford University. If evidence existed to confirm the biblical account of creation, I could find it. I could evaluate it. I was trained to use the scientific method of gathering evidence and evaluating the results.

But it is one thing to apply scientific methodology to records of the past. It is quite another to gather information dealing with creation. *Creation*—the very word had an unfamiliar ring. Before I became a Christian, my world view was that our existence was due to random forces operating within a closed system.

A closed system or a closed Universe excludes the possibility of supernatural forces or divine action. The basic premise of science is that all events must have a *naturalistic* cause. I had felt that nothing could exist outside of or beyond the total cosmic machine. There was no place in this eternal merry-go-round of atoms, molecules, stars, and planets for God. How then could I hope to find theories in support of historical biblical creation from a discipline that seemed to deny the possibility of a Creator? I began to have genuine fears that my new Christian faith would be seriously challenged by research into the latest scientific theories of our origins.

I went to my minister, Jeff Cotter, for help. Jeff researched some key words from the Genesis account in the original Hebrew. We studied Scripture. We prayed for guidance.

As we pondered the problem, two fresh insights emerged. The first insight involved focusing on the *scientific evidence* actually discovered as opposed to the *theories* that sought to explain that evidence *solely in terms of naturalistic causes.* My study should concentrate on the events in the Earth's history for which science has reasonably firm and well-documented evidence. Let us compare the scientific history of our origins with the biblical account *without regard* to *causation.* Perhaps modern science and the Bible are presenting the same record of historical events.

The second fresh insight involved looking at the problem of *causation* in an entirely new way. The traditional conflict between creation and evolution is so intense and so bitter precisely because it is attempting to answer the wrong question. The question is not *creation* versus *evolution.* The real question, the truly vital issue is *Creator* versus *no-creator.*

We owe our existence either to the creative acts of God or to *random chance.* When the question of existence is framed in this way we are able to look at and evaluate the evidence of modern science in a new light. The mists of the conflict begin to clear. My task in this book was therefore to present the latest scientific evidence in such a way that the readers could decide for themselves which was most valid, *Creator* or *no-creator*—*Creator* or *random chance.*

I began my search for the latest scientific information by visiting college geology departments. I asked professors to recommend the latest and best textbooks. My sources had to be impeccable and they had to be up-to-date. I read the recommended books and was truly astonished by the changes that have occurred in science in the past twenty-five years. *Piltdown Man* was gone—a hoax! I, and two generations of students, had learned that the missing link had been found. Now, he was not only lost, but he was revealed to have been a clever scientific forgery. What a shock!

I learned that there had been exciting new discoveries in Africa by Richard Leakey and Donald Johanson. Their finds represent possible new candidates for the missing link lineup. But Johanson's finds, in particular, reveal something else. His research indicates that *Australopithecus africanus*, which had been charted as man's ancestor in popular and scientific texts published up to six years ago, is now to be placed outside man's evolutionary path. So another missing link bites the dust. Textbooks must once again be changed and revised.

Johanson's book *Lucy* is also enlightening in another respect. Although he thinks he has found a potential new missing link in Lucy, he is very honest about the lack of specimens and the gaping holes which exist in the fossil record. The number of specimens is so sparse that there are more scientists studying the problem than there are specimens.

Further, I was astounded to learn that scientists cannot even trace the evolution of chimpanzees and gorillas to their modern forms. The fossil record of primitive ape forms is evident until 8 million years ago; it then vanishes. Modern apes are simply here today. They have no yesterday. The fossil record of their recent past does not exist. Or have scientists been incorrectly interpreting the fossil record?

My quest for scientific knowledge of creation continued. New theories abound as to why the dinosaurs vanished 63 million years ago—the latest is that a giant meteorite from outer space struck the Earth. The resulting dust and debris either choked the dinosaurs to death or caused climatic changes that the dinosaurs could not tolerate. Following the extinction of the dinosaurs, the mammals diversified, multiplied, and filled the Earth.

And what of animal life in the sea? A few traces of organisms have been found prior to the Cambrian explosion of marine life, but the Cambrian period in historical geology is still the basic beginning of the fossil record. The curtain in the drama of animal life rises abruptly 570 million years ago. The waters of the Earth quite suddenly teemed with swarms of living creatures.

I went back farther in geologic time, to a time before the ozone screen transformed sunlight from a lethal killer to a source of beneficial energy, back to the beginning of the first vegetative life. What exactly was the primordial soup? How did the first life come into being? Did it happen by random chance? Or was there some presently unknown selective, directive, or creative force involved? Do scientists feel Darwin's theory of evolution is still valid? Or does it need a major modification to make it fit the latest evidence?

I searched farther into the remote past. When did the first continents rise above the surface of the sea? Was the Earth once completely covered with water? I found that it had been, and that there had been a time before that when there was no water on the Earth at all. And a time before that when there had been no atmosphere. The Earth used to look like the moon—a naked body of cratered rock without air or water.

And where did the planet Earth come from? What about the stars, the galaxies, the Universe? Have they always existed, as some scientists convincingly argued thirty years ago? Or was there truly a beginning? Where did energy, matter, space, and time come from? Did the Universe truly begin with light?

This book will attempt to answer these questions in the light of current scientific

A NOTE TO THE READER ON TIME

Some readers may have trouble with the concept of time used in this book. I have chosen to use the time frame accepted by modern science throughout this presentation. For those readers who may have difficulty with this choice, I suggest reading Chapter 12, entitled "Ages and Days," and Chapter 14 "His Way, His Time," before proceeding with the historical presentation.

knowledge. My purpose is also to provide information useful to those Christian students who are unnecessarily confused or intimidated in today's science classroom. For those readers who are still searching for meaning and purpose in their lives, I hope light will be shed on the question of ultimate causation: Do we exist because of *an accident that just happened* or because of *creation by God?*

Further, does the scientific evidence validate the historical accuracy of Genesis 1? Is there a *Genesis Connection?*

To search for these answers I have presented the scientific account of our origins in the same order as the creation account in Genesis 1. As the book closes, I will attempt to correlate the current findings of modern science with Scripture. I do this both as a Christian firmly committed to the authority of Scripture, and as a scientist firmly committed to thoughtful ongoing inquiry.

CHAPTER 1
THE CREATION OF THE UNIVERSE

In the beginning God created the heavens and the earth.

Genesis 1:1

Is the Universe infinite and eternal? Have galaxies, stars, and planets existed forever? Or did they have a definite beginning in time and space?

The answers to these questions carry very important religious as well as scientific implications. If the Universe has existed forever, throughout eternity, then there was no beginning. The direct implication is clear: *no beginning implies no creation.*

On the other hand, if the Universe has not been in existence forever, then it must have had a beginning point in time. If it had a beginning, the direct implication is again clear: *there was a creation.*

Some scientists are uncomfortable with the concept of a beginning to the Universe. It conflicts with a basic creed of science which is that every event has a natural cause. According to internationally known astronomer, Robert Jastrow:

> They [scientists] believe that every event that takes place in the world can be explained in a rational way as the consequence of some previous event. If there is a religion in science, this statement can be regarded as its main article of faith.[1]

The critical point is that if the Universe had a beginning, then the chain of cause and effect terminates. At the point of a beginning, there can be *no discoverable cause! There can only be a creation!* The implications for pure rationalism are awesome.

It is no wonder that secular scientists have resisted the concept of a beginning to the Universe. It has been much more comfortable to accept the age-old argument of Aristotle that matter is eternal.

Therefore, until recently, many scientists believed that the Uni-

FIGURE 1.1.

Aristotle

FIGURE 1.2.

The Milky Way Galaxy. A top view and a cross section of this gigantic rotating disk of gas, dust, and stars.

verse was infinite and eternal, that it had no beginning. They expressed their conviction in a theory called the *steady state* or *continuous creation theory*. This theory held that the Universe had no beginning in space and time, but rather existed in a steady state condition with new matter being continuously formed from that which was already present. According to this theory, the Universe had just existed in this way throughout all time.

But science is a rather fluid discipline. Its great virtue is the ability to change or adjust its theories when new evidence is discovered. And new evidence began to accumulate as new telescopes and measuring instruments were used to probe the distant stars.

Astronomers found that stars are not distributed uniformly in space, but are grouped into more or less coherent units called *galaxies*. Most galaxies are composed of billions of stars. Galaxies are generally spiral in configuration, and rotate around a compact central region (see figure 1.1). They are thought to be held together by the force of gravitational attraction pulling inward and kept from collapsing by the centrifugal force of rotation pulling outward.

Our Solar System is located in one of the outer spiral arms of the Milky Way Galaxy and rotates around the nucleus of the galaxy, requiring 250 million years for a complete circuit. The presently observable Universe is thought to contain over 100 million galaxies.

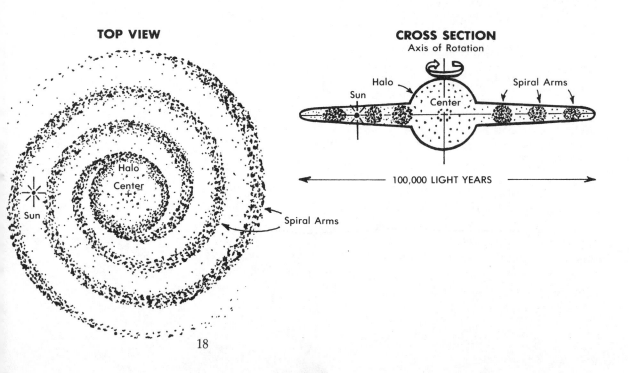

18

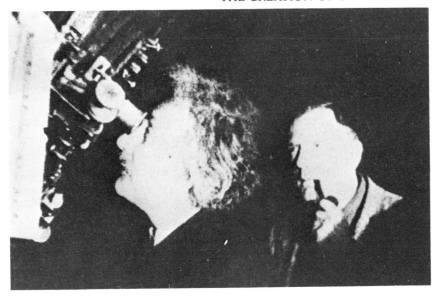

FIGURE 1.3.

Albert Einstein and Edwin Hubble at the Mount Wilson Telescope.

Between 1913 and 1965, a startling series of discoveries was made in astronomy, physics, and chemistry. The first piece of key evidence that the Universe had a beginning came from astronomers.

The Universe Is Expanding. In 1914 Vesto Slipher presented slides to the American Astronomical Society that gave the first hint of an expanding universe. Like many great breakthroughs in science, Slipher's discovery was accidental. He was looking for something else when he found that nearby galaxies were moving away from the Milky Way Galaxy at enormous speeds.

Slipher missed the implications of his observations, but others did not. A great scientific partnership began at the Mount Wilson Observatory in California. Between 1925 and 1930, Edwin Hubble and Milton Humason trained their giant telescope on distant clusters of stars. They measured the speeds and distances of vast numbers of galaxies. Their careful observations and precise accumulations of data proved that *other galaxies were moving away from our galaxy at increasingly rapid rates of speed* in proportion to their distance from our galaxy.

The implications of these observations were profound. If all galaxies are moving away from each other, *the universe is expanding!* The picture that emerges is one of a gigantic inflating balloon with small coins stuck on the surface of the balloon to represent the galaxies. The inflating outer skin of the balloon represents the finite but expanding boundary of the universe.

The fact that the galaxies are moving away from each other necessarily means that they had to be closer to each other in the past. In fact, as we chronologically reverse the picture of the expanding universe, the galaxies come closer and closer together. We eventually come to a point where all the galaxies are compressed together in a space the size of a football field.

As we continue the compression process, we reach a point where all the untold billions of stars and planets in the Universe fit into a space the size of a milk bucket. The Universe then reaches a point of infinite density where matter and energy cease to exist. Space and time are no longer meaningful concepts. We are at the beginning of the Universe. Science can gather evidence no farther back. We are at the beginning!

The observations and proofs of the astronomers at last convinced the great Albert Einstein that the Universe had a beginning. That he held out for so long is often attributed to his personal discomfort with the implications of this conclusion. The odd thing is that it was Einstein's very equations that predicted an expanding universe. But Einstein had made a simple mathematical error that the renowned mathematician, Alexander Friedmann, had to correct. Even when Einstein finally acknowledged his own mathematical error, he was reluctant to admit its implications. In the end he bowed to the weight of both his own equations and the work of the Mount Wilson astronomers. He admitted the Universe had a beginning.

The Depletion of Hydrogen. Another important piece of evidence that the Universe had a beginning involved the chemical composition of stars. It was found that stars are composed mainly of hydrogen, the lightest element, which is consumed throughout the star's lifetime, creating other elements in the process. When the hydrogen is depleted, the star begins to die.

A few very large and massive stars end their lives by collapsing which in turn creates a catastrophic explosion. This exploding star is called a *supernova* and is responsible for converting lighter elements into the heavier elements of which planets such as Earth are composed. Once hydrogen has been burned within a star and converted to heavier elements, it does not return to its original state. This irreversible change, the constant decrease in the supply of fresh hydrogen in the Universe, indicates that the Universe is, in effect, being depleted of the chemical base for the composition of matter.

But discomfort persisted with the idea that the Universe had a beginning. In 1948, three British astronomers, Hermann Bondi,

FIGURE 1.4.

Einstein at the blackboard at the Mount Wilson Observatory in January 1931. The world-famous scientist and mathematician is shown writing the equation for the density of the Milky Way.

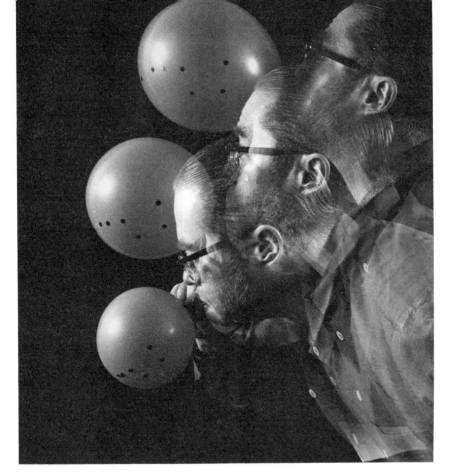

FIGURE 1.5.

The expansion of the Universe is demonstrated by the black dots on the surface of a rapidly expanding balloon. The nature of the expansion in the three-dimensional real world is more difficult to conceive, but the principle is the same.

Thomas Gold, and Fred Hoyle, proposed a new model of an eternal Universe. It became known as the *steady state* or *continuous creation theory* mentioned above. It accounted for the expanding galaxies and the depletion of hydrogen by stating that new matter was being continuously created. As the galaxies expanded outward, new galaxies were created to fill the vacant spaces.

But how was new matter created? Bondi, Gold, and Hoyle proposed the existence of an undiscovered energy field called the C-field (Creation-field) in an attempt to provide a physical and mathematical foundation for their theory. The continuous creation theory enjoyed widespread public and scientific support. It became an equal rival to the theory that the Universe had a beginning.

The problem with the continuous creation theory was that, although novel and appealing, there was no observed data to support it. The debate between a beginning versus an eternal Universe continued until 1965. New evidence then came to light.

Cosmic Radiation. In 1965, scientists at Bell Laboratories were annoyed with static in their sensitive instruments. Searching for the

21

source of this unexplained static, they discovered pigeons in their huge horn-shaped receiving device. The pigeons and their litter were removed, but the unexplained static persisted. Nothing had changed!

The scientists continued to look for the cause of their problem and startled the scientific world with their results. They observed that the Earth is bathed in a diffuse glow of cosmic radiation. This faint glow does not come from the Sun, the Moon, or any single star. The entire Universe seems to be the source.

The cosmic radiation measured by the Bell Lab's scientists is in the form of invisible microwave radiation. This microwave radiation is thought to emanate from the dying ashes of the initial fire of creation. It indicates that the entire Universe was fiery hot and filled with light many billions of years ago.

We can visualize this scientific extrapolation back into time by observing the dying coals in our fireplaces. Red hot coals indicate that the fire burned very recently. As time passes, the coals become progressively duller in color. From the flames of the initial fire until the coals lose their color, we are detecting heat radiation as visible light. Even after the coals have ceased to glow, we can still detect heat radiation by passing our hand over the ashes. The heat we feel radiating from the ashes is called infrared rather than visible radiation.

If we shift from the ashes in our fireplaces to the ashes of the Universe's creation 15 billion years ago, the ashes are very, very cold. They no longer emit infrared radiation, but they still emit radiation in the form of microwaves which can be detected by sensitive instruments.

FIGURE 1.6.

Dr. Arno Penzias, *left*, and Dr. Robert Wilson, 1978 Nobel-Prize recipients, accidentally discovered the Universe's cosmic background radiation while searching for the cause of static in the Bell Lab receiver. This cosmic radiation is strong evidence that the Universe began in an explosive blaze of light.

This microwave radiation or energy exists in the form of *photons* (particles of light). The present temperature of this residual cosmic radiation around the Earth measures three Kelvin degrees which approximates the temperature predicted by physicists for the residual radiation of a universal explosion of long ago. Scientists are now convinced they are witnessing the fading warmth from the ashes left by the primordial furnace of creation.

The presence of this universal background of microwave radiation indicates not only that the Universe had a beginning but that the beginning was, as physicists had predicted, a gigantic explosion. This initial explosion of unimaginable light and heat is termed the *Big Bang*.

Most, but not all, scientists were now convinced the Universe had a beginning. In 1974 another piece of confirming evidence arrived.

The Universe Is Expanding at a Decreasing Rate. If the Universe had a beginning in a Big Bang, then one would predict that the galaxies would be slowing down in their speed of movement away from one another. The gentle tug of gravity by one galaxy on another would cause them to slow down in speed.

For fifteen years Alan Sandage of Palomar Mountain Observatory in California made detailed observations and measurements. In 1974 he reported the results: *the galaxies are moving away from each other at decreasing rates of speeds.*

This deceleration of the galaxies indicates that the Universe is like a clock that was once wound up. It is now slowly running down as the galaxies slow down in their movement away from one another. The Universe had a beginning! And this beginning was a gigantic explosion of light and energy.

THE BIG BANG THEORY

Most scientists now believe that our Universe was created quite suddenly and abruptly more than 15 billion years ago in a cataclysmic explosion termed the *Big Bang.* In the initial cosmic fireball, energy was converted into matter and the results flung far out into the void to construct, in effect, atoms, molecules, gases, stars, planets and space itself. All the matter and energy in the Universe, including the physical elements of which you and I are composed, had their beginnings in the cosmic fireball of creation. According to this theory, our physical bodies are the product of pure energy and star-dust.

How did it begin? What was there before the beginning? From whence came the unbelievable power that created the galaxies, the stars, the planets, and life on the planet Earth? The answer from science is a very simple one: it cannot be determined. And, in fact, science will probably never know, because the scientific evidence, if any, was destroyed in the furnace of creation. In his book, *Cosmos, Earth and Man*, Preston Cloud states that this ultimate question of first causes "transcends the bounds of science."[2]

SOME IMPORTANT RAMIFICATIONS

Since the time of Aristotle, the conventional wisdom of science has held matter to be eternal. As recently as 1965, many scientists believed in an eternal Universe that had no beginning. However, advances in science and technology have accumulated the following evidence of a beginning:

- The Universe is expanding outward—it was once compressed to a point beyond imagining.
- Hydrogen is being depleted—the basic chemical element of matter in the Universe is running out.
- Cosmic radiation permeates the Universe—such radiation can only be the remnant of the initial explosion.
- The Universe is expanding at a decreasing rate—it is like a wound-up clock that is running down.

The Big Bang theory is now the accepted theory of origins by most scientists. All evidence points to the *creation* of the Universe at a definite instant in time, in a colossal explosion of dazzling brilliance. *There was a beginning!*

Modern science and Scripture are in agreement that the Universe is not eternal: it had a definite beginning. And there is only one word that aptly describes this beginning: *creation.* In his landmark book, *The Runaway Universe*, Paul Davies writes: "The Universe cannot have existed forever—there must have been a creation."[3]

Robert Jastrow echoes this view:

What is the ultimate solution to the origin of the Universe? The answers provided by the astronomers are disconcerting and remarkable. Most remarkable of all is the fact that in science, as in the Bible, the world begins with an act of creation.[4]

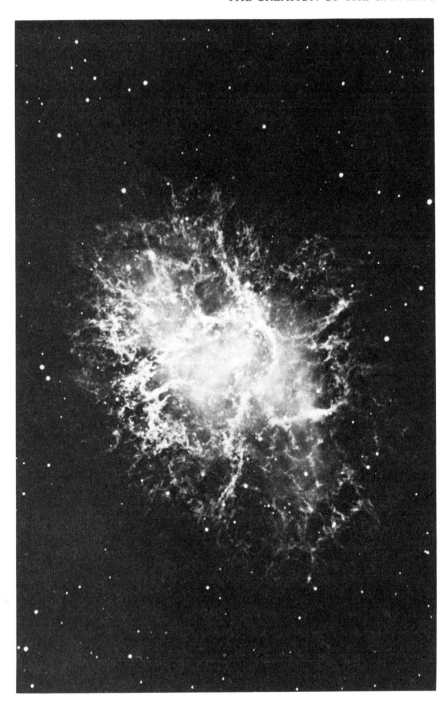

FIGURE 1.7.

The "Crab" Nebula in Taurus. This spectacular collapsing star is identified as the remains of supernova of AD 1054. (Courtesy Palomar Observatory, California Institute of Technology.

Science and Scripture are in harmony—there was a creation! Yet science can say nothing other than that a beginning occurred. Science cannot tell us how or why the Universe came into existence. The question of first cause is not one science can answer on the basis of empirical evidence. But the first words of the Bible proclaim the ageless answer: "In the beginning God created the heavens and the earth" (Gen. 1:1).

CHAPTER 2
BEFORE THE BEGINNING

And the earth was formless and void, and darkness was over the surface of the deep; and the Spirit of God was moving over the surface of the waters.

Genesis 1:2

Cosmologists are scientists who study the Universe as a whole entity. That is, they look for the big picture—the overall patterns of the Universe—not simply at individual stars and planets. Many cosmologists believe that the Universe did not exist at all before its moment of birth in the Big Bang. In their view, the Universe-to-be was once total darkness and nothingness. Darkness, nothingness, emptiness, and total void are difficult concepts to grasp. Space and time are simply not meaningful concepts before the instantaneous birth of the Universe.

IS THERE A DESIGN?

There is a view held by some cosmologists called the theory of the *Pulsating* or *Oscillating Universe.* This theory holds that the Universe eternally oscillates between expansion, starting with a Big Bang, and contraction, resulting in a *Big Crunch.* In the Big Crunch, all matter in the Universe is squashed together in a fiery apocalypse due to gravitational attraction. This could result in either a meltdown or, as the proponents of the oscillating Universe suggest, another Big Bang.

In either case, all matter would be destroyed in a furnace of unimaginable heat. The cremation of the world would leave no ashes. Would another Universe, either past or future, have the same physical properties as ours? Many scientists feel that matter would have vastly different chemical, nuclear, electrical, and gravitational properties in either past or future universes. Even a small change in any

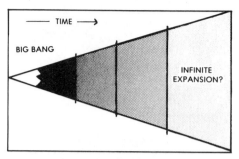

(a) BIG BANG

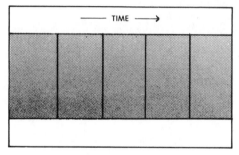

(b) STEADY STATE

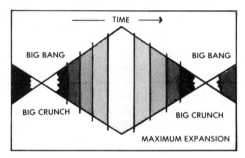

(c) OSCILLATION

FIGURE 2.1.

Three theories of the origin of the Universe: (a) big bang; (b) steady state; (c) oscillation. Dots represent galaxies.

one of these properties would render any life improbable and life as we know it impossible.

Probably the most profound question about the Universe we live in is *why* it is the way it is. Some scientists are even beginning to ask if the Universe were somehow designed for us. There are some very fundamental and unique properties in our Universe that raise important questions about the existence of life itself. For instance:

- Why are there ninety-two naturally occurring elements? Why not only two? Or why not five thousand?
- Why do the galaxies and stars have the particular sizes they have in the Universe?
- Why is the proton 1,836 times heavier than the electron and not heavier or lighter?
- Why does the heat radiation from the Big Bang have the present value of three Kelvin degrees? Why not three hundred Kelvin degrees?

According to theoretical physicist Paul Davies, "The laws of physics do not seem to determine the values of physical quantities, or the

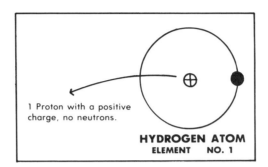

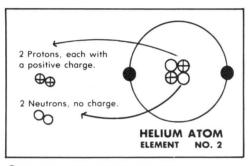

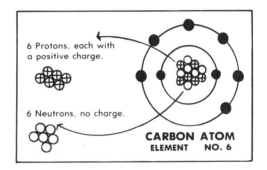

⊕ **PROTON, ONE POSITIVE CHARGE**

○ **NEUTRON, NO CHARGE**

● **ELECTRON, ONE NEGATIVE CHARGE**

sizes or numbers of things; nor do they determine the organization of the world. These features are apparently imposed on top of the physical laws with values that seem to have no particular significance."[1]

The implication is that the Universe is designed and created. For whom? For us. You see, the very existence of life in the Universe is dependent on the "proper" elements, the "correct" forces, the "right" temperatures, or what Davies calls the *imposed order*. This is true not only for the existence of life on Earth but for anywhere in the Universe.

Is there life on other planets? We do not know the answer to this question. We have detected no life on Mars, Venus, or other planets in our Solar System. Further, our current research has not even confirmed the existence of *planets* outside our own Solar System.[2] The reason some scientists speculate that there may be other planets and life upon them is because of the vast number of stars observed in the Universe. But if extraterrestrial life does exist in our Universe, it is dependent upon this same *imposed* order—the same very unique

FIGURE 2.2.

The atomic structure of the hydrogen, helium, and carbon atoms. In the carbon atom there are six protons packed together in the nucleus of the atom. The mysterious force which holds these repelling positive charges together is called the *nuclear* or *strong force*.

FIGURE 2.3.

A molecule of water (H₂O). Chemical combinations of elements are made possible either by the exchanging or sharing of electrons. If the *force of attraction* between the electron and proton were much stronger than it is in our Universe, the electrons would be pulled inside the nucleus of each atom. Chemical bonding of atoms into molecules such as water would consequently be impossible. Even the bond angle of 105° is very specific so that water remains a liquid within a relatively narrow temperature range.

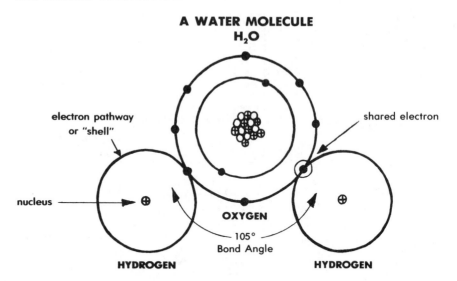

universal properties—that makes life possible here on Earth. We are talking not just about unique conditions on the planet Earth, but about the fundamental laws and properties which science believes govern the entire Universe.

Consider just a few of these so-called "natural laws" or "natural properties" or values which we take for granted. Let us first consider the world of the atom.

Atoms are composed of protons, neutrons, and electrons (see figure 2.2). Protons carry a positive charge (+) and electrons a negative charge (−). Neutrons are electrically neutral. Positive and negative charges are attracted to each other. Like charges repel each other.

One of the early mysteries of atomic physics was the nature of the force that kept two or more protons packed together in the nucleus. Their positive charges repel each other. It was like putting two male lions together in a single cage. Add more male lions and the action really heats up. In this same manner, the protons should be fighting to get away from each other. The cage keeps the male lions together. What keeps the protons together in the atomic nucleus?

The Nuclear Force. Nuclear physicists call the force that binds the protons and neutrons into the atomic nucleus the *nuclear force* (also known as the "strong" force). Without the existence of this mysterious force, the nucleus of an atom would simply explode like an atomic bomb.

The strength of this nuclear force is one of the basic values that is fundamental to the existence of life. Consider what conditions would be like if this force were either weaker or stronger.

If the nuclear force were slightly *weaker,* the protons would fly away from one another. Only elements such as hydrogen and possibly helium could form. The heavier elements could not exist because their protons, like the male lions, could not be brought together. Without the heavier elements, especially carbon, the possibilities of life become highly remote.

Conversely, if the strength of the nuclear force were slightly *stronger,* then all atomic nuclei would have to contain a minimum of several particles because a single proton would attract others. This would mean that hydrogen could *not* form. Without hydrogen there could be no water (H_2O). Life without water is difficult to conjure by even the best of wizards.

The Electromagnetic Force. Another basic value we take for granted is the force of attraction between a proton and an electron (the electrical attraction between positive and negative charges). If this force of attraction were much stronger, then the electrons orbiting around the nucleus of an atom would be pulled into the nucleus and scrambled with the protons and neutrons already there. Without electrons in the outer shell of an atom to share and exchange with other atoms, it is hard to see how molecules could form (see figure 2.3). Stable chemical bonding would become impossible, and it would be impossible for life to exist under such circumstances.

Let us now turn from the infinitesimal world of the atom and its highly critical forces to consider the gigantic world of the Cosmos. Are there critical values imposed that might affect the basic formation of stars and planets?

The Cosmological Conditions. I live about fifteen miles from Vandenberg Air Force Base. Space probes and satellites are frequently launched in full view of my front porch. At night the spectacle is something to behold. The rockets leave a trail of white, orange, and blue as they soar into the heavens on their directed mission.

The space engineers at Vandenberg insist that it is very important to power these rockets properly. The amount of fuel is critical. The rate of burning is carefully calculated and designed. If not enough power is put into a rocket, it will go only a short way and then crash to Earth under the pull of gravity. Conversely, if too much initial power is put into a rocket, it will either destruct or soar off into the void of space, never to be heard from again.

The cosmological condition that determines the rate of expansion

FIGURE 2.4.

The launching of the Columbia space vehicle for its final orbital flight test, June 27, 1982. The attached solid-rocket boosters fire to lift the vehicle into a precise circular orbit. (Courtesy NASA.)

of the Universe is as critical a value as the amount of power in a rocket. If the Big Bang were less powerful, the rate of expansion would be much slower. The pull of gravity would quickly take over and bring the galaxies crashing back together in a Big Crunch. There would not be enough time for stars to burn and cool to form heavier elements which make up planets like Earth. The crash would occur before even the basic elements of life could be formed.

Similarly, if the Big Bang were more powerful, the initial rate of expansion would be too fast. The energy and material would blast away so rapidly that gravitational attraction could not bring clumps of matter together to form stars and galaxies. Like a rocket that is too powerful, the mission would be lost in empty space.

Alan Lightman, writing in the October issue of *Science 82* emphasized the importance of the cosmological condition: "Since living structures apparently require complex atoms, and complex atoms were made in stars, the cosmological parameter in a life-supporting universe could not have been much different than it is."[3]

Other seemingly "determined" parameters are the gravitational coupling constant and the residual heat radiation from the Big Bang. If either of these mysterious conditions varied in essential orders of magnitude, it would drastically change the life-supporting capabilities of the Universe.

Have there been other universes in the past? There is no evidence whatsoever. Will a new universe exist in the future? Science can only speculate. But what has emerged out of the theoretical investigation is highly relevant. There are many very fundamental properties that our Universe "just happens" to possess. There is no logical reason or statistical probability that has determined these basic conditions to be what they are, except one: we are here. And we are asking questions such as: Who instituted the critical cosmological conditions so that they would be exactly right to produce galaxies, stars, and, more importantly, at least one habitable planet? Who designed the nuclear and electromagnetic forces to produce just the "right" atoms with the "proper" characteristics that could be chemically combined into water and the compounds of carbon that form organic molecules?

The evidence now suggests that hypothetical universes that could sustain even a semblance of life are statistically very improbable. The evidence is that our Universe is one of a kind. And its fundamental laws and properties seem not only to be determined, but also designed for us. With this in mind, let us now consider research on the mysterious origin of our Universe.

THE SEARCH FOR THE BEGINNING

Cosmologists have systematically reversed the chronology of the Universe, much as we would run a home movie in reverse, to find the instant of birth in the Big Bang. At that point, however, there is no longer any past from which to learn. All evidence had to have been destroyed in the unimaginable heat and light of that initial blast. Physicists can measure forces and particles; they cannot measure nothingness.

Consider for a minute the problem faced by scientists as they attempt to construct models of the early Universe. At first, the process is on sound scientific grounds. Theoretical physicists have constructed a mathematical model to test. Most importantly, astronomers can make actual observations. They can take actual pictures of our more recent past. Due to the speed of light and the vast distances involved in the heavens it is possible to see a picture of an event that occurred, for instance, two billion years ago in a distant galaxy. An analogy may be useful.

During a thunderstorm you notice that lightning flashes dramatically in the sky. A few moments later you hear the crashing sound of thunder. This tells you that:

1. An event happened—the electrical discharge of the cloud.
2. The light from this event traveled to your eyes.
3. The sound from this event traveled to your ears.
4. You saw the light before you heard the thunder.

A scientifically correct conclusion is that light travels faster than sound.

Suppose that you are inside a house on a dark and rainy night. The curtains are drawn and you cannot see outside. But you hear the sound of thunder. Is the instant you hear the sound the same instant that the event is taking place? No, your ears are telling you of an event that took place in the past, at least a few seconds before you heard the thunder. This is because it took time for the sound waves to travel from the storm cloud to your ears.

The speed of sound is relatively slow: 1088 feet per second. The speed of light is unbelievably fast: 186,000 miles per second. This means that if an event occurred 186,000 miles away, we would see it one second later. The light we see on the Earth from the Sun was actually generated on the Sun about eight minutes earlier.

This time gap is important in obtaining pictures of what the Universe looked liked in the past. This only becomes apparent when we consider the vast distances between Earth and galaxies in far-off space. With modern telescopes we can look at a galaxy that is 2 billion light years away from Earth. Since what we see is the light itself, and since it took 2 billion years to travel to the telescope on Earth, we are actually seeing a picture of an event that happened 2 billion years ago. Similarly, we can look at another galaxy that is 4 billion light years away, or twice as far back in the past.

In this manner, scientists can actually obtain relics of past events. This observed data is correlated with mathematical models and projected farther back in time.

The farther back in time we go, as we approach the time of the Big Bang, the closer the galaxies come together. The pictures from telescopes become dimmer and theoretical physics takes over. The galaxies of stars become a muddled mass as they are compressed together. Matter, as we know it, disappears. Temperatures become so intense that elements and atoms no longer maintain their structure. The atoms break apart into subatomic elementary particles—electrons, positrons, neutrinos, and photons; then quarks, leptons, and gluons. We have entered the realm of plasmas and particle physics. The orderly harmony we observe in the present Universe is gone. We are in the era of fiery primeval chaos.

As we go farther back in time, all matter, space, and energy become theoretically compressed into a volume smaller than a baseball. We are at the beginning: the threshold of creation! Beyond this point space and time, as we know them, cease to exist. Matter, energy, space, and time are simply not meaningful entities before the moment of creation.

The picture stops. There are no more relics, no footprints in the sand. There is no experiment that can be performed in the laboratory. Science has reached the barrier beyond which it cannot penetrate. We are at the beginning of creation and all is in darkness.

THE STUNNING IMPLICATIONS

Let's go back to our original question. *Why does the Universe possess the highly unique properties conducive to the existence of life?* This is perhaps the greatest mystery in modern science. All so-

called "natural laws" or "natural forces" originate in scientific mystery.

The scientific method has a great deal to teach us about what happened after the initial cosmic explosion, which will be explained in the following chapter. However, it is important to grasp the magnificence of the creation *event*. All energy, elements, materials, stars, and planets can be theoretically traced back to their origin in the initial cosmic event which, for want of a better term, is called the Big Bang—the moment of creation.

The materials and natural forces required by all evolutionary theories originated in the creation of a unique Universe, one that appears to be beyond the realm of statistical probability. Moreover, all the physical laws and constants which scientists have discovered and which we now take for granted were also determined during the initial creation event. If these critical physical laws had been created with slightly different values, it is a virtual certainty that the Uni-

FIGURE 2.5.

The Whirlpool Galaxy in the constellation *Canes Venatici*. Galaxies of this order contain approximately 100 billion stars and additional unorganized gas and dust. (Courtesy Palomar Observatory, California Institute of Technology.)

35

verse and the Earth as we know it would not exist. We would not even be here to contemplate it. The Universe definitely appears to have been designed for mankind.

The most we can say scientifically about "before the beginning" is that we know nothing about it. The scientific quest has reached a barrier it cannot penetrate. Time and space have no meaning or existence. We must turn to the Scriptures at this point. "And the earth was formless and void, and darkness was over the surface of the deep; and the Spirit of God was moving over the surface of the waters" (Gen. 1:2).

This points up the very fundamental difference between science and religion. Science arrives at its conclusions by human observation, experimentation, and interpretation of the results. The Christian finds an answer to the question of ultimate causation through revelation, which does not require a human observer. God has spoken and His people believe Him. Thus, "By faith we understand that the worlds were prepared by the word of God, so that what is seen was not made out of things which are visible" (Heb. 11:3).

At the instant of creation, science has reached a barrier it cannot penetrate. Scientifically speaking, we must be content with the statement that the Universe "just came into existence." The question of ultimate causation is one that science cannot answer.

Christianity presupposes God is true. Thus Christians should not expect science to prove God or to give answers to the meaning and purpose of life. To expect science to answer such questions would make God and phenomena subject to the limitations of the human mind. We should expect, however, that as science accurately explores the wondrous mysteries of God's creation, ultimately the weight of evidence will be in harmony with Scripture. The results and phenomena of creation which are all around us will force us to face the reality of the creation.

Science now fully agrees with the Bible that there was a beginning to the Universe. Before the beginning our physical Universe is shrouded in darkness. The stage is set. God is ready to begin the creation.

CHAPTER 3
THE BEGINNING

Then God said, "Let there be light"; and there was light. And God saw that the light was good; and God separated the light from the darkness.

Genesis 1:3–4

Light is the key to all life in this world. It is the form of energy that is necessary for all life on Earth. It is an imperfectly understood gift that behaves as both a wave and a particle to provide the energy upon which all life ultimately depends.

In classical physical theory, energy radiates or travels as electromagnetic waves. Scientists have also discovered that light consists of high energy particles known as photons. Photons are discrete particles without mass (matter). According to quantum theory, light is composed of photons. The filament in an ordinary light bulb emits or radiates enormous quantities of photons which we perceive as visible light.

The Universe began at a sharply defined instant in time in a fiery explosion of intense brilliance. In the beginning, pure energy was transforming itself into matter. One of the greatest contributions of nineteenth-century physics was the statement of the law of *conservation of energy*. In essence this law says that energy can change form, but it is never destroyed. Thus in the Big Bang, pure energy would alter itself into forms of matter about which we can only theorize. The first particles to emerge were photons (particles of light) and neutrinos (subatomic particles that travel through solid bodies at the speed of light). These were almost instantaneously followed by electrons, positrons, protons, and neutrons. Initial temperatures were beyond comprehension, such as one hundred thousand million degrees. The Universe was filled with light.

It is difficult to describe the details of the initial fireball radiation and its more immediate aftermath without dealing with the princi-

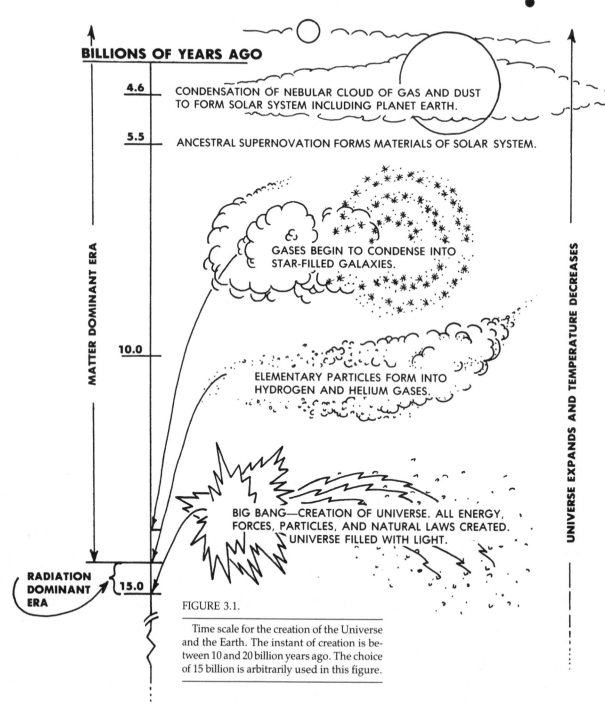

BILLIONS OF YEARS AGO

4.6 — CONDENSATION OF NEBULAR CLOUD OF GAS AND DUST TO FORM SOLAR SYSTEM INCLUDING PLANET EARTH.

5.5 — ANCESTRAL SUPERNOVATION FORMS MATERIALS OF SOLAR SYSTEM.

GASES BEGIN TO CONDENSE INTO STAR-FILLED GALAXIES.

10.0 — ELEMENTARY PARTICLES FORM INTO HYDROGEN AND HELIUM GASES.

BIG BANG—CREATION OF UNIVERSE. ALL ENERGY, FORCES, PARTICLES, AND NATURAL LAWS CREATED. UNIVERSE FILLED WITH LIGHT.

RADIATION DOMINANT ERA

15.0

MATTER DOMINANT ERA

UNIVERSE EXPANDS AND TEMPERATURE DECREASES

FIGURE 3.1.

Time scale for the creation of the Universe and the Earth. The instant of creation is between 10 and 20 billion years ago. The choice of 15 billion is arbitrarily used in this figure.

38

ples of quantum physics and ionized plasmas (the world of sub-atomic particles). But for our purposes, the creation of the Universe can be divided into two basic eras: the radiation dominant era and the matter dominant era (see figure 3.1).

Radiation Dominant Era. The light or radiation dominant era began with the instant of creation and lasted for the first several hundred thousand years. It was characterized by extremely high temperatures and was dominated by energy radiation in the form of light. Energy radiation was so powerful that aggregations of matter were broken up and dispersed faster than they could form. Matter played only the role of a negligible contaminant, and the omnipresent light was so dense that it is best described as a luminous cloud of enormous brilliance.

Matter Dominant Era. The Universe continued to become cooler and less dense as the headlong flight of energy and unorganized matter continued outward into the void. At the temperature of about 3,000°C a striking transition occurred from a *radiation dominated* to a *matter dominated* Universe. Electrons joined with nuclei to form the first atoms of hydrogen and helium. The Universe became transparent and darkness again prevailed.

The enormous energy radiation of the early Universe had been lost by the shift of photon (light) wavelengths to the red end of the spectrum, leaving what was previously a minor contamination of nuclear particles and electrons to grow into vast cloud clumps of gases, then into galaxies of stars. As stars came into existence, they began to convert their hydrogen into helium in a kind of giant nuclear fusion reactor. The stars began to burn and shine with intense

FIGURE 3.2.

The Andromeda Galaxy as seen from the Palomar Observatory. As viewed from Earth, this galaxy lies in a flat plane.

brilliance. The Universe again had a source of light with darkness prevailing in the vast oceans of space between the stars.

Stars, Galaxies, and the Solar System. The main feature of the matter dominant era was the formation of stars within their galaxies. Stars formed from clumps of hydrogen and other materials condensing under the influence of gravitational attraction, rather like a snowball growing in size while rolling downhill.

FIGURE 3.3.

A possible way the Solar System formed: (a) A huge dispersed nebula of interstellar gas and dust condenses under its own gravitational attraction. (b) Nebula contracts, begins to rotate perceptibly, and flattens. Most material falls into the rapidly accumulating central protosun. (c) Nebula rotates faster and flattens further. Protosun becomes distinct from surrounding disk. Particles condense and rapidly accrete in disk eddys. (d) Protosun heats further and becomes an infrared star. Disk still consists mostly of gases, but planets are largely formed. Warped magnetic fields transfer momentum to planets. (e) Contracting sun begins to shine visibly; intense solar wind at this stage drives off gases in the surrounding disk. (f) Sun begins burning hydrogen and is now stabilized. Planets and asteroids are virtually all that remain of disk.

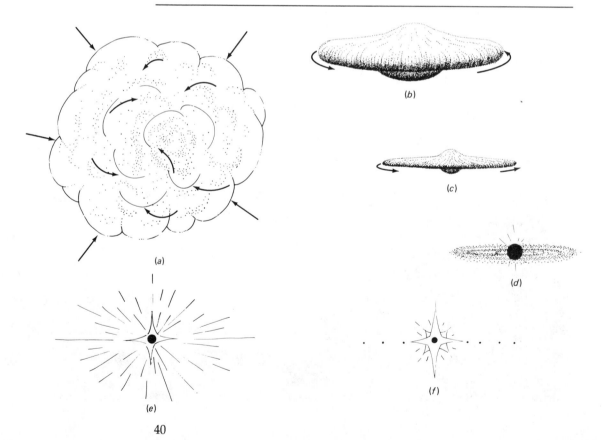

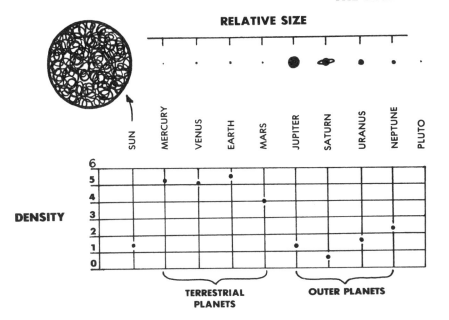

RELATIVE SIZE

SUN MERCURY VENUS EARTH MARS JUPITER SATURN URANUS NEPTUNE PLUTO

DENSITY

6
5
4
3
2
1
0

TERRESTRIAL PLANETS   OUTER PLANETS

Model of Solar System drawn to approximate size. The nine planets orbit around the Sun in the same direction and in nearly the same plane with clockwise regularity—implying a common origin. The density chart shows the relative densities of the Sun and its planets; the density (ratio of mass to volume) of water is 1.0. The Earth has the highest density—5.5. The Sun contains 99.9% of the total mass of our Solar System! Thus, the planets are held in orbit by virtue of the Sun's gravitational attraction.

The terrestrial or inner planets consist chiefly of the earthy materials (silicon, magnesium, iron, etc., combined with oxygen), while the outer planets consist mostly of gaseous and icy materials. The terrestrial planets are thought to have lost considerable mass and size due to their gaseous components being driven off by solar winds.

Stars are born, live, and die within their galaxies. Toward the end of their lives, a few very large stars will collapse and then explode into supernovas.

One or more such supernova explosions, scientists believe, manufactured the basic elements of which the Solar System, including planet Earth, is composed. About 4.6 billion years ago, the Solar System is thought to have condensed from the nebular cloud of gas and dust particles produced by its most recent ancestral supernovation. The basic formation of any solar system includes a dominating, central proto-sun which is surrounded by lesser planets that have also condensed from the original disk-shaped nebular cloud.

The Sun, of course, is the star of our Solar System. It is a giant nuclear reactor, which by its constant conversion of hydrogen to helium supplies energy to Earth. Figure 3.4 depicts the Earth's position in the Solar System and helps visualize the giant mass of the Sun which holds the planets in captive orbit around it through the force of gravitational attraction.

The Planet Earth. Earth is in many respects a very special cosmic body. Most stars appear to be composed chiefly of hydrogen and helium, while the Earth is composed largely of heavier elements.

Moreover, while the Earth appears to have received an allotment of materials not greatly different from that of its close neighbors, the

FIGURE 3.5.

The relative sizes of the planets in relation to a portion of the Sun.

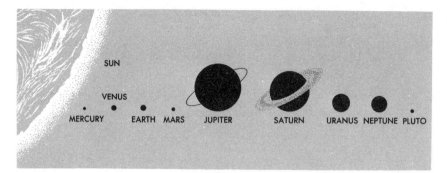

differences were critical. The full importance of these differences may not be apparent until we discuss in later chapters how the Earth obtained its atmosphere, water, and land. But three critical key differences of the Earth's materials must be listed at this point, because they are so basic to the understanding of the Earth's unique development. The Earth received from the nebular cloud:

1. *A large component of metals, especially iron.* Later in the Earth's history this iron formed into a central core with important electrical and magnetic effects. This iron core with its solid *inner* and fluid *outer* components transformed the planet into a giant magnet. The magnetic effects reach out into space itself, helping to shield the Earth from cosmic radiation and the solar wind. The solar wind consists of blasts of ionizing radiation, rich in high-energy protons, that spread in all directions from the Sun. The Earth's neighboring planets of Venus and Mars appear to lack magnetic effects.

2. *A slightly higher amount of radioactive elements.* The decay and heat generation of these radioactive elements were of great importance in the early remelting of the Earth. Today, these elements are believed to be the heat source which keeps the upper layer of the mantle plastic and viscous. The importance of this hot semi-molten layer to renewing the lands of the Earth will become apparent in Chapter 5.

3. *A slightly higher component of water-forming (hydrous) compounds.* From these compounds an extensive supply of water would later be added to the planet's surface. Water is not only the basic component of life, but also is of great importance in protecting our planet from extremes of heat and cold. In addition, water appears to have been a critical component that facilitated the later remelting of the Earth (see chapter 4). Water continues to lubricate the Earth's dynamic, ongoing geological processes. Without water the Earth would be a lifeless planet.

Besides its material makeup, the Earth's distance from the Sun is highly important. On Venus, for example, in a position closer to the

Figure 3.6

Periodic table of the elements.

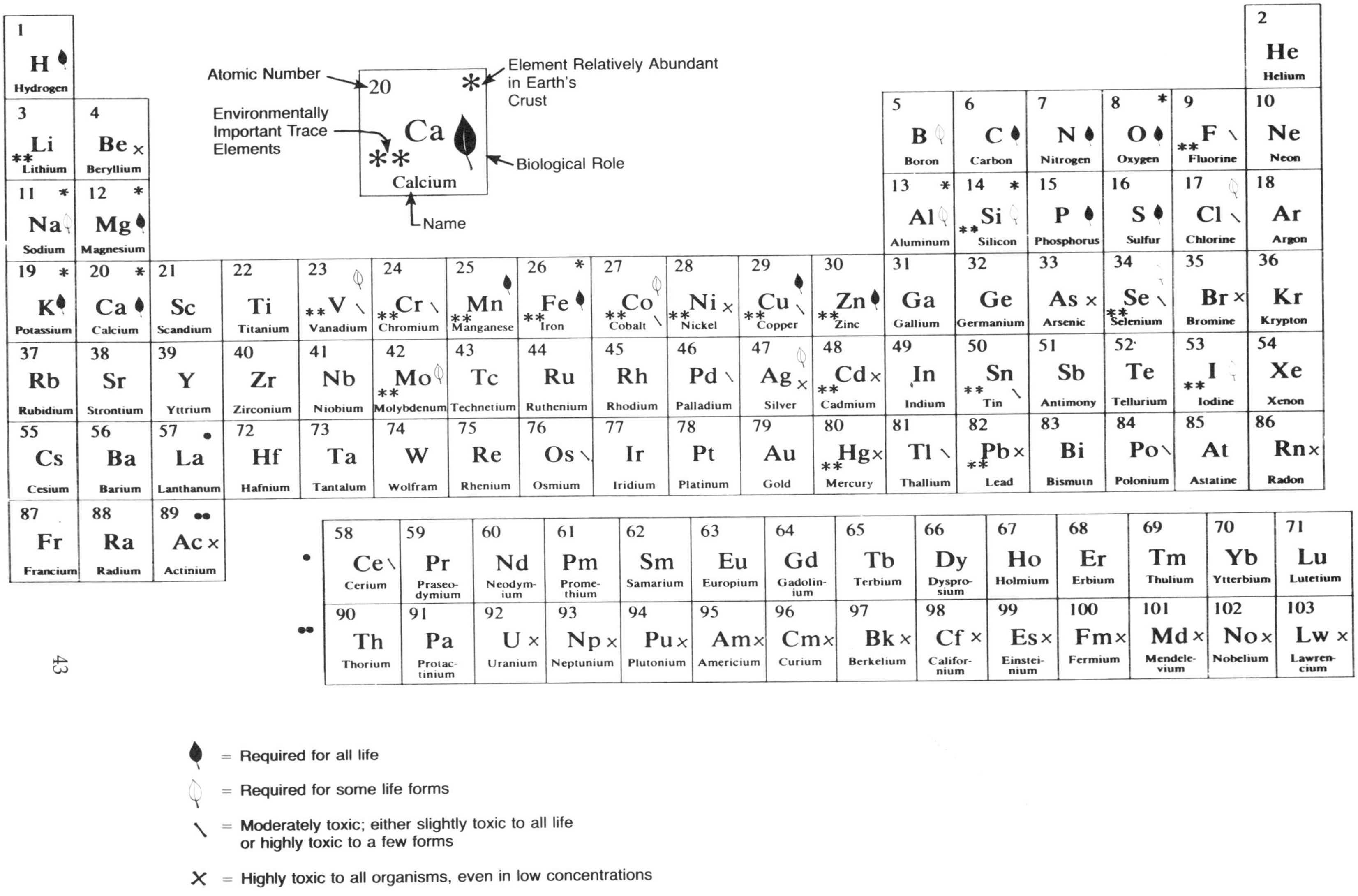

Atomic Number → 20

Element Relatively Abundant in Earth's Crust

Biological Role

Ca
Calcium ← Name

Environmentally Important Trace Elements

• = Required for all life

◌ = Required for some life forms

\ = **Moderately toxic; either slightly toxic to all life or highly toxic to a few forms**

X = Highly toxic to all organisms, even in low concentrations

43

Sun, water is vaporized. On Mars, located farther out, water is mostly frozen. The Earth's distance is such that the heat from the Sun generates exactly the right temperature range for water to exist as a stable liquid. Thus, a slightly different distance from the Sun would have resulted in water's existing either as steam or ice.

Also, the Earth's mass is not large enough to retain the light element of hydrogen through gravitational attraction. It must therefore keep most of its hydrogen locked in heavier molecules of water. However, the Earth's mass is sufficient to retain oxygen, an obviously critical component for the later development of animal life.

LET THERE BE LIGHT

This chapter has covered the initial creation of the Universe from its instantaneous beginning in a blaze of light to the formation of the Solar System which includes the planet Earth. These events took a minimum of ten billion years. The importance of Earth's special location in the Solar System and its unique material composition has been outlined. The concepts contained in the initial creation are so important to the understanding of subsequent events that a review is in order.

The Universe was created at the sharply defined beginning of time in a fiery explosion of dazzling brilliance. Robert Jastrow writes: "Picture the radiant splendor of the moment of creation. Suddenly a world of pure energy flashes into being; light of unimaginable brilliance fills the Universe."[1]

In the beginning, the Universe was filled with energy in the form of light. This radiant energy was largely transformed into matter as the Universe expanded and cooled. All the energy, forces, and particles that subsequently filled the immensities of space with gases, elements, stars, and planets were created in the initial Big Bang explosion.

It would be difficult to find a scientist who disagrees with the statement: The Universe began with light. Interestingly, however, there are rarely direct statements about the presence of light at the beginning of the Universe in textbooks. Instead, textbooks refer to the enormous temperatures of the gigantic initial explosion using such terms as "cataclysmic explosion that hurled matter and radiant energy outward,"[2] or, ". . . exploded violently to initiate the expansion that is still in progress today."[3]

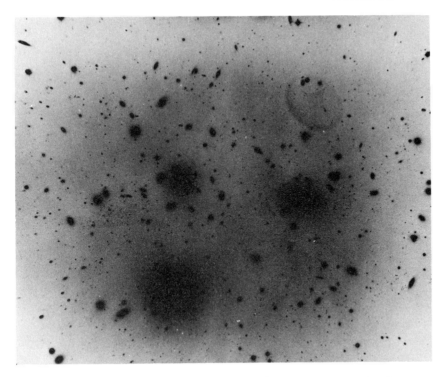

FIGURE 3.7.

The Heart of the Coma Cluster. This picture of a group of galaxies is shown in reverse with the sky light and the galaxies in black. Astronomers study the far reaches of space in this way because the galaxies show up much better for study in black.

It appears that writers or editors of public school textbooks consciously attempt to avoid a statement that might tie too closelv to the Bible. However, science writers who write for the general public are not bound by either textbook editors or Supreme Court rulings. Thus, in books written to explain science to the general public there are such statements as:

> At Point Zero, somewhere in space, all those billions of years ago, the Big Bang went off. At one second after blast-off the temperature was 5,000,000,000°K. At this time the Universe was flooded with a light that was denser than matter.[4]

Is it not reasonable to include in the textbooks our students read a scientifically accurate statement such as that quoted above? Science now fully agrees with the Bible that the Universe began with light. It is time our textbooks reflected the harmony of science with the first creation command in Genesis: "Then God said, 'Let there be light'; and there was light" (Gen. 1:3).

CHAPTER 4
THE FIRST ATMOSPHERE
AND WATER

Then God said, "Let there be an expanse in the midst of the waters, and let it separate the waters from the waters."
And God made the expanse, and separated the waters which were below the expanse from the waters which were above the expanse; and it was so.

Genesis 1:6–7

The Earth as we know it today is a very special planet. There may be others like it in the Universe, but the possibility does not seem as likely as it once did. Space exploration of the other planets in our Solar System has led us to a greater appreciation of some of the Earth's very special features. What is so different about the planet Earth?

For one thing, it is just the proper distance from the Sun so that it is neither too hot nor too cold. Like Goldilocks's response after tasting Little Bear's porridge in the children's story, the temperature of the Earth is "just right." Life as we know it is only possible within a very narrow temperature range, essentially between the freezing point and the boiling point of water. This range is only 1–2% of the total range between absolute zero and the temperature at the surface of the Sun.

The temperature of the Earth is kept in the critical range for life not only because the Earth is the correct distance from the Sun, but also because the Earth's size is "just right" and because it has the "right" rotational speed so that the Earth rotates about its axis every twenty-four hours, exposing one-half of the surface at the equator to the Sun for twelve hours at a time. If the Earth rotated much more slowly (perhaps ten days instead of twenty-four hours for a complete rotation), one half of the Earth would bake while the other half froze. Venus, the closest planet to Earth in size, rotates at the extremely slow rate of only once in 243 Earth days.

Temperature extremes are also evened out on Earth by its special

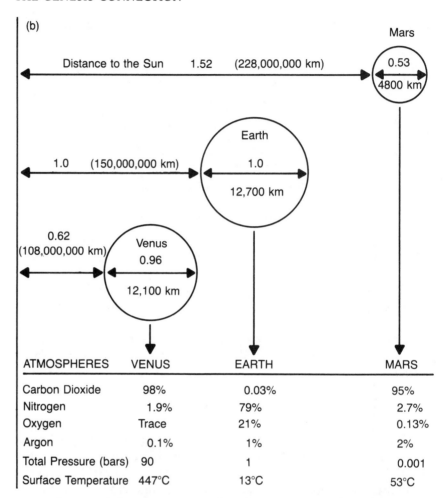

FIGURE 4.1.

A comparison of Venus, Earth, and Mars. This diagram depicts Earth's unique qualities as a habitable planet based on its distance from the Sun, the composition of its atmosphere, and its surface temperature.

ATMOSPHERES	VENUS	EARTH	MARS
Carbon Dioxide	98%	0.03%	95%
Nitrogen	1.9%	79%	2.7%
Oxygen	Trace	21%	0.13%
Argon	0.1%	1%	2%
Total Pressure (bars)	90	1	0.001
Surface Temperature	447°C	13°C	53°C

atmosphere and large quantity of surface water. Furthermore, these temperature extremes are distributed not only daily, but also seasonally between winter and summer as the Earth tilts on its axis.

The critical size of the Earth is also important. If it were much larger, the size or mass of the Earth would have retained through gravitational attraction a heavy, smog-like cover of harmful gases. If the Earth's mass were much smaller, it could not exert enough gravitational force to retain its present atmosphere, especially the oxygen component so critical to life.

It is fairly obvious to most people that the planet Earth has a special atmosphere and water supply at its surface. What is not so obvious is the special nature of the Earth below its surface. Basically,

48

the Earth contains a delicately balanced heat engine that runs on radioactive fuel. Like the engine in a car, it has to run at just the "right" speed to accomplish some amazing feats. One of the remarkable accomplishments of this finely tuned heat engine is the production of the Earth's magnetic core. Another is the production of the Earth's special atmosphere. The Earth's atmosphere and its magnetic field act as a shield—a kind of protective blanket. They act as a barrier against most of the damaging radiation from space that would otherwise strike the Earth and threaten life.

The Earth's special atmosphere also helps protect the Earth from meteors. The gases in our atmosphere act as a cushion to brake and soften the blows from these celestial projectiles that hurtle at us from space. The pockmarked surface of the Moon indicates what the Earth would look like without its protective blanket. The Earth is a very special and pampered planet.

But it was not always this way. When the Earth originally condensed from its nebular cloud of gas and dust particles into a solid planetary body, it looked very different from its appearance today. It

FIGURE 4.2.

An oblique view of the lunar far-side shows a crater of approximately 50 miles, surrounded by numerous smaller craters in the basaltic lava surface which makes up most of the Moon's basic landscape. (Courtesy NASA.)

resembled the Moon, a naked body of rock. There were no oceans, no plains, no towering mountains. There was no life of any kind. The initial gases surrounding the Earth are thought to have been swept away by powerful solar winds. There was no protective atmosphere. There was only desolation.

WATER, WATER EVERYWHERE

Coleridge's ancient mariner was right: there is water everywhere. It lies frozen in glaciers and polar ice. Water covers more than two-thirds of the surface of our planet. Water also exists beneath our feet, occupying the spaces in pores or cracks in soil and rocks of the Earth. This is called groundwater. When rocks contain substantial water,

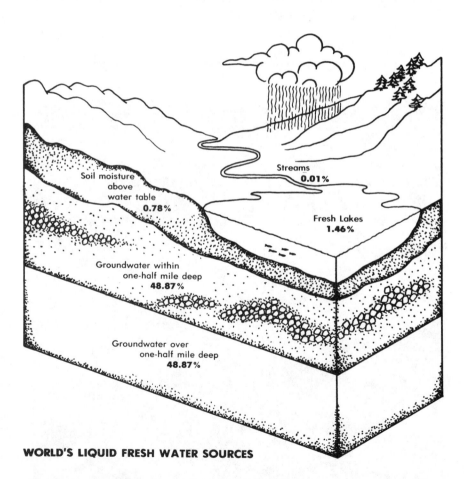

FIGURE 4.3.

The total water distribution (including salt water) on the Earth is: oceans, 97.3%; glaciers and polar ice, 2.1%; underground aquifers, 0.6%; lakes and rivers, 0.01%; and the atmosphere, 0.001%. The percentages indicated in the illustration refer to the percentage of fresh water from the various sources.

Soil moisture above water table
0.78%

Streams
0.01%

Fresh Lakes
1.46%

Groundwater within one-half mile deep
48.87%

Groundwater over one-half mile deep
48.87%

WORLD'S LIQUID FRESH WATER SOURCES

50

they are called aquifers. Some aquifers remain fairly constant in the quantity of groundwater they contain. They are replenished each year by seasonal rainfall. Others, particularly in the more arid western United States, are being slowly depleted as their water is used for irrigation. Geologists estimate that some of these underground supplies are the result of millions of years of rainfall seeping through the ground to accumulate in these underground reservoirs.

One of the tragic side effects of draining these underground reservoirs is subsidence. As the water is pumped out, the reservoir slowly collapses because water no longer occupies the spaces or pores between the rocks. This effect is especially noticeable in cities that deplete their underground supplies for domestic and industrial use. The city of Venice, Italy, is the best-known example where subsidence has lowered the ground level to the point that high tides inundate streets and historic landmarks.

Water is a substance that is familiar to us in its three basic forms: a liquid, a solid and a gas (see figure 4.5). Water comes in its gaseous form from a boiling tea kettle. We see it as condensed vapor in clouds that float in the sky. In its solid form we see it as snow and ice.

Water has some unusual physical and chemical properties that make it different from most substances. Most compounds shrink in size and become denser when they congeal from a liquid to a solid state. Not so water. Water expands when it freezes. It occupies more space and becomes less dense (lighter). It is for this reason that ice cubes float to the top of a glass of water. It is for this reason that

FIGURE 4.4.

A view of the rising Earth just above the lunar horizon. Earth is 240,000 miles away. (Courtesy NASA.)

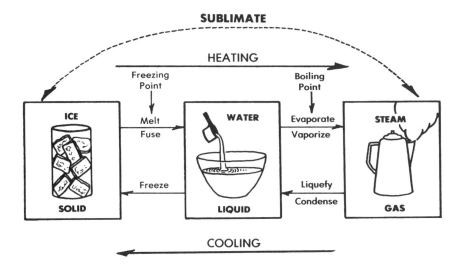

FIGURE 4.5.

The three basic forms or states of matter as exemplified by water: solid (ice), liquid (water), gas (water vapor or steam).

icebergs float in the oceans of the world. It is also the reason why aquatic wildlife can continue to live in water under the winter ice.

Water is also very stable as a liquid. It has unexpectedly low freezing (0°C) and high boiling points (100°C). Without water, the Earth would have no climate, only arid desolation. The Earth's oceans serve as vast heat sinks, storing the heat from sunlight and releasing it at night. In the Northern Hemisphere, the oceans accumulate heat in summer and release it in winter. The oceans are huge reservoirs that moderate the climate throughout the globe.

The molecules of water have an unusual capacity for sticking together, whether into raindrops or snowflakes. Water also has curious electrical properties in its solid state. Most electrical currents in solids are conducted by means of electron flow. Not so in ice. In ice, electricity is conducted by means of the positively charged protons of its atoms.

Water is the primary constituent of protoplasm and comprises 80% to 90% of all living matter. More than 70% of our physical bodies consists of molecules of water. Water is also the universal solvent. Practically everything we make is either mixed with or cleaned with water. Bread may be the staff of life, but it would not exist without water. It takes 136 gallons of water to grow the wheat for a single loaf of bread.

Water is the most common substance on Earth. To obtain our water, we turn a faucet. Water is so common, so much a part of our everyday lives, that we take it for granted.

American astronauts returning from their space mission to the Moon must have thought of water as the source of new life and hope. One has only to contemplate the dry, lifeless surface of the Moon, the frozen ice of Mars, or the inferno of Venus to view the waters of the Earth with reverence.

It was the astronauts who gave the Earth a new nickname—"The Blue Planet"—because two-thirds of the planet is presently covered by our blue oceans. This was not always so. In the Earth's early history it had no water or atmosphere at all. It looked like the Moon, a naked and lifeless body of rock. But, by 3.5 billion years ago, the Earth was completely covered by water.

OUTGASSING OF THE ATMOSPHERE

How did the Earth produce the atmosphere and water that are so vitally necessary for life to exist on any planet?

FIGURE 4.6.

Mount Saint Helens, May 18, 1980. Through such eruptions the earth outgasses its hot primitive atmosphere of noxious gases and water vapor from sources deep within its rocks.

The first part of the answer relates to the basic components of the planet. Earth is thought to have received a larger proportion than its neighboring planets of hydrous (watery) compounds from which a sufficient quantity of surface water could be produced.

The second part of the answer to this question comes from a process inherent in the Earth's formation. When the Earth first condensed and congealed into a solid body, it trapped gases and water vapor in tiny pores within its rocks. Given enough heat, the rocks could release the water vapor and gases into the atmosphere in the same way that baking an apple releases steam. This process is known as *outgassing*. This same process operates today when volcanoes belch out huge vaporous clouds of gases from molten sources deep within the Earth. The initial outgassing of the Earth is thought to have been immense with much volcanic activity. Huge quantities of water vapor and other gases were released from the Earth's interior to produce a dense continuous black cloud which surrounded the Earth.

The third part of the answer is the Earth's temperature, which allowed the water to remain in a liquid form. The Earth's temperature is neither so hot that the water turns to a gas nor so cold that it turns to ice.

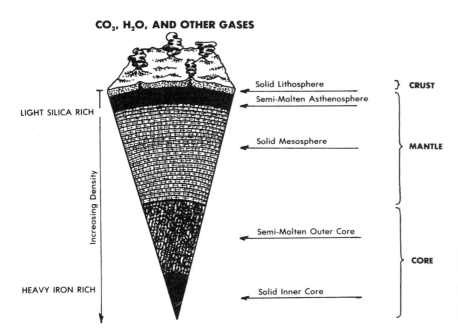

CO_2, H_2O, AND OTHER GASES

LIGHT SILICA RICH

Increasing Density

HEAVY IRON RICH

Solid Lithosphere — } **CRUST**
Semi-Molten Asthenosphere —

Solid Mesosphere — **MANTLE**

Semi-Molten Outer Core — **CORE**

Solid Inner Core —

FIGURE 4.7.

The Earth's interior after it had been stratified (sorted) by density 3.8 billion years ago.

FIGURE 4.8.

The three sources of heat thought to have been responsible for the great melting or rebirth of the Earth between 4.2 and 3.8 billion years ago. Radiation heating, through the decay of radioactive elements, may have caused a slow but steady heat buildup since the planet's formation of 4.6 billion years ago. Gravitational heating through the frictional heat of particles moving past each other, together with compression into a small volume, would have been another important heat source. The principal catalyst for the great melting was probably cosmic bombardment. The impact of giant meteors would have generated enormous heat as their energy of motion was converted. Evidence from moon rocks indicates that a cosmic bombardment of major proportions struck the planets about 4 billion years ago.

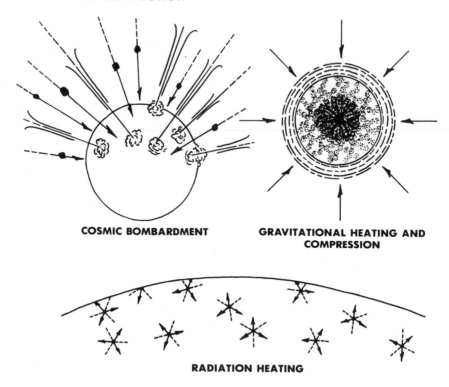

COSMIC BOMBARDMENT **GRAVITATIONAL HEATING AND COMPRESSION**

RADIATION HEATING

THE EARTH IS REBORN

The key to understanding the production of the Earth's atmosphere and water is to understand that our planet has been quite literally reborn. When the Earth first condensed from its nebular cloud of gas and dust, the planet was largely homogenous. That is, the Earth's interior from surface to center was unsorted. Both heavy and light materials are thought to have been distributed rather evenly throughout the cross section of the planet.

The cross section of the Earth today is illustrated in Figure 4.7. Note that the heavy materials such as the iron-rich core are at the center. Toward the surface or crust, the materials become lighter, less dense. The materials of the Earth have been stratified and sorted by density. For this to happen, it was necessary that the original Earth melt into a liquid or at least a semi-molten state. Geologists believe that the entire planet was melted about 4 billion years ago. This catastrophic event is termed the great melting (or remelting). There are three heat sources thought to have been involved in melting the entire planet and causing its dramatic transformation: *radioactive heating, gravitational friction,* and *cosmic bombardment.*

Radioactive Heating. As the radioactive elements such as uranium and thorium present in the body of the Earth decayed, they released heat as a byproduct. This heat slowly accumulated during the half billion years preceding the great melting. Initial heating from this source is thought to have been far greater than it is today because the radioactive elements have decayed through time.

Gravitational heating. As the Earth slowly began to heat up from the accumulation of radioactive heat, it is thought that the denser (heavier) materials began to sink toward the center. The lighter materials would tend to rise toward the surface. The gravitational friction

FIGURE 4.9.

"Great Scott" rock. This lunar sample, a brownish-grey vesicular mare basalt, is the largest collected up through the Apollo 15 mission. (Courtesy NASA.)

FIGURE 4.10.

Meteor crater near Flagstaff, Arizona, is the result of a large meteorite impact in prehistoric times. (Courtesy U.S. Geological Survey.)

of the heavier materials moving down and the lighter materials moving up generated enormous heat as the materials slid past each other. The quantities of hydrous (watery) compounds which the Earth contained are thought to have lowered the melting point of rocks and also to have lubricated this process. The heaviest materials such as iron settled at the Earth's core. The descent of the iron core may have been a catastrophic event which generated enormous heat.

Cosmic Bombardment. The third heat source which may have functioned as the triggering agent for the great melting of the Earth was cosmic bombardment. It is thought that giant meteors generated substantial heat as they struck the Earth with tremendous force. This probably occurred before the Earth's protective atmosphere existed to cushion the blows from these huge meteors. As these objects from space struck the Earth at speeds approaching 100,000 miles per hour, they would have punched into the crust, vaporized, and exploded. Their energy of motion would have been converted almost instantaneously into enormous heat.

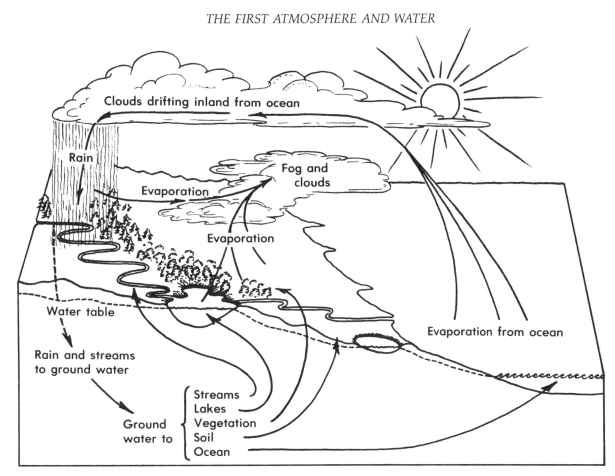

Clouds drifting inland from ocean

Rain

Evaporation

Fog and clouds

Evaporation

Water table

Evaporation from ocean

Rain and streams to ground water

Ground water to
{ Streams
Lakes
Vegetation
Soil
Ocean

Evidence from the Moon indicates that a cosmic bombardment of major proportions struck the planets about 4 billion years ago. Some moon rocks brought back by the Apollo mission date at 4.5 billion years old. This indicates that the Moon was only partially melted by the cosmic bombardment. In contrast, the Earth's oldest known rocks date at 3.7 billion years old indicating that the entire crust of the Earth was melted prior to this time.

WATER VAPOR CONDENSES TO FORM SEAS

The three heat sources—gravitational friction, radioactive heating, and cosmic bombardment—are thought to have combined to outgas

FIGURE 4.11.

The recycling of water (hydrologic cycle). The illustration does not include the cycle in the polar regions where snow falls to form snowfields and ice. Water vapor evaporates or sublimates from snow and glaciers to reenter the atmosphere. Ice and snow also melt to flow into streams, lakes, and the oceans. Although the oceans are permanent features of our planet, the water in them is recycled through the atmosphere and fresh water systems about once every 2 million years.

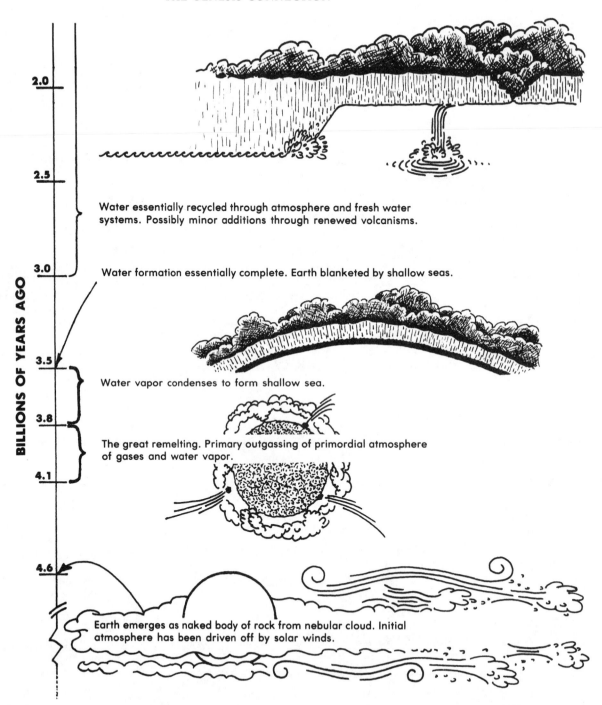

BILLIONS OF YEARS AGO

2.0

2.5

Water essentially recycled through atmosphere and fresh water systems. Possibly minor additions through renewed volcanisms.

3.0 — Water formation essentially complete. Earth blanketed by shallow seas.

3.5

Water vapor condenses to form shallow sea.

3.8

The great remelting. Primary outgassing of primordial atmosphere of gases and water vapor.

4.1

4.6

Earth emerges as naked body of rock from nebular cloud. Initial atmosphere has been driven off by solar winds.

the water vapor and other gases trapped in the pores of the Earth's rocks.

Initially, water in liquid form could not exist since the extremely hot molten surface of the Earth prevented water vapor from condensing. It is generally thought that this vapor, together with smog-like gases (primarily carbon dioxide) formed a hot, dense, continuous cloud surrounding the Earth.

In the gradual but continued cooling of the Earth's crust, the air temperature finally lowered to the point (100°C) where the condensation from water vapor to liquid water took place. At first, rain began to fall only to be reheated to new clouds of steam by the hot crust. Further crust cooling took place and sheets of rain fell from the sky to accumulate on the cooling surface. Volcanic action continued to outgas water vapor to the atmosphere and gigantic cloud bursts sent the water back to Earth. The water accumulated into shallow seas.

By 3.5 billion years ago, the Earth is thought to have been covered by a shallow sea. At this point, water formation was essentially complete. In his college textbook, *Essentials of Earth History,* W. L. Stokes comments: "There is good evidence that sea water accumulated rather rapidly during the early stages of the earth's history and has remained almost constant in quantity for the past 3.5 billion years."[1] Since this time, the waters of the Earth have basically been recycled through the atmosphere and fresh water systems. Minor additions may occur from time to time from new volcanic eruptions, but this also may represent recycling as will be seen in the subsequent chapter.

FIGURE 4.13.

The eruption of Halemaumau in the Kilauea quadrangle, Hawaii, in May 1924. (Courtesy U.S. Geological Survey.)

A LOOK BACK AT GENESIS

Genesis 1:6–7 says, "Then God said, 'Let there be an expanse in the midst of the waters, and let it separate the waters from the waters.' And God made the expanse, and separated the waters which were below the expanse from the waters which were above the expanse; and it was so."

In the biblical account, God has turned His attention from the Universe as a whole to the planet Earth. These verses and those following are therefore descriptive of events on Earth.

Ronald Youngblood, an Old Testament scholar specializing in Semitic languages, describes the *expanse* as "the visible atmosphere or sky, characterized by the layer of clouds that contain the water above it."[2] The *expanse* is the same space in which the birds fly (Gen. 1:20).

It thus appears that Genesis 1:6–7 is describing the initial water and atmosphere formation on the Earth. This suggests that science and Scripture are again in harmony since they both describe the first significant event to take place in the early history of the Earth as water and atmosphere formation.

The succeeding verses (Gen. 1:8–9) lend further support to this view. In verse 8, "God called the expanse heaven." God's second day or epoch then ended. Verse 9 takes up the next significant event in the Earth's history: "Then God said, 'Let the waters below the heavens be gathered into one place, and let the dry land appear.'"

CHAPTER 5
THE FIRST LAND

Then God said, "Let the waters below the heavens be gathered into one place, and let the dry land appear"; and it was so.

Genesis 1:9

Today, both continents and ocean basins are part of the Earth's crust. Continents are relatively high and ocean basins are relatively low because the continents consist of lighter (granitic type) rocks than the heavier, denser (basaltic type) rocks underlying ocean basins. Basically both the continents and the rocks underlying oceans float on a hot semi-molten plastically deforming underlayer. The continents float higher because they are lighter than the heavier basaltic rocks underlying the ocean basins.

THE GLOBAL SEA

Continents and deep ocean basins have not always been present on the planet Earth. At the end of the era of water formation 3.5 billion years ago, virtually the entire surface of the globe was under water, covered by a shallow sea (see figure 5.1). The surface of the Earth was essentially flat and level. The seas spread over this relatively even surface, blanketing the globe to a depth of about one mile.

About 3.5 billion years ago, huge dome-like blocks of granite welled upward from the depths of the mantle. These intrusions were more than twenty-five miles in height and formed the enduring core or *cratons* of the continents. The precise cause of these granitic (lighter rock) cratons thrusting up from the mantle below is unknown, but most geologists think that the enormous heat energy required was produced primarily by radioactive nuclides in the upper mantle. Also, residual effects from cosmic bombardment may

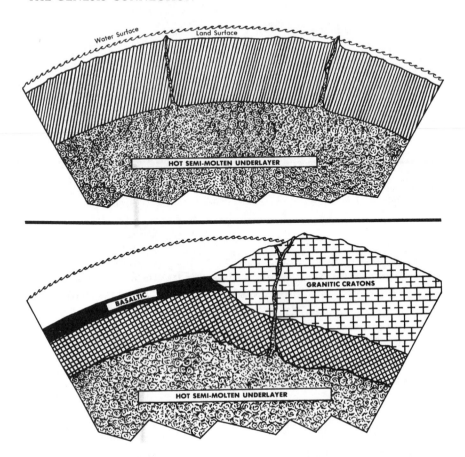

FIGURE 5.1.

The sketch, *top above*, shows a cross section of the Earth's surface prior to 3.5 billion years ago when the crust was relatively flat and covered by water.

The lower sketch shows the surface of the globe after the great vertical separation of the Earth's crust into two distinct types of rocks. The heavy (dense) basaltic rocks formed deep interconnected basins into which the waters were gathered. The lighter granitic rocks rose to form the continents.

have been involved. It is thought that enormous thermal convection currents within the upper mantle were initiated as the Earth attempted to cool itself. These forces somehow combined to differentiate the Earth's crust into light continents and heavy ocean basins. Although a general picture emerges as to how this separation may have been accomplished, the exact cause and mechanisms remain undetermined.

In any event, geologists believe that during the period from 3.5 to 2.5 billion years ago, the worldwide building of continents through successive intrusions of granitic rock took place. At the end of this period, the continental cratons stood as high platforms above the surrounding basins into which the waters of the Earth had been gathered. For the most part, the era of great vertical movement of the Earth's crust had ended. Henceforth, erosion, uplift, and the essen-

tially lateral movement of the Earth's crust would govern the shape of the land.

Fault block mountains. A view from the Panamint Mountains, California, across to the Sierra Nevada (skyline). The Argus Range, *left middle*, is an upfaulting of Plio-Pleistocene basalts. (Courtesy W. Hamilton.)

THE FLOATING CONTINENTS

An obvious question needs to be asked at this point. If erosion has been wearing down mountains and carrying their sediments to ocean basins for the last 2.5 billion years, why haven't the mountains become flat plains and the ocean basins filled to the brim with sediments? Why isn't the surface of the Earth one continuous mud flat?

Part of the answer lies in the buoyancy of the continental plates. When the upper layers of the mountains are stripped away by erosion, load (weight) is removed, and the mountains move higher. They are floating on a semi-molten underlayer.

This principle can be observed as a ship is unloaded in the harbor. As heavy cargo is removed, the ship floats higher above the water. This process in continental plates is best visualized in the faultblock mountains of Nevada and Utah and has given the area the distinctive name of Basin and Range Country. The mountains in effect grow as fast or faster than erosion can lower them. Growth and erosion are in such good balance that continents are essentially permanent features.

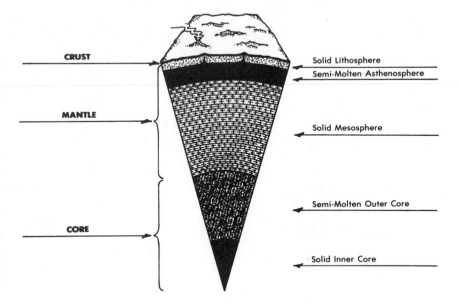

CRUST

MANTLE

CORE

Solid Lithosphere
Semi-Molten Asthenosphere

Solid Mesosphere

Semi-Molten Outer Core

Solid Inner Core

FIGURE 5.3.

The Earth's interior with new geologic descriptions on the right. The older terms on the left, which are still useful, are: the core; the mantle, which is comprised of the mesophere, the asthenosphere, and all of the upper lithosphere except the crust; and the crust, the top skin where the obvious action takes place.

PLATE TECTONICS

The other part of the answer to the question of why the surface of the Earth isn't flatter is to be found in the dynamics of plate tectonics. This theory also explains why the continents change their shape and geographical positions over time.

Plate tectonics and the ideas of continental drift came into prominence in the field of geology in the 1960s. Geologists now use this term to explain the dynamic movement of the Earth's upper layer and many bizarre observations that have been puzzling for centuries.

The Earth's upper layer (lithosphere) is divided into about eight major plates and a dozen or so smaller ones. They extend into the Earth for distances that vary between thirty to ninety miles where they float on the semi-molten underlayer (asthenosphere). Most plates bear both continents and oceans, and a few are essentially oceanic (see figure 5.4).

The plates are best visualized by imagining the cracked shell of an egg with the plates being separated along the lines of the cracks but able to move in relation to each other. The movement of the plates is

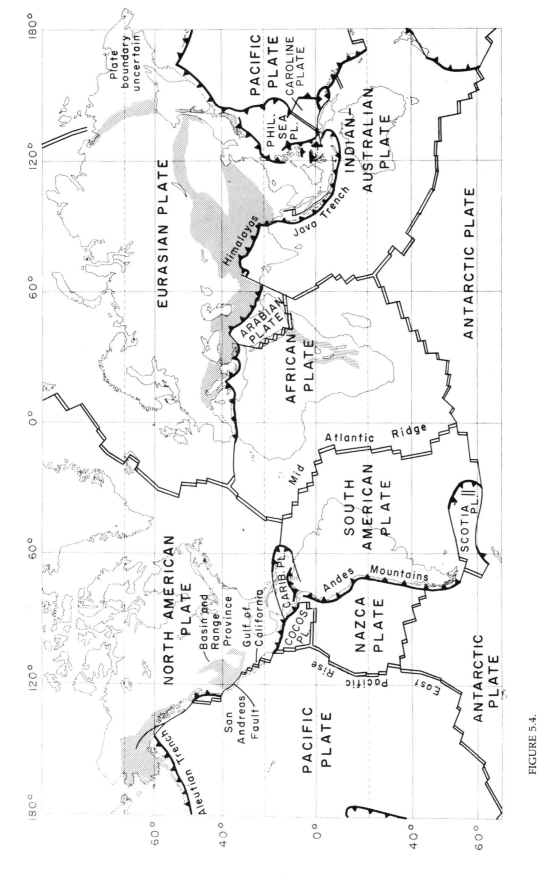

FIGURE 5.4.

Lithospheric plates of the world showing boundaries that are presently active. The double line indicates a zone of spreading where plates are moving apart. Line with barbs indicates a zone of underthrusting at which one plate is sliding beneath another. Single line indicates a strike-slip fault, where plates are sliding past one another. Shaded areas are parts of continents, exclusive of a plate boundary, which are undergoing active faulting. (Courtesy U.S. Geological Survey.)

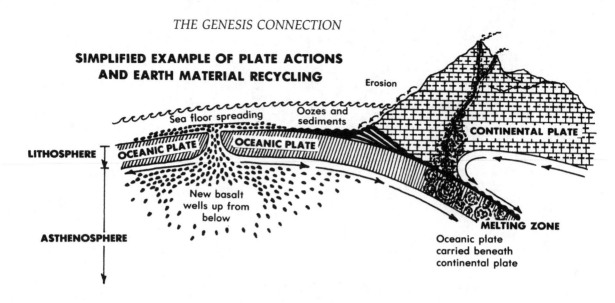

SIMPLIFIED EXAMPLE OF PLATE ACTIONS AND EARTH MATERIAL RECYCLING

Erosion

Sea floor spreading

Oozes and sediments

CONTINENTAL PLATE

OCEANIC PLATE

OCEANIC PLATE

LITHOSPHERE

New basalt wells up from below

ASTHENOSPHERE

MELTING ZONE

Oceanic plate carried beneath continental plate

OTHER TYPES OF PLATE BOUNDARIES AND PROCESSES

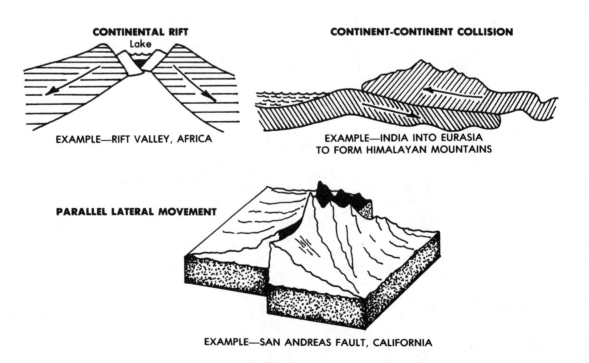

CONTINENTAL RIFT
Lake

EXAMPLE—RIFT VALLEY, AFRICA

CONTINENT-CONTINENT COLLISION

EXAMPLE—INDIA INTO EURASIA TO FORM HIMALAYAN MOUNTAINS

PARALLEL LATERAL MOVEMENT

EXAMPLE—SAN ANDREAS FAULT, CALIFORNIA

Figure 5.5

essentially lateral, and they appear to have moved in many different directions in the last 2.5 billion years. It is rather like a game of bumper cars, only without the bumpers. When continental plates collide, they wrinkle and buckle up the crust to form mountains. When a heavy oceanic plate collides with a continental plate, the oceanic plate is carried beneath the lighter continental plate to be remelted. The continental plate is lifted or jacked up to form huge mountain chains like the Andes of western South America (see figure 5.5). Some remelted material from the oceanic plate may also be carried upward through cracks to form new coastal mountain volcanoes or add material to old ones.

Heat sources in the upper mantle create new basaltic sea-floor material in a process known as *sea-floor spreading.* This process is thought to initiate the various plate movements. Remember that the interior of the Earth is a giant heat engine that is slowing down as its radioactive fuel continues to decay. Like a hot car engine, it must be cooled. One of the ways the Earth's engine cools itself is to vent hot molten basaltic magma from the mantle to the crust. This magma rises through cracks in the crust to create new sea-floor material. As the magma cools, it fills the rift in the crust left by the movement of plates away from one another.

The Mid-Atlantic Ridge is a current example of this sea-floor spreading process (see figures 5.6 and 5.7). The land masses of the Americas are effectively being moved away from Europe and Africa.

At the other end of the outward moving oceanic plates, deposited sediments and oozes are carried beneath the lighter continental bearing plates to be reheated to form new continental material (see figure 5.5). Thus, much of the Earth's crust, with the exception of the stable continental cratons, is recycled over time in the same way that the

FIGURE 5.6.

Stages in the development of a divergent junction and sea-floor spreading. The lithosphere breaks, *left*, and a rift develops under a continent. Molten basalt from the asthenosphere spills out. The rift continues to open, *right*, separating the two parts of the continent—in this case, America and Africa. The active rift is marked by a mid-ocean ridge, with earthquakes and volcanism as characteristic features. (After "The Breakup of Pangaea" by R. S. Dietz and J. C. Holden. Copyright © 1970 by Scientific American, Inc. All rights reserved.)

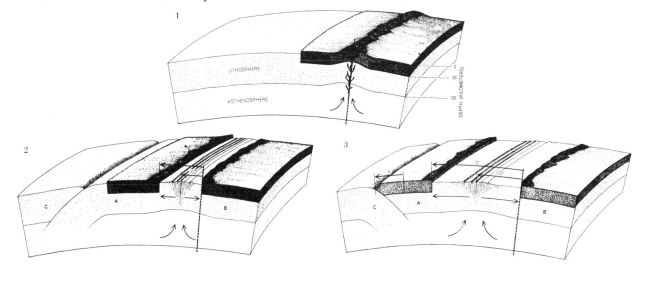

FIGURE 5.7.

The Mid-Atlantic Ridge is pictured in the center of this topographical painting by Heinrich Berann. Numbers are in feet above or below sea level. (Courtesy Aluminum Company of America.)

FIGURE 5.8.

Coal beds in Lignite Creek, Alaska. (Courtesy U.S. Geological Survey.)

waters of the Earth have been recycled since 3.5 billion years ago.

Plate tectonics has enabled us to understand some phenomena that we were formerly unable to explain. For example, movement of continent-bearing plates helps to explain the deposits of coal in Antarctica and Alaska. Since this fossil fuel is derived from organic materials that are normally characteristic of warmer climates, it is assumed that these polar continents must have at one time been closer to the equator. Also, similarities between fossil animals of different continents can now be explained if it is assumed that these continents were once joined together.

Although much ancient geography is unclear, the large continent-bearing plates are thought to have been one coherent land mass or aggregation about 200 million years ago (see figure 5.9). This giant super continent is called *Pangaea* (all lands) and was surrounded by a single world ocean called *Panthalassa* (all seas). The continents then drifted apart to form the world's present seven continents and seven seas.

FIGURE 5.9.

The changing position of the world's continents.

**200 MILLION YEARS AGO
PANGEA**

**135 MILLION YEARS
AGO**

TODAY

FIGURE 5.10.

The Arabian Peninsula on the right, pulling away from Africa on the left, has opened the great rifts flooded by the Red Sea and forming the Gulf of Suez and the Gulf of Aqaba. (Courtesy NASA.)

FIGURE 5.11.

A new ocean may be in the process of formation along a rift in the Earth's crust running from the Rift Valley of Africa up through the Red Sea. This rift is thought to extend into the Dead Sea and Jordan River Valley, which are substantially below sea level.

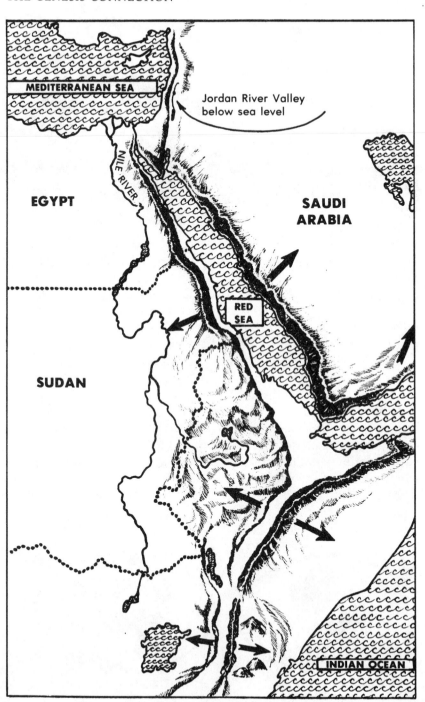

The Atlantic Ocean was formed during this separation by sea-floor spreading. This theory explains why the coastline of Africa fits rather neatly into that of the Americas, like pieces in a jigsaw puzzle, especially when their continental shelves are taken into account. Many suspect that a new oceanic rift is in its initial stages along a line running through the Rift Valley of Africa and the Red Sea. A branch of this rift in the Earth's crust extends into the Dead Sea and the Jordan River Valley. This crack in the Earth's crust is evidenced by the general subsidence of the area (the entire Jordan River Valley from the Sea of Galilee through the Dead Sea is below sea level) and by earthquakes that have been recorded in recent times.

NEW MOUNTAINS AND EARTHQUAKES

New oceans are formed when continent-bearing plates are moved away from one another by sea-floor spreading. Conversely, when plates are pushed against one another, mountains are formed. In recent times, geologically speaking, the collision of plates is thought to be responsible for some of the world's greatest mountain chains. The subcontinent of India is thought to have moved from its position in the southwestern Pacific Ocean and collided violently with south-

FIGURE 5.12.

The rugged mountains near the Bedretto Valley, Switzerland, are a young mountain belt. (Photoswissair)

FIGURE 5.13.

The lateral movement of plates along the San Andreas fault in California. Displacements of distinctive geologic formations indicate that during the past several million years, movement has been at a rate of about 1 centimeter (0.4 in.) per year in northern and central California. Measurements of displacement that has occurred during the last century indicates an average rate of recent movement of about 5 centimeters (2 in.) per year.

ern Asia 50 million years ago. The force of this collision wrinkled and elevated the Earth's crust into the Himalayas (continued uplift is still in process today). Similarly, the Alps were probably formed when Italy was driven like a huge nail into Europe by the African plate.

Plates are also known to slip laterally past each other. The infamous earthquake-causing San Andreas fault in California is due, not to the collision of two plates, but to their lateral movement in opposite directions (see figure 5.13). The western plate which includes Los Angeles, Baja California, and the ocean is moving northward. The eastern plate which comprises the continental United States including most of California is moving southward. If these movements continue, Los Angeles will one day, 50 million years from now, be in Alaska. It will pass what is left of San Francisco on the journey north. Lest southern California real estate investors became nervous about the climate in Alaska, it should be pointed out that their real estate is moving only at the snail's pace of less than one inch a year.

Californians should be far more worried about earthquakes. The plates don't appear to move at a uniform rate along their boundaries at the fault line. Instead they build up tension and stress like a spring or rubber band. When the frictional bond finally breaks, the elastic strain of energy is released in the form of intense seismic vibrations called an earthquake. The last truly large movements along the San Andreas fault were felt in the destructive San Francisco earthquake of 1906 and the earthquake of 1940 in the Imperial Valley in southeastern California. Geologists predict that another large quake is in the offing in the near future.

Earthquakes and volcanic activity are most common at or near plate boundaries. The famous "ring of fire" around the volcanic island arc of the eastern Pacific Ocean is a good example of such a plate boundary. Peru and Chile also lie on an active plate boundary and are known for devastating earthquakes.

In a broad sense, nothing is fixed in place. We have seen in Chapter 1 that all the galaxies in the Universe are moving away from each other at enormous speeds. Our Solar System is revolving about the center of the Milky Way Galaxy, and the Earth is revolving around the Sun. The Earth itself is spinning around its own axis requiring twenty-four hours for a complete rotation. Here on Earth the oceans of the world have changed position over time. The water molecules themselves have been recycled through the atmosphere and fresh water systems about once every 2 million years.

FIGURE 5.14.

The California earthquake of 1906, due to slippage along the San Andreas fault, left an offset of more than 8 feet in this fence near Bolinas, California.

The crust of the Earth is divided into plates which move about the surface of the globe while floating on a semi-molten underlayer. The ocean floor itself is changing. New basaltic ocean floor material wells up from the mantle at the Mid-Atlantic Rift. Where it meets a continent-bearing plate at its other end, the heavy oceanic crust dives beneath the lighter continental plate to be remelted by the hot asthenosphere below. Some of the oceanic crust's lighter materials may be welded onto the continent, or rise from the depths to create volcanoes, or simply add material to the bottom of the continent to elevate it higher above the oceans.

Continents themselves grow by the contributions from these oceanic plates and by adding sediments of their own as erosion wears down the mountain ranges. The Mississippi delta is constantly growing. The ancient city of Ur in southern Iraq, hometown of Abraham, was once almost a coastal town. Now that the delta of the Tigris and Euphrates rivers has extended into the Persian Gulf, Ur is many miles inland. Similarly, the great trade center of Ephesus was dependent upon its Mediterranean seaport. As the harbor filled with silt, the city lost its vital harbor and declined in importance.

We know that mountains and valleys and rivers and seas change their positions over time. We also know that the continents themselves slowly move about the globe. But can the moving continents themselves be considered essentially transitory features? Do they too disappear to be recycled?

The answer is basically no. In contrast to the crustal floor of the ocean whose oldest known age is 160 million years, the continents contain at their centers great granitic bases that date between 2.5 and 3.5 billion years ago. Where these granitic bases or cratons are exposed to the surface they are called shields. The extensive Canadian Shield of eastern Canada is the best-known geologic example. These basement rocks extend under a major portion of the United States.

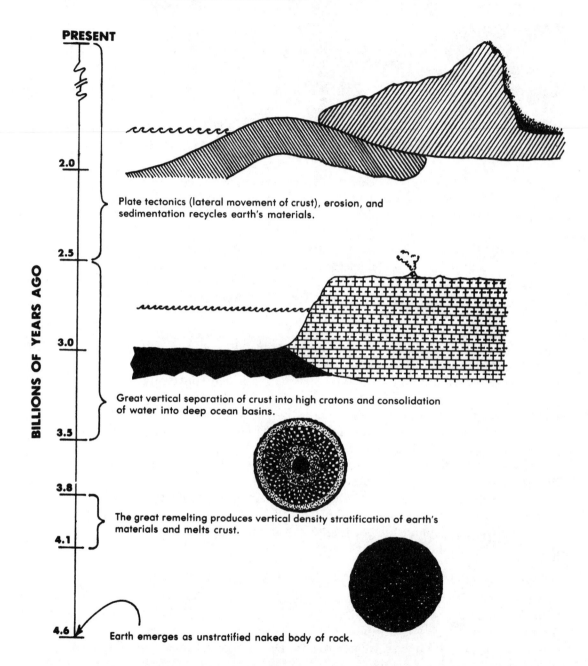

Figure 5.15 Time Scale of the Earth's Land Formation

They are not visible because they are buried by sediment or covered by overthrust mountains.

These granitic continental cratons form the enduring core of the continents. Thus, while continents are added to or reduced on their margins by erosion and collisions, and while they move in relation to each other, they have remained essentially permanent features since their creation during the great vertical movements of the crust 2.5 to 3.5 billion years ago.

WHAT ALL THIS MEANS

Geologists feel they have found the answer to recent geologic and geographic events in the theory of plate tectonics. It should be borne in mind, however, that this process is apparently dependent on unique concentrations and densities of elements and materials in rather specific locations in the core, mantle, and crust of the Earth. The concentration of specific elements in the total Earth is unexplained, but it is apparently connected with the initial formation of the planet Earth from its nebular cloud of gas and dust. The *vertical* separation of material by density so that the heavier materials sink toward the core of the Earth and lighter materials rise toward the crust is in accordance with the law of gravity.

The crucial question is what caused the *lateral* separation of materials at the crust of the Earth into light granitic continents and heavy basaltic ocean basins in the first place. Gravity can account for the separation and sorting of materials in a *vertical* plane. But how did the *lateral* separation of the heavy oceanic material and the light continents occur at the Earth's crust? Until the massive granitic cratons appeared and formed platform-like continents, the process of plate tectonics could not begin.

What caused the first land to appear? We can speculate that, like the later operation of plate tectonics, the explanation has something to do with cooling the Earth's finely tuned heat engine. But the fact is we simply do not know why the first lands appeared. There is no observed, similar process operating today, and synthesizing granite in the laboratory remains unaccomplished. Perhaps scientific thinking is faced with a "gap" or unexplained cause that only God's creation command "Let the dry land appear" can answer.

What would the surface of the Earth look like without the lateral separation by density into the light high-riding lands and the heavy

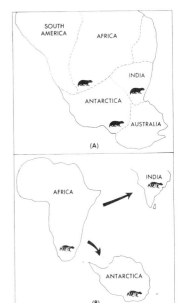

FIGURE 5.16.

Evidence that continents were once joined together is provided by the fossil remains of *Lystrosaurus,* a medium-sized reptile with distinctive skeletal characteristics that included large downward-pointing tusks. *Lystrosaurus* lived during the early Triassic period (about 200 million years ago) and neither it nor its close relatives could have crossed the oceans that now separate the continents of India, Africa, and Antarctica. Yet the fossilized remains of *Lystrosaurus* are found in Triassic formations on each of those continents.

FIGURE 5.17.

Foundation failure of buildings designed to withstand
earthquakes. The structures
toppled intact during the earthquake of 1964 in Niigata, Japan.

deep ocean basins? Essentially it would be a nearly even rock surface. Little or no erosion and uplift of lands could occur, and the
planet would be incapable of its constant cycle of geological renewal
through plate tectonics.

More importantly, the relatively even surface would be overlaid by
an outer layer of water and ice that would cover the entire surface of
the Earth to a depth of more than one mile. This is essentially the
picture of the planet Earth before the creation of the first lands and
the gathering of the waters into deep connecting ocean basins. The
Earth with its towering mountains, deep valleys, and mighty oceans,
and with its continual process of geological renewal may be a very
special planet in the Universe.

The creation of the first lands took place in real time in scientific
history. The surface of the Earth was blanketed by water. The shallow
seas were then gathered into interconnecting deep ocean basins and
the dry land did in fact appear. How beautifully Scripture reflects this
reality when it says: "Then God said, 'Let the waters below the
heavens be gathered into one place, and let the dry land appear'; and
it was so" (Gen. 1:9).

How timely that in this age of cynicism scientific evidence should
concur so perfectly with God's Word.

CHAPTER 6
THE SEEDS OF LIFE

Then God said, "Let the earth sprout vegetation, plants yielding seed, and fruit trees bearing fruit after their kind, with seed in them, on the earth;" and it was so.
Genesis 1:11

At the end of the first billion years of the Earth's history the surface of the planet had been transformed from a naked body of rock to one covered by a shallow sea. This blanket of water was in turn surrounded by a dense atmosphere of carbon dioxide, nitrogen, and water vapor.

At approximately the same time as the first land rose up out of this shallow sea, life made its appearance. This radical new factor—the appearance of living things—is so important and its origins so controversial that it will be dealt with at length later in this chapter. First, however, it is necessary to explore what the fossil record has to reveal about the progressive development of vegetation on the planet Earth.

THAT CURIOUS BLUE-GREEN ALGAE

The fossil record of the first life begins 3.5 billion years ago with structural traces of bacteria and bacteria-like blue-green algae, organisms still with us today. Fossil evidence for the possible existence of these microscopic organisms at this early date comes from the sedimentary rocks of western Australia. Examination of thin sections of these rocks under high-powered microscopes has revealed remnants that some scientists have identified as simple filamentous bacteria (see figure 6.2). These remains are identified today by the presence of *stromatolites*. Stromatolites are not actual organisms, but are deposits thought to have been laid down by blue-green algae. We are able to observe blue-green algae laying down similar deposits today in tidal mud flats (see figures 6.1 and 6.3). The discovery of scattered algae

bodies within these fossil stromatolites indicates the ancient presence of blue-green algae in the waters of the Earth.

Blue-green algae are single-celled microscopic organisms. More than 1500 species are presently in existence exhibiting many different forms and structures (see figure 6.4). Some are present in single cells, others as small colonies, and others as multicellular filaments. Their cell walls are very similar in composition and structure to those of bacteria. In fact, blue-green algae are sometimes called *cyanobacteria* (blue-colored bacteria) because of this close similarity.

Blue-green algae differ from bacteria in one very important respect: blue-green algae are endowed with the remarkable capability of releasing oxygen through *photosynthesis*. (The importance of this

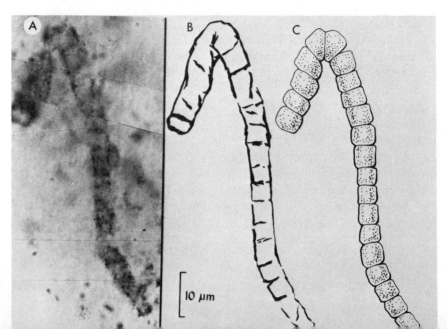

process in changing the atmosphere and preparing the way for subsequent life will be covered in chapter 7.) For much of the first 2 billion years of the history of life, mats of blue-green algae may have floated like rafts in the oceans of the world. Until slightly more than 1 billion years ago, blue-green algae and other forms of bacteria-like microscopic cells were the dominant and virtually exclusive life forms on Earth. These life forms are called *prokaryotes*.

Biologists make a major distinction at the cellular level between life forms. Cells such as bacteria and blue-green algae that lack an organized nucleus are known as *prokaryotes*. Prokaryotes reproduce by simple asexual division wherein the cell simply divides into two new identical cells (binary fission). This process is also known as vegetative reproduction.

The other biological classification at the cellular level is known as *eukaryotes*. Other than the plant-like blue-green algae, all plants and animals are eukaryotes. Their cells contain an organized and well-defined nucleus. Organisms classified as eukaryotes generally contain many cells (multicellular), which may be different in both form and function. Our own bodies, for example, contain billions of diverse and complex cells.

Eukaryotes are generally both larger and vastly more complex than simple prokaryotes. The cells of eukaryotes also contain chromosomes which make them capable of sexual reproduction with the potential to provide more varied life forms through genetic interchanges. Eukaryotes made their appearance in the form of red, green, and brown algae about one billion years ago.

LAND-DWELLING PLANTS

The fossil record indicates that land-dwelling plants appeared about 400 million years ago in the form of horsetails, club mosses, and ferns. These plants were restricted to moist wetland environments and reproduced through spores rather than seeds. Lush tree ferns and giant palm-like evergreens formed a rich swampy vegetation whose remains have benefited mankind in rich deposits of coal. The first seed-bearing plants appeared shortly thereafter in the form of seed ferns and conifers familiar to us today as pine, cedar, and fir trees.

Until 130 million years ago the Earth's landscape was a leafy vastness of monotonous and drab greenery. Not a single flower blossomed. Then, in an incredibly brief span of 10 million years, the *Big*

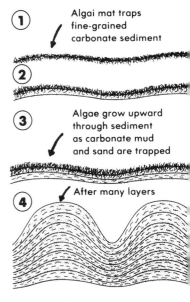

FIGURE 6.3.

Stages in the growth of stromatolite formed by the sediment-trapping action of algae. As the sediment accumulates, the previously deposited layers become cemented and lithified. The convex upward structures range in size from a few centimeters to more than a meter in diameter. The laminae are typically a few millimeters thick. (From *Earth*, 3rd ed., by F. Press and R. Siever. Copyright © 1982 by W.H. Freeman and Co. All rights reserved.)

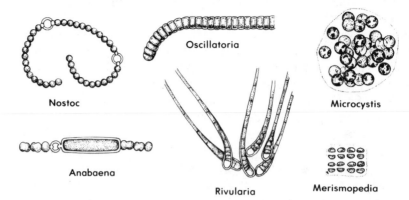

Bloom, the explosion of the flowering plants or *angiosperms* took place. Later, about 62 million years ago, grasses appeared to complete the roster of our modern vegetative types. The landscape had changed from its initial monotonous greenery of ferns, mosses, and pines to its present panorama of varied colors and radiant beauty.

THE QUESTION OF SOURCE

Blue-green algae and bacteria appeared in the fossil record several billion years ago. How did they come into existence? How did vegetative life begin? Science has no consistent answer to this question.

First of all, there is no fossil record of how life began. Secondly, there is obviously no evidence from direct observation for no human

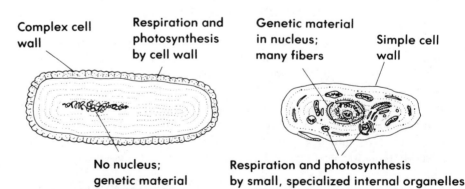

FIGURE 6.5.

Prokaryotic and eukaryotic cells.

80

beings were there to see it. Thirdly, although scientists can suggest possible answers to the question of how vegetative life began, the theoretical problem is both difficult and extremely complex. Many hypotheses have been proposed. All of them have their problems, and as a result there is no standard theoretical "model" for the origin of life.

Nevertheless, there have been some impressive experiments performed in the laboratory. Graduating high school and college students often have the impression that these experiments demonstrate that life evolved "naturally" by random chance on the planet Earth.

In fact, primordial life has not been created in the test tube. Science has not come close to creating initial life. It is true that amino acids (the building blocks of protein) have been created from organic and inorganic compounds, and there have been some other impressive experimental results. But those who think science has come even reasonably close to solving the problem of the creation of initial life simply do not understand the problem.

FIGURE 6.6.

Leaf impressions of the extinct fern-like plant *Callipteris conferta* from the Hermit Shale. (From *Geology Illustrated* by John S. Shelton. W. H. Freeman and Co. Copyright © 1966.)

FIGURE 6.7.

Reconstruction of a coal-forming forest of the Pennsylvanian period. (Courtesy Field Museum of Natural History, Chicago.)

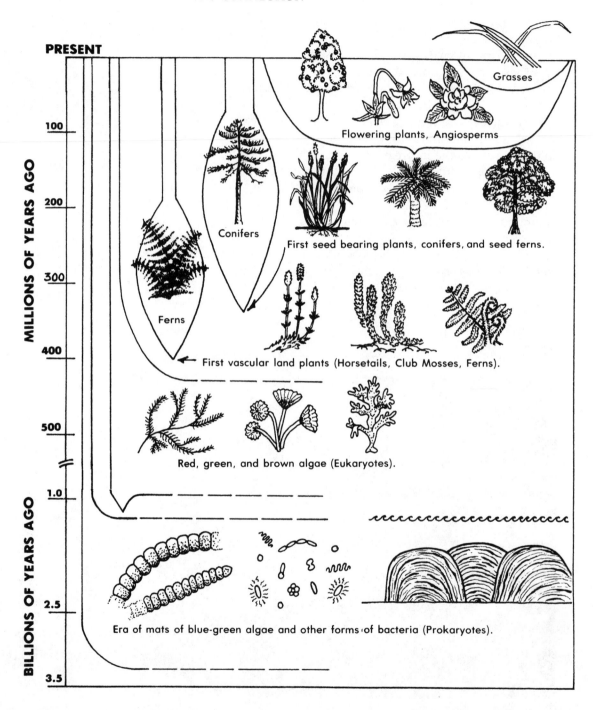

Figure 6.8 Time Scale of the Earth's Vegetation

MAKING THE FIRST CELL

The creation of the first living cell or biological unit of life will be broken down into seven stages as follows:

1. Basic raw materials.
2. Energy source and proper environment.
3. Monomers (basic organic molecules): amino acids, sugars, phosphates, and organic bases.
4. Polymers: polypeptides and polynucleotides.
5. Clumping: microspheres and coacervates.
6. Completed components: proteins, enzymes, and nucleic acid.
7. First living cell.

These stages are shown schematically in Figure 6.9.

Stage 1. *Basic Raw Materials.* Through volcanic processes the Earth outgassed its atmosphere of water vapor and dense gases. As the Earth's crust cooled, the water vapor condensed to form shallow seas. Many gases were retained by the Earth in its atmosphere. In addition to water vapor, these included carbon dioxide (CO_2), carbon monoxide (CO), methane (CH_4), ammonia (NH_3), together with nitrogen (N) and hydrogen sulfide (H_2S).

The list of materials above sounds like a formula for acid rain, and some of these components were undoubtedly condensed into the primeval seas as the rains fell. Not only were these raw materials present in the waters and atmosphere of the early Earth, but recent studies of interstellar space have indicated that many of these compounds exist there as well. In addition, meteorites that have fallen to Earth also contain carbon-rich compounds. The origin of life involves many unsolved problems, but the presence of abundant raw materials is not one of them.

Stage 2. *Energy Source and Proper Environment.* To transform the raw materials of life to the next stage and beyond requires energy. Available energy existed in several forms, one of which was energy from the Sun. This source was a mixed blessing. While it could supply energy, it could also destroy biological life that was not shielded from its ultraviolet rays because the Earth was not protected by an ozone screen during the formation of early life. Moreover, recent observations of young stars suggest that our primordial Sun

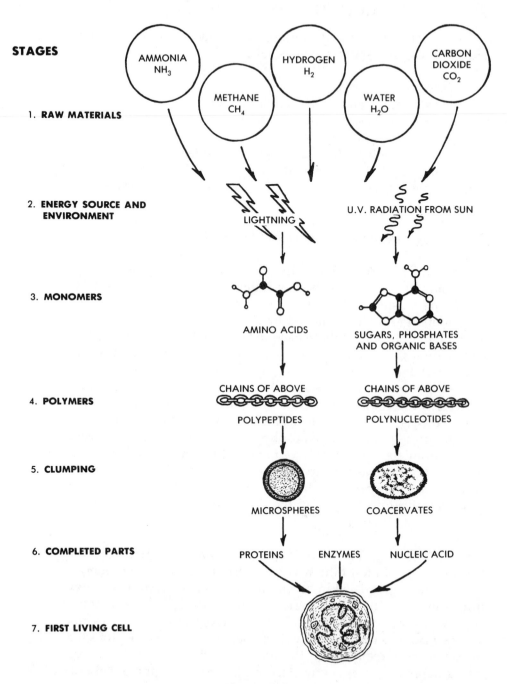

STAGES

1. **RAW MATERIALS**

2. **ENERGY SOURCE AND ENVIRONMENT**

3. **MONOMERS**

4. **POLYMERS**

5. **CLUMPING**

6. **COMPLETED PARTS**

7. **FIRST LIVING CELL**

Figure 6.9

may have emitted up to ten thousand times more ultraviolet radiation than it does today.[1] Life-destroying ultraviolet rays were therefore a constant threat to early life.

Energy sources also existed in the form of lightning from the numerous storms that must have racked the Earth during primeval times. Electrical energy is a source used often in experiments. Thermal energy from hot springs and volcanoes was also present and could possibly have supplied the necessary energy for life.

An essential component for life is, of course, water. Water comprises 80% to 90% of all living matter. We know that the surface of the Earth was virtually covered with water so that a plentiful supply was available. Mixing processes existed in the form of water currents, waves, and tides. Wind and volcanic action may also have been important in distributing and mixing various chemical elements and compounds.

Even though it could not sustain life as we know it today, the smog-like atmosphere of carbon dioxide, methane, and ammonia was perfect for the beginning of life. Life could not have begun in the oxygen-rich atmosphere we presently enjoy. It would simply have burned up (oxidized) the organic compounds through chemical combination with them.

Energy sources and the oxygen-free environment necessary for primitive life on the early Earth were present. They will be discussed in detail in the following chapter. With the important exception of the life-destroying ultraviolet radiation from the Sun, they present no severe problems for the origin of life.

Stage 3. *Monomers (basic organic molecules).* Monomers are simple organic molecules, sort of molecular sub-units, from which, by repeated linking actions, polymers (chains of monomers) can be made. Amino acids are monomers that form polypeptides. Sugars, phosphates, and organic bases are monomers that combine to form polynucleotides.

Amino acids. To account for the formation of amino acids is not difficult. In 1953 Stanley Miller, a biochemist working in the laboratory of Nobel Prize chemist Harold Urey, conducted significant experiments using the apparatus pictured in Figure 6.10. The gases used were those thought to have been present in the primordial atmosphere, and he used intermittent spark discharges to simulate lightning. The result was the synthesis of several common amino acid molecules.

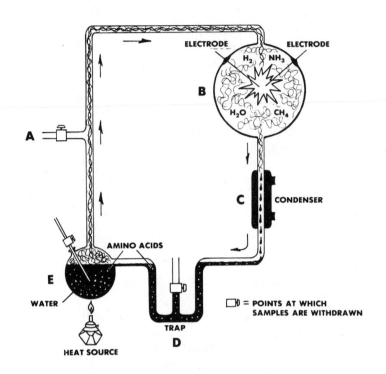

FIGURE 6.10.

The Miller-Urey apparatus for synthesizing organic compounds. Various mixtures of gases thought to have been present in the Earth's primordial atmosphere are introduced at point A. They are subjected to a spark discharge at point B to stimulate the energy input of lightning. A heat source at point E boils water to force a continuous circulation of gas through the system. Amino acids and other organic compounds collect primarily at point D. The final formation of amino acids is the result of a series of consecutive intermediate reactions typically requiring about a week's time. Further, after amino acids are formed they must be isolated from the energy source or it will cause them to disassociate.

These experiments have since been repeated by Miller and others using a variety of gases and also substituting ultraviolet radiation for the spark discharges. Many common forms of amino acids found in proteins have been produced.

It should be noted that recent work performed by Joel Levine of NASA's Langley Research Center suggests that the laboratory experiments of the past thirty years have been conducted using the wrong mixture of atmospheric gases.[2] Levine's computer model simulations suggest that the primary components of the primordial atmosphere were water vapor, carbon dioxide, and nitrogen with a small amount of oxygen also present. The methane and ammonia used by Miller and others is thought to have been chemically unstable and therefore very short-lived, if indeed these compounds existed at all. While the yields are less using Levine's carbon dioxide, water vapor, and nitrogen mixture, some complex organic molecules essential for the formation of life have been produced in laboratory experiments.

There are twenty kinds of amino acids found in biological proteins today. One of the interesting sidelights of laboratory experiments has been the production of numerous types of amino acids that are not part of present biological systems. Why the particular twenty amino acids are the only ones used to form proteins is unknown.

Another interesting aspect of the chemical synthesis of amino acids in the laboratory is that an equal number of what are known as left-handed and right-handed molecules are produced. Yet proteins in all living systems use only left-handed molecules, or to use a hardware analogy, a left-threaded system of nuts and bolts for linkages. Right-handed threads on a bolt will not fit into a nut with left-handed threading. In the same way, the two systems of molecules are incompatible for building chains of amino acids. Yet the molecular components of both systems are produced in equal numbers in the laboratory.

There are two implications to these observations. One is that life arose only once. For if life had arisen many times we would expect to find right-handed systems in proteins as well as left-handed ones. The second implication is that some selective force or mechanism was involved in the selection of the standard twenty amino acids used to construct proteins in existence today.

ORGANIC COMPOUNDS AND THE DEFINITION OF LIFE

The difference between organic and inorganic compounds is basically a chemical distinction. An organic compound is one in which the element carbon is directly united with hydrogen or nitrogen. Organic compounds are the chemical materials of which living things are composed. Of themselves, they are not life. Methane (CH_4) is an organic compound. It is obviously not life nor is it living.

There are several important characteristics of life such as the capacity to respond to outside stimuli and spontaneous movement (locomotion). However, for an object to be alive, it must have at least two key characteristics. First, it must have *metabolism*—it must exhibit internal chemical activity whereby nutrients are utilized for growth, repair, and maintenance. Second, it must have *reproductive capability*—it must be able to produce new individuals like itself. If an object possesses both these capabilities, it will probably be judged to be alive.

Table 6.1

Sugars. Theoretically, it is not difficult to account for the synthesis of sugars under prebiotic (pre-biological life) conditions. The raw material (formaldehyde) is thought to have been present, and the chemical process is relatively simple. Balancing the national budget is also very simple in theory. The problem is achieving this balanced budget in the "real" world. The same holds true for the synthesis of sugar under prebiotic conditions. Sugars are very unstable and chemically reactive substances especially in an aqueous (watery) solution. To date, no sugars have been recovered in the laboratory under the requisite prebiotic conditions.

Organic Bases. Some of the organic bases have been produced under prebiotic (pre-life) laboratory conditions. *Adenine* is the best-known example, and it is remarkably stable and resistant to destruction. Other bases have not, to my knowledge, been successfully synthesized in the laboratory. These are known as the *pyrimidine* bases: *thymine, uracil,* and *cytosine.* Their chemical structure differs in that pyrimidine bases have a six-sided ring with nitrogen at the 1 and 3 positions.

Before completing the discussion of the formation of monomers (the molecular sub-units of life), it may be well to summarize what has been accomplished in the laboratory under prebiotic conditions. Some of the amino acids needed for proteins have been synthesized. Some of the organic bases needed for nucleic acid have been synthesized; others have not. Sugars have not been synthesized in the laboratory under what are thought to be prebiotic conditions.

This indicates that more than 30% and maybe up to 40% of the non-living sub-units for life have demonstrably been synthesized by "natural" processes in the laboratory. But there is no such thing as a potential 40% life. Matter is either 100% alive or it is not alive. And we are not yet talking about life; we are talking about non-living organic molecules that make up the building blocks of life. But let us assume for now that all the organic molecules have been brought into existence. Let us further assume that some presently unknown force is selecting only those relatively few organic molecules known to be useful in constructing living systems. Now the truly difficult part begins.

Stage 4. *Polymers—polypeptides and polynucleotides.* The first problem with bringing about the formation of polypeptides (chains of amino acids) and polynucleotides (chains of organic bases and sugars) is in forging this linkage. A water molecule must be driven off at each link in the molecular chain. Yet water is presumably needed as both a mixing and solution medium to bring the molecules together. Driving off the water molecule at each link in the chain in order to forge the linkage requires energy. Furthermore, nucleotides are high-energy molecules which would probably not exist for any length of time in a water solution.

In present-day biological linkages this energy is transferred by what is called the Krebs cycle, which is essentially a sequence of enzymatic reactions that involve the oxidation of a two-carbon acetyl molecule unit resulting in carbon dioxide and water, which provide energy to increase ADP (adenosine diphosphate) to ATP (adenosine triphosphate) and back again. The problem is that in experiments to create the first life, the Krebs cycle and the ATP which it requires do not yet exist.

The second problem in forming polypeptides and polynucleotides is known as the "concentration gap." This is basically the problem of concentrating the essential biologically active compounds in "primordial soup" from a diluted to a concentrated state. The monomers could then come into close contact and increase their chances of connecting into polymers, but there is no known natural mechanism to bring this about. Brownian forces would actually cause diffusion of concentrated solutions into dilute ones.

Further, while it is possible to imagine a simple process of polymerization whereby monomers link up to form chains of polymers, it should be noted that if a polymer comes into contact with water, the molecules are likely to dissociate, break the chain, and yield the original amino acids. In fact this polymer to monomer reaction known as hydrolyzation requires no energy. In the presence of water it can occur spontaneously.

The problems of dehydration and concentration are generally solved by proposing that the primordial soup existed in a "warm little pond" that evaporated. This would both concentrate and dry out the monomers so that the polymer chains would have a chance to form. There are two major problems with this scenario. The first is that the numerous other molecules present would also concentrate, greatly lessening the chances of the "correct" molecules coming into contact. Too many other molecules of the "wrong sort" would be in the way.

This negative concentration effect would be especially pronounced in sea water. One has only to visit the Great Salt Lake near Salt Lake City, Utah, to see the effects of evaporation in salt water. Salt molecules would greatly outnumber amino acid molecules (10,000 to 1 by some estimates[3]). Further, high salt concentration is destructive to life. The Dead Sea is lifeless because of its salt concentration, not because of lack of water.

The second major problem with the synthesis of polymer chains in the evaporating primordial pond is that as the pond dries out, it exposes organic molecules to ultraviolet raditation which destroys them. How is this problem solved?

A great deal of thought has been given to clay as the medium for concentration, dehydration, and protection from ultraviolet radiation. Mineral-bearing clays are an attractive medium because they contain many sheets and layered surfaces that absorb organic molecules quite effectively. They also exhibit a degree of selectivity, that is they tend to absorb some molecules more easily than others.

It is also thought that the minerals in clays may have served as inorganic primitive catalysts that selectively speeded up certain reaction rates. The control of the rate of such reactions is highly important in successful polymerization. An Israeli scientist, Aharon Katchalsky, has shown that montmorillonite clays tend to promote the formation of some amino acids into protein-like polypeptide chains. Mineral-bearing clays could have been the templates upon which life was forged and assembled.

But like other mediums for concentration, clay has its limitations, including the fact that materials in clay tend to be subject to ultraviolet degradation. Nevertheless, clay remains a promising area for research.

Stage 5. *Clumping: microspheres and coacervates.* Assuming that polypeptides and polynucleotides could be produced from scratch in the laboratory, the next problem is that of isolating them into bound cellular units with a chemistry and identity of their own. The problem of isolation and concentration has been approached by Sidney Fox of the University of Miami. Fox has heated dry mixtures of amino acids to moderate temperatures and produced what he calls thermal *proteinoids*. When heated in a concentrated aqueous solution they have grouped spontaneously into *microspheres* (see figure 6.11). Under certain conditions they have also been known to bud in a manner similar to bacteria.

The Russian biochemist Alexander Oparin, who originally proposed that life arose spontaneously from the "primordial soup," also produced polymer-rich colloidal droplets in his Moscow laboratory. He found that various combinations of biologic polymers suspended

FIGURE 6.11.

Structured proteinoid microspheres. (From *Molecular Evolution and the Origin of Life*, by S. Fox and K. Dose. Copyright © 1972 by W. H. Freeman and Co.)

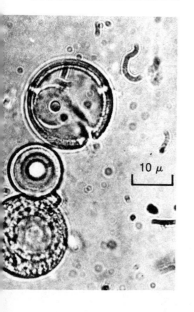

10 μ

in water will join together spontaneously into polymer-rich colloidal droplets called *coacervates.*

The major problem with both the Fox and Oparin experiments is that they don't represent the "real" world. Fox starts with dried and concentrated powders of amino acids. Oparin starts with biologic polymers and adds biologic enzymes for stabilization. How would these have occurred in the "real" world? Further, neither experiment has come anywhere even remotely near to producing life, only objects that are similar or analogous to some aspects of life. Nevertheless, the experiments are useful in demonstrating natural properties of substances. They suggest possible pathways for the original grouping of substances if properly dried and prepared and then placed in water.

Stage 6. *Completed Components: proteins, enzymes, and nucleic acid.* As we have proceeded through the stages in the hypothetical origins of life, we have encountered many problems and we have found laboratory solutions to only a few of these. Imaginative and wishful thinking has supplied speculative solutions to some of the other problems. But the simple fact remains that no prebiotic proteins, enzymes, or nucleic acids have been produced under simulated primordial conditions. Why not?

To understand perhaps the central problem involved in building proteins, enzymes, and nucleic acids we need to examine Table 6.2 on page 92, the critical components of life. The magnitude of the problem of stage 6 becomes apparent. We see that we must have all three components to make life: proteins for structural materials; enzymes to assemble the components, in effect as tools; and genes, nucleic acid (DNA and RNA), for blueprints and direction. There are four very basic problems involved.

The first problem is that we need to assemble the amino acids into proteins so that we can have structural material. The problem is that the tools (the enzymes) we need to use for assembly are composed of the same structural material we are trying to make. To use an analogy, you can't make steel (the structural material) without tools which are also made of steel.

The second major problem involves the construction of the nucleic acid (DNA)—the blueprints. The paradox is that DNA cannot be assembled without specific enzymes (the right tools), and the enzymes can't be made or at least duplicated without DNA (blueprints). Until there is DNA, there can be no biological duplication

CRITICAL COMPONENTS OF LIFE

Components	Assembled Organic Compounds	Function
Structural Materials	Proteins (assembled from amino acids)	Construction (shape and mobility)
Tools and Machinery	Enzymes (special forms of proteins)	Metabolism (growth and maintenance)
Blueprints	Genes–Nucleic Acid (DNA and RNA)	Reproduction (information and directive function)

A living cell is made up of a number of enormously varied proteins and nucleic acids. All components are highly specific to each other. For example, only a highly specific enzyme can assemble a particular protein from amino acids (the right wrench sizes must be used for the right bolt sizes). Also, only highly specific enzymes can be used to assemble a particular nucleic acid.

Proteins, the base materials of life, are made from specific numbers and kinds of organic building blocks called amino acids. There are about eighty amino acids in nature, but only twenty are important to present life as we know it.

DNA (information) and RNA (transfer and coding) are made from four kinds of molecules (nucleotide bases). These must be strung together in very precise linear arrays on spiral chains of sugars and high energy phosphate molecules. The resulting nucleic acids provide the basis for the coding and transfer of the genetic information necessary for replication.

Table 6.2

and therefore no "natural selection." The basis of biological evolution cannot operate without a mechanism for biological duplication.

The third problem is the need for the special organic material known as lipids to enclose and protect the first living cell. To my knowledge these have not been produced in the laboratory by what are assumed to be prebiotic methods.

The fourth problem is the need for some form of mutual recognition between the structural proteins, the enzymes, and the nucleic acids so they will function together as a living cell. Engineers designing computers are well aware of the need for compatible parts that communicate in a common "language." Who designed this compatibility into the component parts of the first biologic cell?

Scientists have three speculative though possible answers to these problems. The first answer is that life began by means of more simple precursor molecules that we know nothing about. While this is certainly possible, it leaves us with a new problem—How? We need a new hypothesis and laboratory experiments to test it. The mystery remains.

The second answer is that the first tools (enzymes) may have been chemical catalysts such as clay minerals. Metal-bearing clays may have played a key role in the origin of life. This too is a possible answer, but validation must await successful experiments.

The third possible answer is that all three assembled components for life simply appeared at the same place at the same time. They somehow recognized each other, fell in love, and embraced. With biological life initiated and a plentiful supply of food and no competition, initial population growth would have been rapid. Once begun, biological life would be virtually impossible to stop. What are the chances of this scenario happening by random chance?

Listen to Robert Jastrow's answer:

> According to this story, every tree, every blade of grass, and every creature in the sea and on the land evolved out of one parent strand of molecular matter drifting lazily in a warm pool.
> What concrete evidence supports this remarkable theory of the origin of life? There is none.[4]

Many scientists believe that the statistical probability of the correct sequence of components and their correct assembly by chance is so small that it would not occur during billions of years on billions of planets, given that each planet was covered with a watery solution of the necessary amino acids.[5] Most scientists who believe in prebiotic chemical synthesis either believe that some presently unknown directive or selective process had to be involved or that life began through presently undiscovered channels.

Although life could have started on Earth as a result of random chance (accidents do happen), the present scientific evidence does not support this conclusion. A tornado may strike a junkyard and the result may be the space shuttle, but most of us would have to see it to believe it.

THE HEART OF THE MATTER

How did life originate on Earth? We don't know, but Robert Jastrow hits the issue squarely, offering us two—and only two—choices:

> Perhaps the appearance of life on the earth is a miracle. Scientists are reluctant to accept that view, but their choices are limited; *either* life was created on the earth by the will of a being outside the grasp of scientific understanding, *or* it evolved on our planet spontaneously, through chemical reactions occurring in non-living matter lying on the surface of the planet.
>
> The first theory places the question of the origin of life beyond the realm of scientific inquiry. It is a statement of faith in the power of a Supreme Being not subject to the laws of science.
>
> The second theory is also an act of faith. The act of faith consists in assuming that the scientific view of the origin of life is correct, without having concrete evidence to support that belief.[8]

The above statements by Robert Jastrow focus our choices into a fundamental decision between *Creator* and *no-creator*. They also emphasize that faith is required in either choice. However, an unnecessary wedge may be driven between science and religion if Jastrow's statements are not given more careful scrutiny.

It is certainly true that those who hold the world view or philosophy of *no-creator* must believe (or have faith) that life arose through *spontaneous* prebiotic chemical synthesis. That is, *causation* for the first living cells must be attributed to *random chance* and *"natural" mechanistic forces*. This position presupposes that there is no Creator involved in the presence of the raw materials, the requisite energy and forces, and in their selective assembly into life.

In contrast to this belief system, those of us who believe in the *Creator*, believe that the *causation* for the origin of life (whether by prebiotic chemical synthesis or by more direct means) is due to the action of God. However, those of us who believe in biblical creation must be very clear what we mean when we say that the origin of life is due to the action of God. Certainly we mean that God, not blind chance or random accident, created life. But do we require God to create vegetative life *ex nihilo* (out of nothing)? Or does the interpretation of Scripture allow for the use of inorganic materials to assemble

---

STATISTICAL PROBABILITY OF LIFE ORIGINATING BY RANDOM CHANCE

Statement 1: Referring to the view of scientists who have rejected the idea of spontaneous biogenesis, W. Lee Stokes writes:

"The problem of synthesizing one simple protein of about 300 amino acids has been cited. It is assumed that the protein must be synthesized, by a gene with at least 1000 nucleotides in its chain, the nucleotides being the four basic chemical units of which genes are built—adenine, thymine, guanine, and cytosine. A chain of 1000 nucleotides made of the four basic units might exist in any of 41,000 ways, but only one will form the protein being sought. The chance that the correct sequence would be achieved by simple random combination is said to be so small that it would not occur during billions of years on billions of planets, each covered by a blanket of a concentrated watery solution of the necessary amino acids."[6]

Stokes then comments that there are other biologists who think life may have originated with smaller, less complicated duplicating entities that would have a greater chance of occurring spontaneously.

Statement 2: In dealing with the subject of origin in natural selection, the critical paradox of the problem becomes apparent. As the classic work *Evolution* by Dobzhansky, Ayala, Stebbins, and Valentine states:

"Both nucleic acids and proteins are required to function before selection can act at present, and yet the origin of this association is too improbable to have occurred without selection."[7]

It appears neither nucleic acids nor proteins could have occurred by themselves under the laws of statistical probability. It's the chicken or the egg problem.

Table 6.3

vegetative life? In other words, does a literal rendering of Genesis 1:11–12 preclude God's use of the preexisting materials and the energy sources He had created in His previous creation commands? In attempting to answer this question, we must look more closely at the words used in the Genesis account.

Many people are under the impression that each creation command in Genesis states that God *created* (Hebrew *bārā*), as opposed to formed or *fashioned* (Hebrew *yāṣar*), the object brought into being. A close look at Genesis reveals that, in the case of vegetative life, the Hebrew word *bārā*, which translates creation of a new and original object, is *not* used. In fact, the word *bārā* is only used for the creation of the heavens and the earth (1:1), animal life in the sea (1:21), and man (1:27). The implications of the special use of *bārā* (create) will be further explored in Chapter 9. For now it is important to note that with respect to the specific process by which God created vegetative life, Genesis reads: "Then God said, 'Let the earth sprout vegetation . . . .' And the earth brought forth vegetation . . ." (Gen. 1:11–12).

It appears to me that such language does not negate the use by God of inorganic compounds contained in dust, clay, water, etc., for use in the formation and assembly of vegetative life. In fact, I would like to suggest that the words used, "Let the earth sprout . . . And the earth brought forth," give us meaningful insight into His creation process. Scripture appears to be saying that God actually did use materials from the Earth or earthy materials (i.e., inorganic compounds) in His creation of vegetative life.

The scientist and the student of science who are also Christians are therefore on solid scriptural grounds when exploring prebiotic chemical synthesis. What the Christian cannot accept is the no-creator presupposition that the process happened *spontaneously*, i.e., by random chance or fortuitous accident. In fact, many who apparently hold the no-creator philosophy find this particular area a troublesome point in their chosen belief system because there is simply no concrete evidence to support the remarkable occurrence of the origin of life by random chance. Unfortunately, it is the no-creator presupposition or system of belief in random chance that is being taught in the public schools.

In this chapter we have traced the fossil record of plant life through its beginnings in the microscopic blue-green algae of the oceans to the present diverse landscape of flowering trees, shrubs, and grasses. Plants are the base of the pyramid of life, the necessary beginning of the food chain upon which all animal life ultimately depends. The appearance of animal life had to be preceded by suitable plant life.

However, before animal life could be supported, a dramatic change had to occur in the atmospheric blanket surrounding the Earth. Animals need oxygen to breathe, and the rays from the Sun had to be transformed from lethal killers into a beneficial energy source. We shall see in the next chapter how the blue-green algae, the first plant life, were involved in this remarkable transformation.

CHAPTER 7
LIGHT FOR THE EARTH

Then God said, "Let there be lights in the expanse of the heavens to separate the day from the night, and let them be for signs, and for seasons, and for days and years; and let them be for lights in the expanse of the heavens to give light on the earth"; and it was so.
Genesis 1:14–15

The creation of the Sun, stars, and planets was covered in the initial chapters dealing with the creation of the Universe. We then focused our attention on the planet Earth. We learned how Earth received its initial atmosphere, its water, its land, and its vegetative life. It would seem logical to describe next how animal life came to inhabit this planet.

However, before animal life could exist on the Earth, three highly important and interrelated changes had to take place:

1. Light from the Sun had to be transformed from lethal ultraviolet radiation into a beneficial source of energy.
2. Oxygen had to be made available for animals to breathe.
3. The dense clouds of noxious smog-like gases (carbon dioxide, etc.) that shrouded the Earth had to be removed to make sunlight more visible and to improve the air quality of the polluted atmosphere.

In this chapter we shall learn how these transformations occurred.

OUR ENERGIZER AND PROTECTOR

The Sun is the magnificient power plant of our Solar System. It is a giant nuclear reactor that converts hydrogen into helium by fusion and in the process releases the constant radiation energy that makes life possible on the planet Earth. This nuclear energy appears on the Earth as light.

4 HYDROGEN ATOMS

HIGH | TEMPERATURE
AND | PRESSURE

1 HELIUM ATOM + SOLAR ENERGY

+

ENERGY

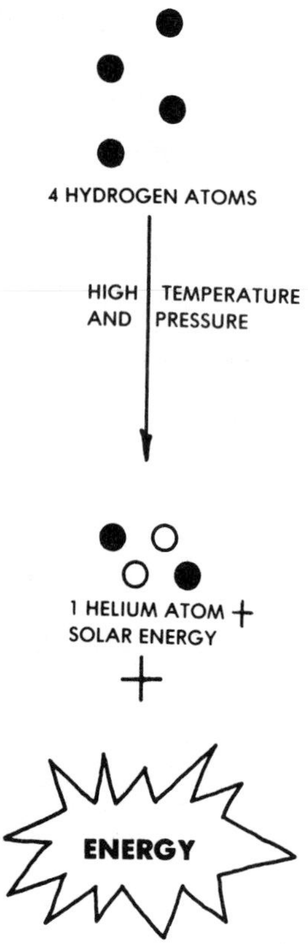

FIGURE 7.1.

Hydrogen fusion. Four nuclei of hydrogen atoms are converted into the nucleus of a helium atom. The one nucleus of helium is lighter by roughly 1% than the four nuclei of hydrogen. The mass deficit is converted to energy in accordance with Einstein's formula, $E = mc^2$. Conversion of 1 gram of hydrogen to 0.99 grams of helium releases energy equivalent to approximately 40 tons of TNT. This mass deficit appears as energy, photons of light, which we perceive as sunlight.

There is one major problem with this nuclear reactor in the sky. Like the nuclear power plants on Earth, it also emits harmful radiation. In fact, at one end of its light spectrum, it emits ultraviolet rays that not only can cause cancer, but also can disrupt the genetic mechanisms of life. What protects Earth from these lethal rays?

The Ozone Screen. The shielding barrier that protects the Earth today from the Sun's lethal radiation is called the ozone screen. It is composed of molecules of O_3 (three atoms of oxygen) and forms a highly concentrated invisible layer fifteen miles above the surface of the Earth. It effectively filters out the harmful ultraviolet rays and lets the remaining beneficial light rays pass through the atmosphere to the surface of the Earth (see figure 7.2). The ozone screen has not always been present in the upper atmosphere of the Earth.

When and how was this remarkable shielding barrier erected? Evidence from fossil marine plant life and oxidized mineral components in sedimentary rocks points to the fact that this barrier was erected about 2 billion years ago, after more than one-half of Earth's history had elapsed. The evidence for this date will be explored later in this chapter. For now we need to consider where the oxygen came from that provided the ozone screen and, much later in time, produced the oxygen-rich atmosphere we enjoy today.

THE SOURCE OF OXYGEN

Atmospheric photolysis. One source of oxygen is water. By at least 3.5 billion years ago the Earth contained an abundant supply of water in the oceans and water in vapor form existed in the atmosphere. Although very stable in both its liquid and gaseous forms, a molecule of water (H_2O) can be split into its chemical elements of hydrogen and oxygen. The high-energy ultraviolet radiation from the Sun in the upper atmosphere provides the energy for this reaction.

$$2H_2O \xrightarrow[\text{radiation}]{\text{solar}} 2H_2 + O_2$$

The process is called *atmospheric photolysis* and is shown in Figure 7.3. The size or mass of the Earth is very important to the success of this process. The gravitational attraction of the Earth's mass is large enough to retain the heavier element of oxygen while small enough to let the light element of hydrogen escape to outer space. Although

98

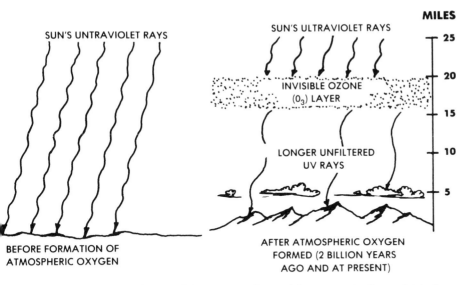

SUN'S UNTRAVIOLET RAYS

SUN'S ULTRAVIOLET RAYS

MILES

INVISIBLE OZONE
(O₃) LAYER

LONGER UNFILTERED
UV RAYS

BEFORE FORMATION OF
ATMOSPHERIC OXYGEN

AFTER ATMOSPHERIC OXYGEN
FORMED (2 BILLION YEARS
AGO AND AT PRESENT)

FIGURE 7.2.

Formation of the ozone shield. Before free oxygen existed in the atmosphere, the ultraviolet rays from the Sun were not barred from striking the surface of the Earth. About 2 billion years ago, enough free (uncombined) oxygen had accumulated to build an invisible layer of molecules of O_3. This ozone shield absorbs most of the ultraviolet radiation from the Sun, protecting life on the Earth's surface from cell-damaging radiation.

the addition to the Earth's oxygen from this source is thought to have been minor compared to biological photosynthesis, it is still thought to have been significant.

Photosynthesis. Evidence suggests the ozone screen was primarily erected by the first plants, the blue-green algae, that also helped to transform the planet's atmosphere from a dense layer of carbon dioxide and other noxious gases into the oxygen-rich atmosphere of today. Photosynthesis is the process by which green plants utilize the Sun's energy to convert carbon dioxide (CO_2) and water (H_2O) into

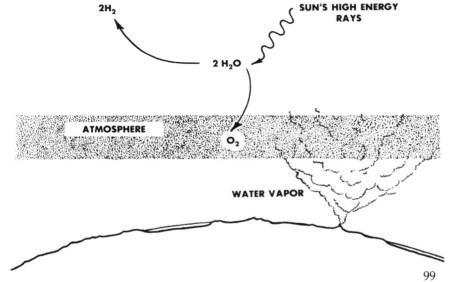

$2H_2$

SUN'S HIGH ENERGY
RAYS

$2 H_2O$

ATMOSPHERE

O_2

WATER VAPOR

FIGURE 7.3.

Atmospheric photolysis. Water vapor (H_2O) rising into the upper atmosphere is split by the Sun's ultraviolet (high energy) rays into its chemical elements of hydrogen and oxygen. The mass of the Earth is small enough to let the hydrogen escape to outer space. The Earth's mass is large enough so that oxygen is retained in the atmosphere through the force of gravitational attraction.

food in the form of carbohydrates. These carbohydrates, principally sugar, starches, and cellulose, provide a fundamental energy source not only for the plants themselves, but also for the animals that eat them. Animals are ultimately dependent on plant sources for their nutrition.

The byproduct of most photosynthetic processes is free oxygen, which is retained in the oceans and in the atmosphere, the latter through gravitational attraction of the Earth's mass. In effect, the Sun's energy has been used by the green plants to split the water molecule into its elements as in the process of atmospheric photolysis. The basic formula for green plant photosynthesis is:

$$6CO_2 + 12H_2O \xrightarrow{\text{solar radiation}} C_6H_{12}O_6 + 6O_2 + 6H_2O$$

carbon dioxide + water $\longrightarrow$ carbohydrates + oxygen + water

Today plants not only serve as the basis of the food chain for all animal life, but also they furnish the oxygen that animals breathe and use to metabolize (convert into energy) the food which the plants provide. The appearance of animals has made a unique interdependence possible.

In their respiratory processes, animals breathe in oxygen and breathe out carbon dioxide for the plants to utilize (see figure 7.4).

FIGURE 7.4.

The interdependence of plants and animals. Plants convert sunlight into chemical energy through the process of photosynthesis. The byproduct is oxygen. Animals inhale oxygen and exhale carbon dioxide (respiration). All the oxygen contained in the atmosphere cycles through plants and animals about once every 3,000 years.

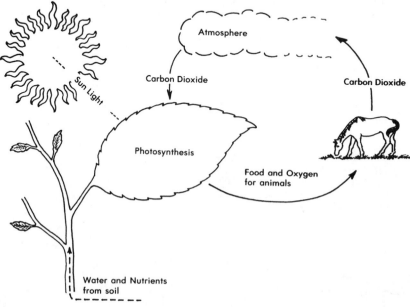

100

This cycle is far more complex than visualized here, but the importance of the interdependence of plants and animals is illustrated. Basically all the oxygen in the present atmosphere is recycled through plants and animals about once every 3,000 years.

Before the first photosynthesizing organisms captured energy from the Sun, primitive organisms had to rely on a limited supply of organic molecules of purely chemical origin for food. Somehow, an unknown ancestral microbe was endowed with the capability of photosynthesis. Energy could then be utilized from the Sun to convert chemical elements directly into food.

With this enormous advantage, the first known photosynthesizing organisms—the blue-green algae—spread through the waters of the Earth. They are thought to have been a key factor in cleaning the air of noxious gases, building the ozone screen and producing oxygen for animals to breathe. They were the hardy pioneers that paved the way for higher forms of life.

THE FIRST POISON—OXYGEN

It seems incredible to us today, as we relish the fresh air which our bodies require, that oxygen should have been a poison to early life, but such was the case. We must remember that the cells of our bodies, like all *eukaryotic* (nucleated) cells, contain oxygen-mediating enzymes that counteract the otherwise poisonous effects of oxygen. But to the *prokaryotic* blue-green algae, oxygen was a poison, a pollutant.

Today there are bacteria that are killed when exposed to oxygen and therefore live deep within the soil. One of the first indications of pollution in rivers and lakes is the appearance of blue-green algae. They indicate a deterioration of the oxygen supply.

It was therefore very fortunate for the blue-green algae that the oxygen supply increased at a slow rate of speed, even by geologic standards. It is actually a rather puzzling situation. The photosynthetic blue-green algae had the enormous biologic advantage of utilizing the Sun's energy for growth and metabolism. Yet they were producing a byproduct that was poisonous to them—oxygen. There were no animals present to convert the oxygen back to carbon dioxide as in today's ecologic cycle. What kept the oxygen produced by the blue-green algae at a low level so they could thrive for 2 billion years?

Part of the answer lies in the fact that as the blue-greens died, some of their remains would have been oxidized—converted back into carbon dioxide. Dead organic matter is oxidized in this manner today (see figure 7.5). But where the organic matter was quickly buried by sediments, its carbon would not have had a chance to combine with oxygen. The oxygen that escaped combination with dead organic matter would have continued to increase the oxygen level in the ocean and thence the atmosphere. Remember that we suspect the blue-greens were alive and well 3.5 billion years ago and that the ozone screen was not erected until 2 billion years ago. What happened to 1.5 billion years of oxygen?

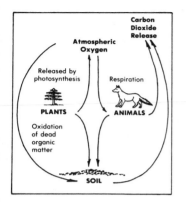

FIGURE 7.5.

The oxygen cycle at present.

THE GREAT IRON AGE

Many would associate iron with our industrial society, for iron is smelted with coal and made into steel, the structural backbone of the industrial age. In terms of structural metals, it could be said that we presently live in the Iron Age.

Students of ancient history may remember that another Iron Age began about 1200 B.C. It was during this period of history that the terrible Hittites swarmed out of what is now eastern Turkey to battle the armies of ancient Mesopotamia and Egypt. The Hittites were such successful conquerors because they had weapons of iron. Armed with iron swords and spears, they cut to pieces armies with the softer weapons of bronze. From mines in Tarsus and the hinterland they had extracted iron ore and learned the secret of smelting and forging it into weapons. The Philistines also learned this secret process and became formidable warriors.

For the geologist, there is another "Great Iron Age" that took place between 2.5 and 2 billion years ago. This geologic age of iron formation answers the riddle of what happened to the excess oxygen produced by the blue-green algae (that missing 1.5 billion years of oxygen). It also explains why geologists conclude that the first accumulation of oxygen in the atmosphere and the erection of the ozone screen occurred 2 billion years ago.

To learn about the great age of iron formation we must travel from the iron mines of Michigan and Minnesota to the Preston Cloud Laboratory at the University of California at Santa Barbara. Preston Cloud, the dean of ancient earth geologists, has been studying particular rock formations known as BIFs (banded iron formations) for many years (see figure 7.6). These rocks exhibit a pronounced layering structure like a finely layered baklava pastry. For the most part, the layers of iron oxide alternate with layers of chert (silicon dioxide). They thus present a layered or varved appearance indicating they were deposited in water (sedimentary rocks). These deposits are located in quantity throughout the world's iron producing regions and constitute the primary source of iron for our industrial age. Although BIFs are known to have existed more than 3.5 billion years ago, almost all commercial deposits date between 2 and 2.5 billion years ago, with the majority dating at slightly more than 2 billion years ago.

Preston Cloud and other geologists have found that these BIF formations are found in association with *stromatolites,* rock deposits formed by blue-green algae. This is our first clue that mineral formation is related to biologic life. It indicates that the oxygen produced in the waters by blue-green algae may have been utilized in the formation of the BIFs. However, to understand how the BIFs were formed we must learn something about mineral chemistry.

When iron in surface rocks of the land is exposed to air or water containing oxygen, it rusts. Iron combines with oxygen to form the compound ferric oxide, rust, which is highly stable and resistant to erosion. Anyone who has tried to remove rusty iron from metal surfaces can testify to its tenacity.

FIGURE 7.6.

Specimen of Precambrian banded iron formation from the Iron River district, Michigan. (Courtesy U.S. Geological Survey; photo by Harold L. James.)

However, in primordial times, the iron present in surface rocks could not have formed into stable ferric oxide because little or no oxygen existed in the atmosphere. Iron exposed to the surface would therefore have been soluble in water. As the rains fell, iron present in surface rocks would have been taken into solution and washed into seas and lakes. The primordial oceans and lakes would therefore have had a major quantity of iron in solution.

What happened to this iron in the waters of the Earth? Remembering that the blue-green algae that lived in these waters were producing oxygen, the answer then is simple—the iron combined with the oxygen thus produced to form ferric oxide. The ferric oxide precipitated and fell to the bottom to form rusty layers on the ocean floor. As seasonal rainfalls weathered newly exposed volcanic land and swept soluble iron out to sea (or as iron stored in ocean basins welled up into shallow water where the blue-green algae lived), a layer of iron oxide would be precipitated and deposited. As the alternating light layers of chert (silicon dioxide) were being continuously deposited, alternating layers of iron-rich and iron-poor chert were formed. This caused the layered or banded appearance of the BIF rocks.

In addition to the episodic introduction of soluble iron to the shallow seas, the rhythmic banding or lamination of the BIFs could have been produced by episodic growth and production of oxygen-releasing blue-green algae. This would have produced a temporary increase in the oxygen supply for combination with the soluble iron. Both the episodic flowering of blue-green algae and the episodic introduction of soluble iron from the land (or its release from storage in deep ocean basins) may have been responsible for the banded layers produced during the great "Age of Iron Formation."

Geologists believe that the great "Geologic Age of Iron" ended 2 billion years ago because by this time the blue-green algae had finally produced enough oxygen to oxidize all the iron then present at the Earth's surface. Thereafter, new iron exposed at the surface would not go into solution. It would rust (convert to stable ferric oxide) immediately on contact with oxygen in the atmosphere or water. Geologists believe that oxygen thereafter began to accumulate in the atmosphere, and thence to build the ozone screen.

Evidence that free oxygen first appeared as a permanent and accumulating component of the atmosphere 2 billion years ago is also seen in the rocks of the Earth. Anyone who has traveled to Utah, Colorado, and Arizona has been struck by the brilliant red rock formations of the Canyonlands. The brilliant red color is due to iron,

FIGURE 7.7.

Chimney Rock at Capitol Reef National Monument in central Utah is a striking specimen of the red beds formed during the Triassic age 200 million years ago. (Courtesy Utah State Historical Society.)

and the formations are often composed of sandstone deposited by wind or in shallow-water, dry-land environments. Once oxygen was present in the atmosphere, it could combine with the iron present in the grains of rocks to form the stable compound ferric oxide, which is resistant to solution. Iron would no longer be easily soluble to be carried to the world's oceans and lakes.

Thus the sedimentary rocks testify to the ancient supply of the world's oxygen. Prior to 2 billion years ago, oxygen as a gas was present only in the world's oceans where it combined with the soluble iron to produce the banded iron formations. After 2 billion years ago, oxygen was free to accumulate in the atmosphere, create the ozone screen, and combine with the iron still present on the land to form the Red Beds of the deserts. Once in the stable state of ferric oxide in the Red Beds, the iron was no longer free to wash into the oceans. Banded iron formations are virtually absent after 2 billion years ago. The land formations known as Red Beds first began to appear about 2 billion years ago, and iron continues to rust in our present oxygenated environment when exposed to water and air.

A critical effect of the increasing accumulation of oxygen in the atmosphere was the creation of the ozone screen. The ozone screen began to filter out the Sun's ultraviolet rays, and advanced forms of photosynthesizing plant life, red, green, and brown algae appeared. As the oxygen supply continued to increase, animal life in the water appeared, then plant life on the land, and finally animal life on the land. The time scale of the changing atmosphere of the Earth is illustrated in Figure 7.8.

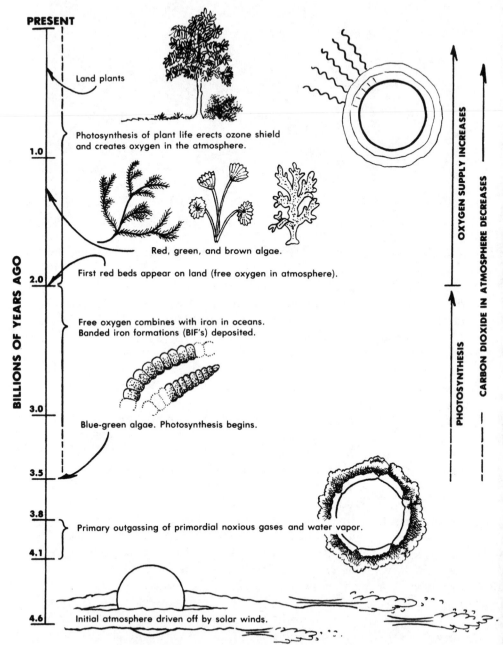

PRESENT

Land plants

Photosynthesis of plant life erects ozone shield and creates oxygen in the atmosphere.

1.0

Red, green, and brown algae.

2.0   First red beds appear on land (free oxygen in atmosphere).

Free oxygen combines with iron in oceans. Banded iron formations (BIF's) deposited.

3.0

Blue-green algae. Photosynthesis begins.

3.5

3.8

Primary outgassing of primordial noxious gases and water vapor.

4.1

4.6   Initial atmosphere driven off by solar winds.

BILLIONS OF YEARS AGO

OXYGEN SUPPLY INCREASES

CARBON DIOXIDE IN ATMOSPHERE DECREASES

PHOTOSYNTHESIS

Figure 7.8 The Changing Atmosphere of the Earth

CLEAN AIR AND SMOG

The unique atmosphere cycle of the Earth today is truly a marvel of design (see figure 7.9). Note that our air is kept breathable through active geologic, chemical, and biologic processes. We are currently adding to this cycle by the burning of the fossil fuels coal, oil, and gas. The carbon in these fuels recombines with oxygen to produce carbon dioxide (CO_2) and other components of the smog so familiar to residents of Los Angeles and other heavily urbanized and industrial areas.

The short-range effect of this smog is very uncomfortable to those living in these areas. The long-range effect may include a rise in the average temperature at the surface of the Earth through what is known as the "greenhouse effect." The Sun's visible light rays are able to penetrate the blanket of smog and are partially converted into invisible heat (infrared) rays as the surface of the Earth is heated. As the infrared heat rays are radiated back into the atmosphere, they are absorbed by the carbon dioxide molecules and reflected back to Earth. This same effect is observed in a greenhouse in which the glass in the greenhouse may be thought of as analogous to the carbon dioxide molecules in the atmosphere. The same effect can also be observed in a car that has its windows shut on a sunny day. The

FIGURE 7.9.

Photosynthesis and respiration in the atmosphere and oceans far outweigh other inputs and outputs. Even if all photosynthesis were to stop, the oxygen supply in the atmosphere would last more than 2000 years. (From *Earth*, 3rd ed., by F. Press and R. Siever. W. H. Freeman and Co., Copyright © 1978.)

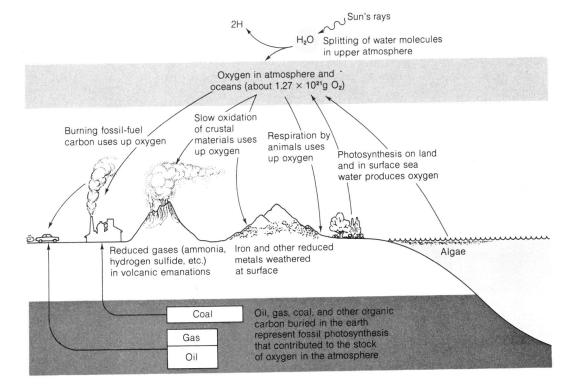

2H

Sun's rays

H_2O Splitting of water molecules in upper atmosphere

Oxygen in atmosphere and oceans (about 1.27×10^{21} g O_2)

Slow oxidation of crustal materials uses up oxygen

Burning fossil-fuel carbon uses up oxygen

Respiration by animals uses up oxygen

Photosynthesis on land and in surface sea water produces oxygen

Reduced gases (ammonia, hydrogen sulfide, etc.) in volcanic emanations

Iron and other reduced metals weathered at surface

Algae

Coal

Gas

Oil

Oil, gas, coal, and other organic carbon buried in the earth represent fossil photosynthesis that contributed to the stock of oxygen in the atmosphere

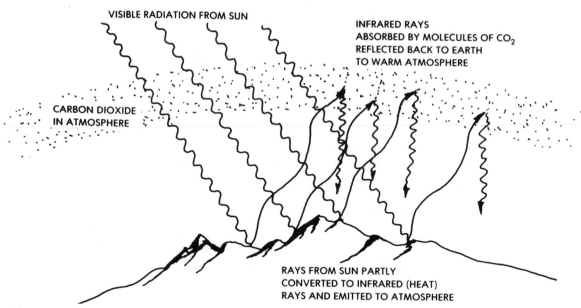

VISIBLE RADIATION FROM SUN

INFRARED RAYS
ABSORBED BY MOLECULES OF CO_2
REFLECTED BACK TO EARTH
TO WARM ATMOSPHERE

CARBON DIOXIDE
IN ATMOSPHERE

RAYS FROM SUN PARTLY
CONVERTED TO INFRARED (HEAT)
RAYS AND EMITTED TO ATMOSPHERE

FIGURE 7.10.

The greenhouse effect. Carbon dioxide in the atmosphere acts in the same way as the glass of a greenhouse. It allows visible light rays from the Sun to pass through, but absorbs and reflects infrared (heat) rays back to the surface of the Earth.

inside of the car will become unbearably hot as the radiated heat rays are trapped within.

The oceans and lakes are currently serving as a sink for some of the excess carbon dioxide being produced. As the carbon dioxide level builds up in the atmosphere some of the excess gas enters the waters of the Earth. The plant life (plankton) in the water is thought to be important in this transfer process. About 50% of the excess carbon dioxide is removed from the atmosphere to be stored in solution in cold water or to combine with calcium to form the mineral calcium carbonate ($CaCO_3$). The remaining excess carbon dioxide continues to increase the carbon dioxide level in the atmosphere.

The long-range effect of this buildup may be to increase the Earth's temperature enough to melt the polar ice caps. This would result in the flooding of low-lying coastal cities and lands as the rise in sea level would be 300 feet or more. Virtually all major coastal cities and most of the state of Florida would be under water. At present there are too many variables to predict the increase in the Earth's temperature with certainty, but it is still a cause for concern.

It is thought that the temperature of the primordial atmosphere may have been warmed by the effects of carbon dioxide and other gases that created a magnified greenhouse effect. To prepare for animal life, the primordial atmosphere had to be purified of the more prevalent noxious gases that existed in those primeval times.

108

CLEANING THE AIR

The great outgassing of the Earth's interior occurred between 4.1 and 3.8 billion years ago. Clouds of water vapor, carbon dioxide, and other noxious gases blanketed the globe. As the rains fell, some of the carbon dioxide was carried into the oceans and some remained in the atmosphere. Oxygen was produced by plant life and to a lesser extent by upper atmospheric chemical reactions. However, we have not accounted for the vast decrease in carbon dioxide that must have taken place since primordial times. How did those clouds of smog

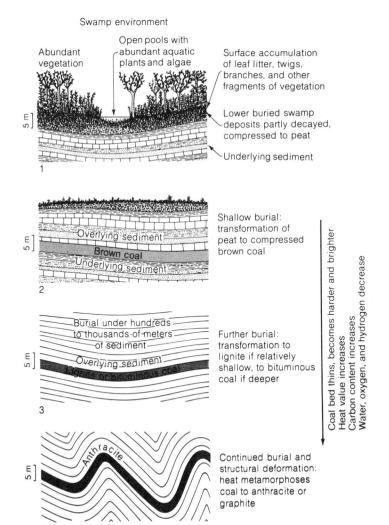

FIGURE 7.11.

The process by which coal beds form begins with the deposition of vegetation. Protected from complete decay and oxidation in a swamp environment, the deposit is later buried and subjected to mild metamorphism, which transforms it into lignite, bituminous coal, or anthracite, depending on depth of burial, temperature, and amount of structural deformation. (From *Earth*, 3rd ed., by F. Press and R. Siever. W. H. Freeman and Co., Copyright © 1978.)

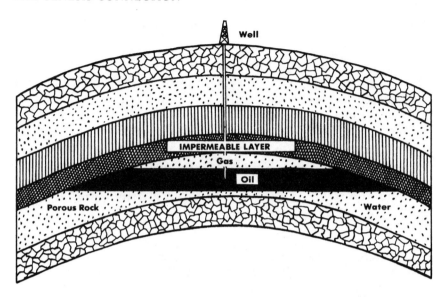

FIGURE 7.12.

A common trap for oil and gas. The original organic matter from which the petroleum was derived may have migrated many miles into the porous formation that constitutes the fossil-fuel reservoir. Note that the lighter gas is on top. Water is heavier than oil and therefore on the bottom. The example shown is known as an anticlinal trap. Traps may also be formed by faults or by stratigraphy wherein the porous layer thins out to an impermeable one.

disappear? As with the increase in oxygen supply, the decrease in carbon dioxide is due to both biologic and chemical processes involving the sedimentary rocks of the Earth.

Biologic Processes. In the process of photosynthesis plants convert carbon dioxide to carbohydrates and release excess oxygen as a by-product. This is one way that carbon dioxide is removed from the atmosphere. However, this process is not a completely effective one; for as the plant dies and decays, its carbon products are recombined with oxygen (oxidized) to again produce carbon dioxide. Only the dead organic matter that is partially buried in the muck of swamps or in the depths of the oceans (where oxygen supply is greatly reduced) escapes this oxidation process. It is this unoxidized carbon that has helped to reduce the CO_2 and to add oxygen to the atmosphere.

Exposed sedimentary rocks testify to the ancient burial of dead organic matter. The carbon-rich shales of Colorado and Utah contain layer after layer of these carbonaceous formations that alternate between layers of other types of sedimentary rocks (sandstones and limestones) laid down in ancient seas. Where organic material from swampy vegetation has been buried in volume, it often forms commercial deposits of coal. Beds of coal are accumulations of fossil plants that thrived in swamps millions of years ago.

Petroleum products such as oil and gas also owe their origin to once living biologic life. Since all life is based on carbon compounds, small amounts of hydrocarbons occur in organisms of all kinds, from

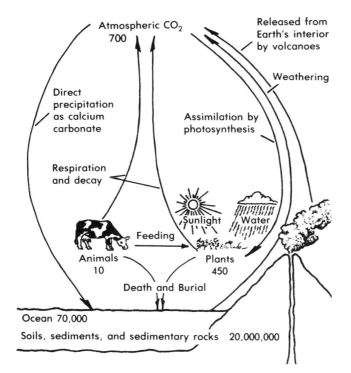

FIGURE 7.13.

The carbon and carbon dioxide (CO_2) cycle as it exists today. The numbers show the present distribution of carbon in billions of metric tons. The bulk of the CO_2 released through volcanic action (outgassing) over geologic time has been dissolved in the oceans and then precipitated as calcium carbonate to form sedimentary rocks such as limestones and dolomites. Additional CO_2 has been removed by the biologic processes of plants and animals with their carbon-rich remains accumulating in sediments and fossil fuels (coal, oil, and gas).

bacteria to elephants. In coastal or inland waters where the productivity of organic matter is high, large numbers of minute organisms thrive, die, and are buried in muds and oozes. Those that escape scavenging and oxidation preserve their carbon content. Over the course of millions of years bacterial and chemical reactions convert the organic remains into liquid and gaseous hydrocarbons.

For commercial deposits of oil and gas to exist, several other conditions must occur. The converted hydrocarbons must be squeezed out of their muddy formations. The pressure to accomplish this comes from overlying sediments that have been deposited on top of the organic bearing layer. Secondly, the liquid and gaseous hydrocarbons must have a porous or permeable formation into which to migrate. Thirdly, there must be an impermeable overlying formation to trap the petroleum or it would escape to the surface. A common type of trap is illustrated in Figure 7.12. This trap must remain relatively undisturbed by metamorphic or volcanic processes that would crack or otherwise severely deform the structure, allowing the petroleum to escape.

Commercial sources of fossil fuels are the legacy of hundreds of millions of years of dead organic matter. In effect, these fossil fuels represent solar energy captured by plants and animals. They are stored through their burial in the sedimentary rocks of the Earth. The oxygen that would otherwise have oxidized these carbonaceous products was free to accumulate in the atmosphere. When these fossil fuels are converted back into carbon dioxide by burning them to obtain heat and power, they again require oxygen for combustion. They are oxidized and carbon dioxide is produced.

Chemical Processes. Much of the original carbon dioxide was removed from the primordial atmosphere and locked up in fossil fuels and deep sea sediments present in the rocks deep beneath the Earth's surface. However, there were other chemical processes that had been operating since the world's oceans came into existence more than 3.5 billion years ago that have had an even greater influence on the reduction of carbon dioxide in the atmosphere and oceans.

To remove carbon dioxide from the atmosphere by chemical means requires, as a first step, that it be dissolved in the oceans and lakes. In the presence of large bodies of water much carbon dioxide in the atmosphere simply dissolves into the water. Here it enters into chemical combination with calcium to form calcium carbonate. This compound is precipitated and forms deposits on the ocean floor. As these deposits thicken, they harden into rocks of limestone and dolomite due to the pressure of overlying sediments. In more recent geologic time limestone and dolomite have been produced biologically. They are formed from the microscopic shells and external coverings of marine animals. It is estimated that the majority of the carbon dioxide produced from the Earth's original volcanic outgassing has been locked up in sedimentary rocks.

To put the amount of carbon dioxide in perspective, we should bear in mind that some quantity of CO_2 is very necessary for the ecologic balance on our planet. Carbon dioxide is one of the basic components used by plants in their photosynthetic process. Further, the element of carbon comprises about 18% of the mass of all living things. The primary source of this carbon is carbon dioxide. Essentially all organic matter, including our bodies, is carbon-based.

The original source of carbon was from volcanoes which outgassed carbon dioxide along with water vapor into the atmosphere. Today, considerably less than 1% of the carbon present at or near the Earth's surface is in the atmosphere and oceans. Almost 100% is contained in the sedimentary rocks of the Earth's veneer. Of this amount about 77% is found in the carbonate rocks of limestone and dolomite. The remaining 23% is carbon-rich material from ancient animals and plants that have been buried in the dark-colored sedimentary rocks known as carbonaceous shales.

What would happen if this large quantity of carbon stored in sedimentary rocks was somehow returned to the atmosphere? The atmosphere of the Earth would be returned to its original primordial state. The Earth would again be shrouded in a cloud of carbon dioxide. This is the state of the atmosphere on the planet Venus today.

It is interesting to note that futuristic proposals for space colonization call for seeding the atmosphere of Venus with blue-green algae. In this way it is hoped that the blue-green algae would convert the CO_2 on Venus to oxygen. This experiment would probably be a failure, because Venus lacks water in liquid form. Bodies of water are necessary for blue-green algae to propagate and for dissolving the CO_2 and forming sedimentary rocks. The unique development of our atmosphere and its constant cycle or renewal is dependent upon volcanic processes from the Earth's interior, our oceans, and geologic, chemical, and biologic processes. It is truly a masterpiece of design and engineering.

THE ENERGY SOURCE FOR INITIAL LIFE

It is obvious today that we need energy for living organisms to exist. Plants capture energy from the Sun and provide animals not only with oxygen but also with the energy they store in their seeds, nuts, fruits, and leaves. In Chapter 6 we discussed some hypotheti-

FIGURE 7.14.

Tube worms, clams, and crabs at a respectful distance from a 350°C (662°F) hydrothermal hot vent on the sea floor at 2600 meters (1.62 mi.) depth near the East Pacific Rise. (Photo by Dr. Thierry Juteau, Universitie Louis Pasteur, Strasbourg, France. Courtesy Stephen Miller, Rise Expedition photo archive, University of California at Santa Barbara.)

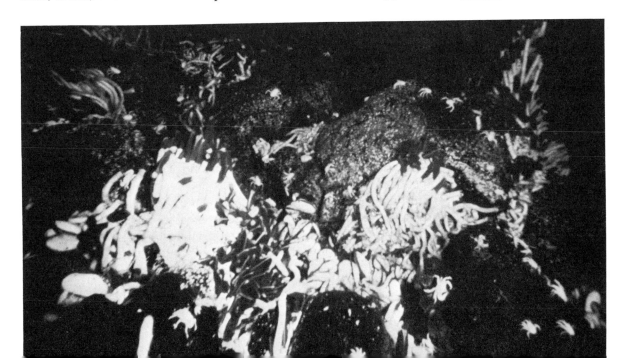

cal means by which the first life could have arisen. Almost all steps in the process require energy.

The energy source for the formation of the first plant life could have been lightning from the numerous storms that racked the planet. It also could have been nuclear radiation from the radioactive material in the Earth's crust. Hot springs that utilize heat from volcanic sources deep within the Earth are favorite sites for investigation.

One of the most exciting discoveries of recent times is the curious life forms that exist around deep-sea thermal vents. These warm-water vents lie more than a mile beneath the surface where there is no sunlight for photosynthesis. The giant clams, white crabs, and large tube worms (up to 5 feet in length) that live near these vents appear to exist on bacteria. The bacteria themselves are thought to utilize hydrogen sulfide, which flows up through the vents, combined with oxygen and carbon dioxide in the sea water to obtain energy.

By far the most important single energy source for the initial steps toward life was ultraviolet radiation from the Sun (see table 7.1). Because there was no ozone shield present in primordial times, the Sun's ultraviolet rays would have struck the Earth with far greater intensity than at present (see figure 7.2). While useful in providing energy to chemically synthesize initial organic compounds in the atmosphere, it must be remembered that this same high energy ultraviolet radiation is destructive not only to living cells, but also to their more advanced (non-living) molecular building blocks. Therefore, life must have begun in a place shielded from the Sun's lethal ultraviolet rays. Such a place could have been beneath moist soil, in tidal mud flats, or under a layer of water.

The fossil record provides evidence that blue-green algae existed on platforms of boulders and rocks submerged in shallow water. These platforms would have to have been deep enough to be shielded from ultraviolet radiation, but shallow enough to receive the light wavelengths essential to photosynthesis. The fact that oxygen levels decrease with increasing water depth together with blue-green algae's known intolerance of oxygen tends to give credence to this hypothesis.

Further, the tolerance of blue-green algae both to limited ultraviolet radiation and to lack of oxygen suggest that it, or perhaps earlier life forms, could have arisen in the primordial hostile environment. Nevertheless, determining the energy source and the shielded environ-

Primordial energy sources in terms of the percentage of average total energy they would have supplied at each point on the Earth's surface.[1]

ultraviolet radiation	99.8 %
electrical discharges	.12%
natural radioactivity	.08%
meteorites	.03%
high-energy particles	.006%
volcanoes	.004%

Table 7.1

ment, like the biochemistry of the first life, will probably remain a highly interesting area of investigation for science.

IN SUMMARY

The energy source for the first life on Earth was probably ultraviolet radiation from the Sun. However, before the Earth could be inhabited by higher forms of life, the Sun's ultraviolet rays had to be screened out by the creation of an ozone layer in the upper atmosphere. In addition, the primordial atmosphere of carbon dioxide and other smog-like gases had to be purified.

The first known plant life was blue-green algae. Endowed with the remarkable capability for photosynthesis, this algae slowly built the ozone screen and provided the air with an increasing supply of oxygen. Light from the Sun was transformed by the first primitive plants into a beneficial energy source for advanced plant life. This advanced plant life continued to create additional oxygen and food, paving the way for animal life in the oceans and later for life on the land.

There are mysteries enough to be sure, such as how the process of photosynthesis came into being. While there are suggested pathways for this development, the present answer is that we simply do not know how biologic photosynthesis originated. We do know that without this process in operation, animals would have nothing to eat. Further, sunlight would be a lethal killer rather than a beneficial source of energy to all life exposed to its rays.

Is the transformation of light from the Sun into a beneficial energy source what Genesis is addressing when it says " 'and let them be for lights in the expanse of the heavens to give light on the earth'; and it was so" (Gen. 1:15)? While we can't be certain of this, I would like to suggest this interpretation as a likely possibility. We do know that scientific history places the appearance of sunlight beneficial to advanced life in the same sequential order as this fourth creation command in Genesis. This event had to occur after the appearance of the first plant life, blue-green algae, and before animal life in the sea and on the land. Science, once again, appears to be in harmony with Scripture.

CHAPTER 8
LIFE IN THE SEA AND IN THE AIR

Then God said, "Let the waters teem with swarms of living creatures, and let birds fly above the earth in the open expanse of the heavens."

Genesis 1:20

LIFE IN THE SEA

The most significant landmark in the geologic time scale occurred 570 million years ago. Almost 90% of the Earth's history had elapsed by that time in what is known as the *Precambrian* era. Algal plant life had held sway in the oceans for almost 3 billion years. A few muffled footsteps and backstage whispers of animal life were heard. Then, quite suddenly, the curtain on the next act in the drama of life was lifted.

This act opened with almost the entire cast on stage. So sudden was the widespread appearance of the primitive forms of almost all major categories of invertebrate animals—worms, trilobites, sea scorpions, jellyfish, starfish—that this event is known to geologists as the *Cambrian explosion*. The waters of the Earth literally teemed with many different living creatures.

From the beginning of the Cambrian period to the present is known as the *Phanerozoic Eon*—the era of manifest or exposed life. The transition from the Precambrian era is marked by a juncture comparable to the invention of writing. Before written history there were only scattered fragments of pottery, a few cave paintings, and tribal legends to tell us about our past. But after the invention of writing, people were able to keep historical records of events. Although there are still gaps in the record, the appearance of fossils has made possible a comprehensive history book, written in the stone pages of sedimentary rocks (see figures 8.1 and 8.2).

The main reason for the great improvement in both the quantity and quality of the fossil record is that many marine animals appeared

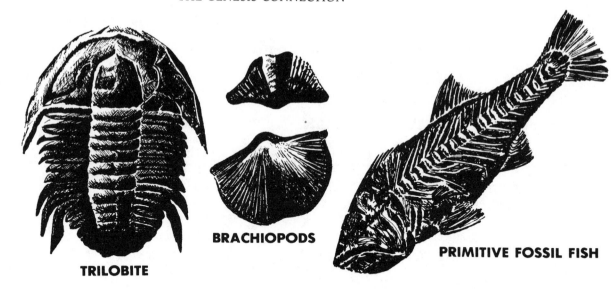

TRILOBITE

BRACHIOPODS

PRIMITIVE FOSSIL FISH

FIGURE 8.1.

Fossil records preserved in sedimentary rock. These may be impressions or chemical replacement of the original parts by more durable material. The original shells or bones are very rarely preserved.

with external coverings in the form of shells and armor made of durable calcium carbonate. Shells are far less subject to immediate decay than soft tissue, internal organs, and other organic parts. They leave a far more durable and complete record.

There was something very different about this new form of life that appeared in the sea. It was multicellular. Animals today are composed of millions and in some cases billions of cells. There are 100 trillion cells in the human body. Furthermore, these cells are organized into tissues and organs with different forms and functions that cooperate to act as a functioning whole unit.

This new kind of life required specialized kinds of cells for different purposes. There are cells for tissues or skin; cells for nerves; cells for fat and muscles; cells for circulation, digestion, excretion, reproduction, and respiration. Even the very simplest kinds of multicellular organisms have several different kinds of cells. The more complicated ones have as many as two hundred different specialized varieties.

The advantages of multicellular organization are several. First of all, the cells can become more specialized and therefore more efficient at their tasks. Secondly, in marked contrast to single-celled organisms, multicellular organisms can replace individual cells, as when your cut finger heals. The only permanent cells in the human body are those of the nerves and the brain. Ten years from now all other cells in your body will have been replaced by new ones.

The third advantage of multicellular organisms is the potential for variety in architectural body forms. Instead of mere single cells that sometimes group into clusters, a fantastic variety of body forms can be constructed: from an elongated worm, to a compact clam, to the more complicated crab and lobster.

Whereas multicelled life in its plant form is thought to have made its appearance more than 1 billion years ago in the form of red, green, and brown algae, the first hints of animals did not arrive until 700 million years ago. These traces of animals consist of casts of worm-like burrows and impressions of jellyfish. These traces or images are rare until the beginning of the Cambrian period in geologic history, 570 million years ago. At this point in history and during the next 50 million years, almost all phyla of invertebrate animals appear abundantly in the fossil record, including sponges; corals and jellyfish; brachiopods (lamp shells); mollusks—snails, clams, and squids; arthropods—insects, trilobites, and crustaceans (crabs, etc.); and echinoderms—sea lilies, starfish, and sea urchins.

These categories of marine animals, with the exception of the ex-

THE CLASSIFICATION OF MULTICELLULAR PLANTS AND ANIMALS

Multicellular organisms are classified into three kingdoms: Metaphyta (plants), Fungi, and Metazoa (animals). This grouping is based on broad differences in modes of life, and in particular the method of obtaining energy. Plants require only organic compounds for nutrients (autotrophy) and utilize the energy from the Sun to create living matter (photosynthesis). Fungi such as mushrooms are plant-like but ingest complex organic material already synthesized for growth and maintenance. Animals (Metazoa) rely on organic material, especially plants, for nutrition. They have nerve cells that coordinate the most obvious characteristic of members of the Animal Kingdom—movement of appendages, which often results in locomotion.

It is useful to note that the prefix "meta" means changed or altered. Thus, Metazoa means "changed animal." A "metamorphic" rock means one that has been changed or altered in form from its original state which could have been either sedimentary (deposited by water or wind) or igneous (of volcanic or melted origin). The "Metazoa" or changed animals are thought by evolutionists to have arisen from the unicelled (single-celled) Protozoa, although there is no fossil evidence to support this hypothesis.

Table 8.1

FIGURE 8.2.

Trilobites may have been the primitive ancestors of crabs, shrimps, and insects. They became instinct 225 million years ago. (Courtesy Lloyd and Val Gunther.)

tinct trilobites, have continued to the present day. They are now more modern in appearance, but since 500 million years ago there have been no new forms or structures introduced in the world of invertebrate animals.

The rapid expansion in both abundance and variety of the shell-bearing marine invertebrates (without internal backbone or skeleton) was shortly followed by the appearance of the marine vertebrates (with internal backbones and skeletons). The first forms with semblances of internal skeletons seemed to have been mainly mud-grubbers. Lacking jaws and teeth, these are called the jawless fishes. Although they are thought to have arisen from the marine invertebrates, there is no fossil record of a transition.

Like the marine invertebrates, the first vertebrates simply appear in the fossil record. The star of the first act walks—or rather swims—onstage without introduction.

The first internal supports of the vertebrates were composed of cartilage rather than bone as is characteristic of the sharks of today. By 350 million years ago all major groups of fish had appeared in the record. Their internal skeletons were composed of bone, and with this structural advantage they became the masters of the sea. The period from 400 to 350 million years ago is known as the Age of Fishes.

While most shell-bearing animals and fish have continued to change in size and diversity up to the present time, their basic form and composition were completed during their early history. Few new characters have been introduced into the drama of life in the sea.

However, radically new life entered the sea about 200 million years ago in the form of fish-like and serpent-like dinosaurs. Except for sea turtles, these great monsters of the ancient seas became extinct about 63 million years ago. They were replaced by the mammals that invaded the sea in the form of dolphins, seals, and whales. The development of the dinosaurs and mammals will be covered in the following chapter dealing with life on the land.

LIFE IN THE AIR

About 400 million years ago, during the Age of Fishes, greenbelts were spreading into low-lying continental terrain. Fern-like trees made their appearance. The first airborne life with wings were flying insects. Because of their small size, they are relatively poorly recorded in the fossil record. Fortunately, there are inherent limitations in size (related to their breathing mechanism) to which insects can grow. These upper limits in size were achieved about 300 million years ago when giant cockroaches were one foot (30 cm.) long, and dragonflies attained wingspans of two feet (60 cm.).

The aerial monopoly of the insects was broken about 200 million years ago with the appearance of primitive gliding reptiles. These were highly modified lizards. The bat-like *pterosaurs* appeared about 150 million years ago. Some gliding reptiles were the size of the familiar sparrow, and others were giants of the sky with wingspans of more than twenty-seven feet (see figure 8.5). Their leathery, membranous wings lacked feathers and are thought to have been used more for gliding than true flight.

Birds and reptiles share the common reproductive habit of laying eggs. However, birds differ from reptiles in important respects. Reptiles have teeth to capture food and tear it into digestible portions. The beak of a bird is used to gather food. It uses its specially constructed muscular gizzard to break up the food for digestion.

Another major difference between birds and reptiles is maintenance of internal body temperature. The warm-blooded birds are highly dependent on feathers for insulation. Flying is an extremely energy-consuming process, and feathers conserve body heat so that energy may be reserved for flight. Feathers are even more efficient

FIGURE 8.3.

Scorpion-like arthropods called *eurypterids* inhabited freshwater habitats from 250 to 500 million years ago. This well-preserved fossil specimen is from 400-million-year-old rocks in western New York state and measures about 20 centimeters (8 in.) in length. (Courtesy Buffalo Museum of Science.)

FIGURE 8.4.

Three fossil forms of clams in sandstone. Fossil at upper left is actual shell. Fossil in center is stone replacement of original shell material which had dissolved after burial. Fossil at upper right is impression or natural mold of original shell.

than fur as insulation. Only the penguin can withstand temperatures of 40° below zero on the Antarctic ice caps.

The true purpose and beauty of feathers is for flight. In addition to being exquisite examples of aerodynamic design, the wings of birds are driven by the powerful engines of the breast muscles. This capability for true flight was a significant advancement. Before birds appeared, it is thought that the reptiles with leathery membranes for wings may have been climbers that used their wings for descent or gliding to the next tree or bush. The presence of front feet is indicated by fossil footprints, and these reptiles may also have been able to run or walk fast to gather speed for takeoff. Because the fossil remains of these flying reptiles lack signs of attachments for powerful wing muscles, it is doubtful that they were efficient flyers. They were probably more adept at gliding.

Current scientific theory holds that birds began their transition from reptiles 140 million years ago. A possible transitional form which has both the bird characteristic of feathers and the reptile characteristic of teeth is known as the *Archaeopteryx* or "ancient bird" (see figure 8.8). The discovery of slightly younger avian or bird-type bones has led some scientists to question whether this "feathered reptile" or reptilian bird is a link between reptiles and birds. However, there is growing evidence that a form of two-legged dino-

FIGURE 8.5.

The flying reptiles called *Pterosaurs*. The Dimorphodon, *left*, is thought to have lived 150 million years ago. It had a wingspan of two to three feet. The giant Pteranodon appears somewhat later in the fossil record and measures 27 feet from wingtip to wingtip.

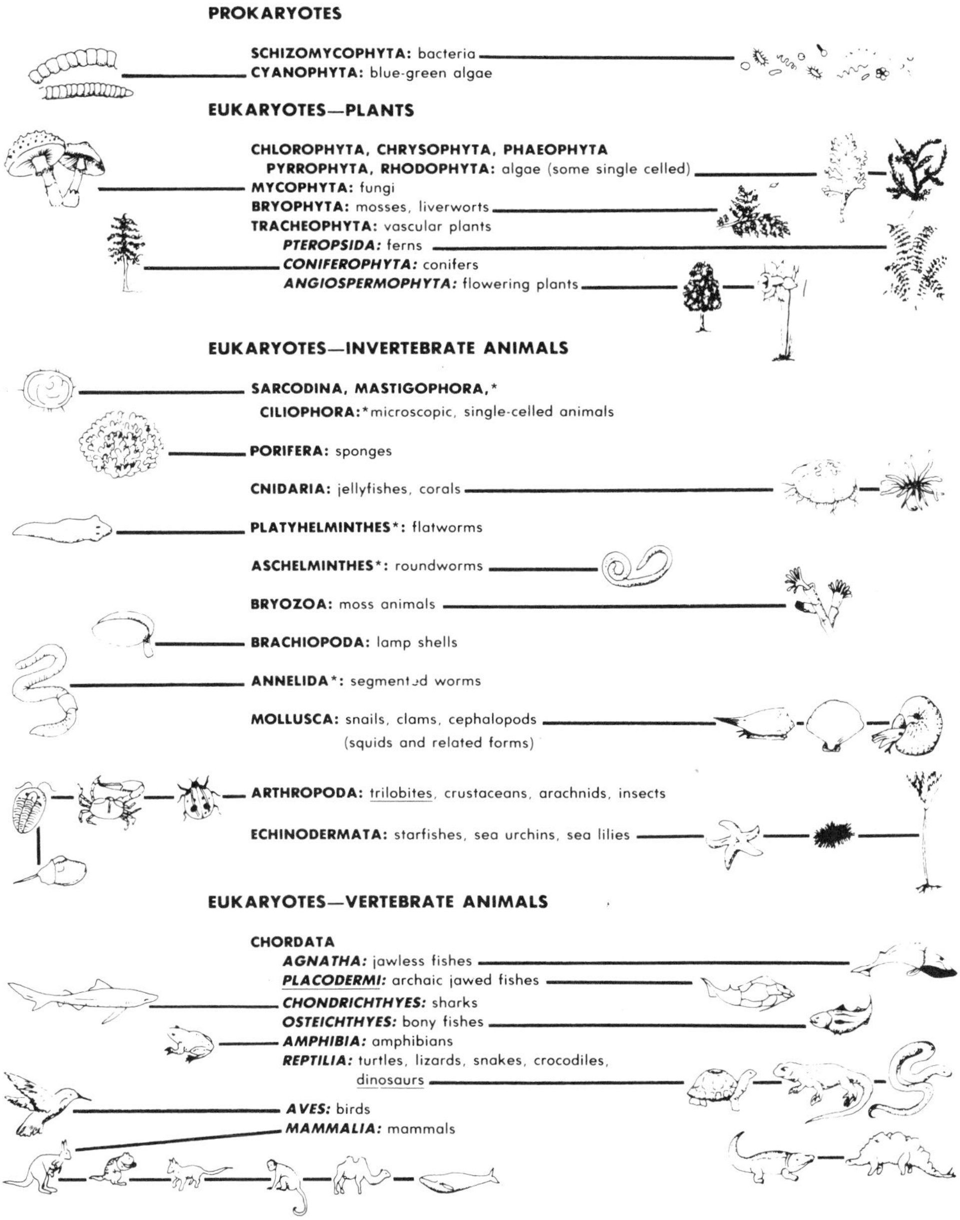

PROKARYOTES

SCHIZOMYCOPHYTA: bacteria
CYANOPHYTA: blue-green algae

EUKARYOTES—PLANTS

CHLOROPHYTA, CHRYSOPHYTA, PHAEOPHYTA
PYRROPHYTA, RHODOPHYTA: algae (some single celled)
MYCOPHYTA: fungi
BRYOPHYTA: mosses, liverworts
TRACHEOPHYTA: vascular plants
  PTEROPSIDA: ferns
  CONIFEROPHYTA: conifers
  ANGIOSPERMOPHYTA: flowering plants

EUKARYOTES—INVERTEBRATE ANIMALS

SARCODINA, MASTIGOPHORA,*
  CILIOPHORA:*microscopic, single-celled animals

PORIFERA: sponges

CNIDARIA: jellyfishes, corals

PLATYHELMINTHES*: flatworms

ASCHELMINTHES*: roundworms

BRYOZOA: moss animals

BRACHIOPODA: lamp shells

ANNELIDA*: segmented worms

MOLLUSCA: snails, clams, cephalopods
  (squids and related forms)

ARTHROPODA: trilobites, crustaceans, arachnids, insects

ECHINODERMATA: starfishes, sea urchins, sea lilies

EUKARYOTES—VERTEBRATE ANIMALS

CHORDATA
  AGNATHA: jawless fishes
  PLACODERMI: archaic jawed fishes
  CHONDRICHTHYES: sharks
  OSTEICHTHYES: bony fishes
  AMPHIBIA: amphibians
  REPTILIA: turtles, lizards, snakes, crocodiles,
    dinosaurs
  AVES: birds
  MAMMALIA: mammals

Extinct groups are underlined. Some important classes are listed for vascular plants and animals.
*Predominantly soft-bodied phyla with little or no fossil record.

Figure 8.6 The Major Subdivisions of Life

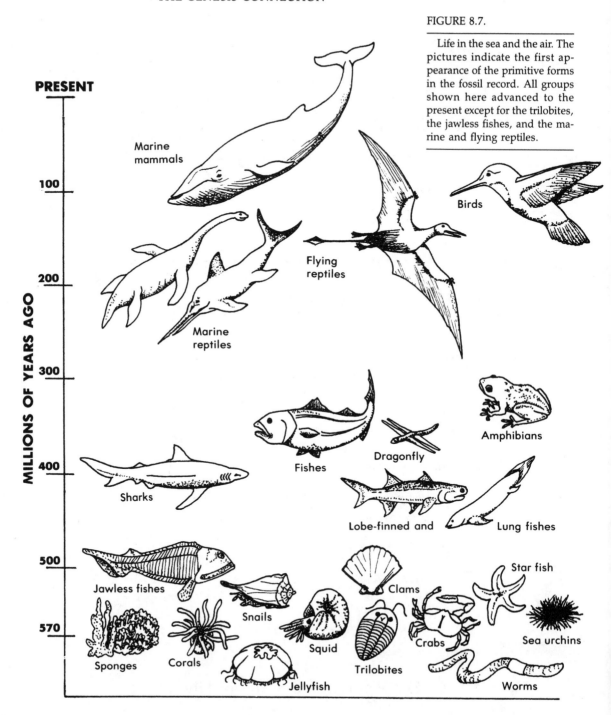

FIGURE 8.7.

Life in the sea and the air. The pictures indicate the first appearance of the primitive forms in the fossil record. All groups shown here advanced to the present except for the trilobites, the jawless fishes, and the marine and flying reptiles.

FIGURE 8.8.

The archaeopteryx, *left*, may be a transitional form between reptiles and birds. A fossil cast is sketched at far left beside the simulated reconstruction. Some scientists hypothesize that the "featherbed reptile" or "reptilian bird" may have evolved into the true birds and that dinosaurs are therefore not extinct. They live on as birds. The primitive reptile, *right*, may be the ancestor of both the dinosaurs and the archaeopteryx.

saur (the *Ornithopod*) may be so closely related to true birds through the Archaeopteryx that they may be placed in the same biological classification. The logical conclusion of such a close relationship is that dinosaurs are not extinct; they live on as birds.

In any event, about 100 million years ago, two types of birds made their appearance. One was a small gull-like bird that was apparently a strong flier. The other, a penguin-like diving bird, was large with powerful swimming legs and only vestiges of wings.

Birds not only have powerful breast muscles for driving their wings, but also have numerous individual feathers for true flight and maneuverability. The individual feathers can be renewed and replaced as needed. If the membrane-like wing of a flying reptile were damaged, the creature was probably permanently out of commission. Birds therefore had great advantages in the air. They replaced the flying reptiles and achieved unparalleled success in the skies of the Earth.

THE THEORY OF EVOLUTION

The Cambrian explosion of marine animals is not only the most dramatic event in the history of life; it is also the best documented. The evidence is there, preserved in sedimentary rocks on every continent in the world. For this reason, it forces us to examine the theory of evolution, the theory which is most commonly thought to explain the fossil evidence of Cambrian marine animals and the development of other forms of life. After studying this theory, we will take a new look at the fossil evidence in an effort to determine if the theory of evolution explains the how and the why of the Cambrian explosion.

FIGURE 8.9.

The peppered moth and its color adaptation to changing environment. The sketch at left shows trees with lichens. Note how difficult it is to spot the well-camouflaged, lighter form in the lower part of the picture. The sketch at right shows the same forms after soot from factories in industrial England destroyed the lichens. The dark (melanic) form then became far more prevalent. This is the classic example of observed *micro-evolution*. It also demonstrates that life has been endowed with an inherent genetic potential for change.

History credits Charles Darwin with originating and developing the theory of evolution. Darwin's theory holds that life forms have changed over time and have developed into the types of plants and animals that are present on the Earth today. According to this theory, all life is related; all life is descended from a common ancestor. The primary mechanism that has determined the direction that life has taken is "natural selection."

In analyzing "natural selection," the term "survival of the fittest" is frequently used. If we picture the world of fang and claw, we can visualize that the fastest zebra escapes the charge of the lion. He or she survives to produce more offspring and thus, over time, the zebras become faster runners. The slow zebras are caught; the fast ones survive to produce offspring. The race in life goes to the swiftest.

We can also look at giraffes and their eating habits. Those giraffes with the longest legs and longest necks can reach higher in the trees to get food. Since they obtain more food when food is scarce, they produce more offspring. In this case, the race goes to the tallest.

The problem with these examples is that they are too simple and therefore scientifically incorrect. To base natural selection on one trait implies zebras would break the sound barrier and giraffes would be as tall as four-story buildings. But as the zebras got faster, so would the lions chasing them. As the giraffes got taller, so would the trees they eat. There are obvious limitations and other factors that make

126

natural selection more complex than the examples shown. Modern evolutionists tend to speak in terms of "ecological niches" and better "reproductive strategies" to incorporate the multitude of factors that determine how life might evolve in one or more different directions.

Nevertheless, the basic principle of natural selection as envisioned by Darwin is still the cornerstone of evolutionary theory: Parents produce offspring that are different; those that are best equipped to survive in the existing environment or to exploit new ecological opportunities thrive and multiply; over time or in isolated areas the changes slowly accumulate to produce new forms of life and new species.

OBSERVATIONS OF EVOLUTION

Do actual observations of changes over time substantiate Darwin's theory of evolution? The answer is both yes and no. Let us first look at *micro*-evolution—variations among different populations of the same species, as in the variation between the different human races of the world. We will then take a look at *macro*-evolution or major changes in life forms as exemplified by the Cambrian explosion.

During the latter half of the nineteenth century, the countryside surrounding the coal-burning factories of England underwent a dramatic change. Air pollution from coal smoke and soot caused the lichens on trees to disappear and the trees turned black. During the same period, the peppered moth underwent a marked change. Prior to the 1840s, the population of peppered moths was made up of individuals that were almost exclusively a speckled gray color (the light form). By 1895, in the areas surrounding the factories, 98% of the peppered moths were almost completely dark in color (the dark or melanic form). Why?

The answer is obvious when one visualizes how easy it is for birds who eat the moths to spot the light form against tree trunks that are black and lacking in the camouflage pattern of lichens (see figure 8.9). The light-colored moths stand out "like a sore thumb." They are easy prey for hungry birds. Thus, over a fifty-year period, the light-colored moths became rare. The black-colored forms had taken their place. This is a classic example of micro-evolution, or small change over time to fit changing environmental conditions.

Another example of observed change over time is improved breeds of milk- or beef-producing cattle. In the first example of the peppered moth, birds carry out the natural selection. In the second example, man is the selector. Both examples show that small changes in life forms can be produced over time due to selection to fit the needs of a changed environment or the needs of man. It also demonstrates that life forms have been created with the inherent genetic potential for change. That is, there is enough potential for variation in the gene pool of the offspring so that when conditions change, a few of the offspring can adapt to the changed conditions and multiply.

All scientists and observers of nature agree on the effects of micro-evolution. But do the same factors account for major changes in life forms such as from a single-celled *protozoa* to a starfish, crab, or lobster, and thence to a fish? Such major changes would be called *macro*-evolution.

Animals are far removed from being simply a cluster of self-sufficient cells. Even the lowly worm is comprised of highly specialized cells organized into unique tissues and organs with functions as diverse as:

- gathering food
- processing and digesting food
- eliminating waste
- external protection
- internal absorption and integration
- circulation of fluids
- reproduction
- perception
- locomotion

How did this miracle happen? A *single cell to an animal*. What an incredible transformation!

If the Darwinian evolutionary theory is correct, then we should hope to find fossil evidence of gradual transitions from single-celled protozoa to a complex, multicellular, multi-organed, completely functioning animal. In addition we should expect to find transitional forms between the eleven or so invertebrate phyla which appear in the fossil record. We should further expect to find some sort of transition from the invertebrate marine animals to the fish. Let's re-examine the Cambrian explosion of marine life to determine if Darwin's theory can be proven when applied to macro-evolution—major changes in life forms.

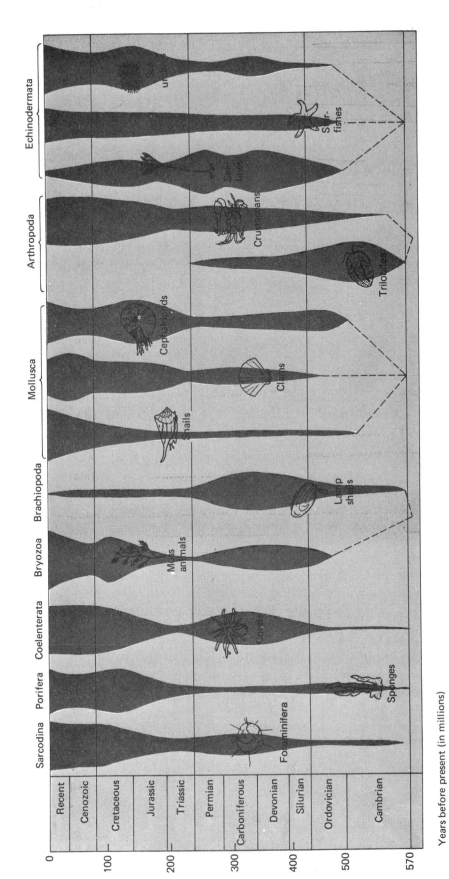

Years before present (in millions)

FIGURE 8.10.

Geologic record of the principal groups of marine invertebrates. The shapes of the vertical areas indicate the approximate abundance of each group. The dashed lines indicate possible relationships.

Varied sedimentary formations rising over 45,000 feet in central East Greenland. These rocks date from the late Precambrian period.

THE MYSTERY OF THE CAMBRIAN EXPLOSION

There are several very important points that one must bear in mind with respect to the Cambrian explosion of marine life. The first point is its suddenness. All the major categories of marine invertebrates appear in the fossil record during the Cambrian period in geologic history.

The second point to be noted is that all these marine invertebrates appear in a fully formed condition. Further, they are essentially unchanged to the present time. While they are presently more modern in appearance than in Cambrian times, there have been no fundamentally new forms or structures introduced. Just as a child changes in appearance as he grows to adulthood, we recognize some changes, but not in basic form or structure. The marine invertebrates of today can be recognized from their ancestors of 500 million years ago.

The third point of importance is that there is no fossil record of any transitional forms between the invertebrate phyla. If Darwinian evolutionary theory is correct, we should expect to find fossils of a common ancestor for fossils of one or more differing types. These should then give rise to other new types or phyla and so on.

There is no fossil record of an ancestor for any one of the invertebrate phyla. Further, there is no fossil record of transitional forms between the types or phyla. The standard college textbook on the subject, *Evolution* by Dobzhansky, Ayala, Stebbins, and Valentine, states, "The origins and earliest evolution of the metazoan phyla cannot be documented from fossil evidence."[1] All the phyla simply appear in the fossil record, fully formed and without ancestors. Where did they come from?

This answer is very simple: we don't know because there are no fossils, no records, no clues of any kind.

Our knowledge of the present ecology of the marine animals tells us that several key conditions had to have been present before they could exist in the waters of the Earth. These conditions are: food source (plants such as algae and other organisms); a supply of oxygen for metabolism; and an ozone screen in the upper atmosphere to screen out the Sun's lethal ultraviolet rays. Scientists believe that these requisite ecologic conditions were in place several hundred million years prior to the Cambrian era, although the percentage of oxygen in the oceans may not yet have reached some critical factor.

Scientists also believe that biological developments such as the nucleated cell (eukaryotes) and sexual reproduction had also been accomplished over one billion years ago. Yet the evidence shows thousands of feet of sedimentary strata underlying Cambrian rock that is identical to the Cambrian strata above it. What then marks the boundary between the Precambrian and Cambrian rocks? The abundant presence of fossils of fully formed marine animals in the Cambrian strata. Where did they come from?

One hundred years ago, the explanation for the gaps or missing links was simple: the transitional forms are there, but have not been discovered. Today this explanation has a hollow ring for we have discovered and examined extensive Precambrian strata throughout the world. What has been found? A few rare traces of possible burrows of worms and impressions of jellyfish. These worms and jellyfish were not transitional forms. The fossil impressions indicate fully formed multicellular animals. The transitional forms have not been found. Do they exist?

If, as Darwin envisioned, life evolved in a slow and gradual way, we should expect that somewhere in the 300 million years of extensive Precambrian sedimentary deposits there should be at least one transitional form leading to the invertebrate animals *(Metazoa)*. But there is nothing. Further, we should also expect in the next 100 million years of the Cambrian period and into the Devonian period (the Age of Fishes) to find transitions within the Metazoa phyla and also something leading up to fishes. There is nothing. There are no transitional forms.

We have no transitional forms at all: none leading up to the Metazoa phyla, none within the Metazoa phyla, and none leading to the fish. The lack of evidence is in direct conflict with the Darwinian theory of evolution. How are these major gaps to be explained?

Some scientists have devoted their whole professional careers to the search for the missing transitional forms, to no avail. Still the traditional Darwinist holds out for discovery of the missing links. He still claims the evidence lies buried somewhere in the fossil records.

Others have faced the facts and feel it is time to modify evolutionary theory to account for the lack of transitional forms in the fossil record. One such modification is the new theory of punctuated equilibrium.

Punctuated Equilibrium. The theory of punctuated equilibrium holds that life did not evolve in the slow uniform method that Darwin envisioned but rather in rapid evolutionary bursts of major change called *adaptive radiations.* The Cambrian explosion of marine life was such an adaptive radiation. We will encounter other adaptive radiations—amphibians, reptiles, and mammals—as we explore animal life on the land in the next chapter. The term will be used solely in a descriptive sense.

This new theory of punctuated equilibrium envisions that life doesn't change at all for very long periods of time. Then in a short period of geologic time, whole new forms of life appear and rapidly radiate into new varieties. Change does not come in small steps, but in giant leaps. When all the ecological niches become occupied by the new life forms, life becomes stable again. It settles down to a long period of static equilibrium. Niles Eldridge of the American Museum of Natural History and S. J. Gould of Harvard are the originators and major proponents of this theory.

The theory of punctuated equilibrium accounts very well for the huge gaps in the fossil record. It does correlate with the evidence. It makes sense. But now we have to face the central question. Does it explain anything? Or are the terms *adaptive radiation* and *punctuated equilibrium* merely well-chosen words to describe the observed evidence?

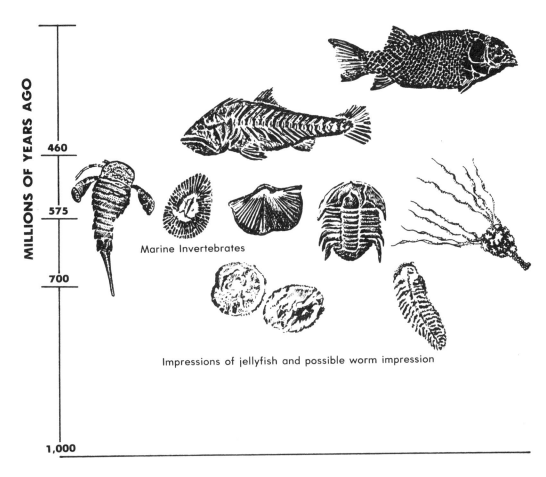

MILLIONS OF YEARS AGO

460

575

700

1,000

Marine Invertebrates

Impressions of jellyfish and possible worm impression

I suspect the latter is true, for the mechanistic causes of these major transformations are not worked out. There isn't a definitive theory or standard model that can be tested. We can consider major environmental changes, such as an increase in the oxygen supply, or the creation of new ecological niches to be occupied. We can also consider the possibility of major genetic changes brought about by cosmic radiation. We can envision species in isolated locations becoming better adapted to specialized environments and subsequently radiating geographically outward to displace existing worldwide populations. But a single cell to a fish? There ought to be some sort of transitional record somewhere in 400 million years of sedimentary deposits.

In the next chapter, dealing with animal life on the land, we will encounter fossil evidence for transitional forms and for changes in

FIGURE 8.12.

The Cambrian explosion. Virtually all the major categories of marine invertebrate animals appear in the Cambrian period (575 to 500 million years ago). Primitive fish appear shortly thereafter. Three mysteries remain: there are no fossil transitional forms leading from single cells to the completely formed, multi-celled animals; none between the invertebrate animals; and none leading to the fish. There are 400 million years of sedimentary deposits with no transitional forms whatsoever.

forms and structures that fit new environments. But as far as evidence for the appearance of animal life in the oceans, the transitional record is a complete and total blank. The lack of intermediate forms in the Cambrian explosion of marine life is the great "black hole" of mechanistic evolutionary theory.

MORE THAN HARMONY

In Chapter 4 we learned how God created the waters and the sky. In this chapter we learned that God filled those spaces with abundant, beautiful, and harmonious life.

Animal life in the waters of the Earth began with the sudden appearance of almost all major forms of marine invertebrates 570 million years ago. This event is known as the Cambrian explosion. The waters literally teemed with swarms of living creatures. Jawless and armored fishes appeared shortly thereafter and the roster of marine vertebrates was complete with the arrival of the true fishes. Giant marine reptiles occupied the sea during the Age of the Dinosaurs and were later replaced by the marine mammals.

Flying insects appeared about 400 million years ago. They were followed by the flying reptiles during the Age of Dinosaurs. True birds appeared in the fossil record more than 100 million years ago. Their feathered wings and efficient flight have given them dominion in the skies of the Earth.

In a very real sense, the scientific record of life in the sea and in the air describes what took place when God said: "Let the waters teem with swarms of living creatures, and let birds fly above the earth in the open expanse of the heavens" (Gen. 1:20).

Science and Scripture are again in harmony. In fact, the scientific term *adaptive radiation* is an apt description of the response to God's command when He blessed them and said, "Be fruitful and multiply, and fill the waters in the seas, and let birds multiply on the earth" (Gen. 1:22).

There appears to be more than harmony here. Could Scripture be supplying the answer to causation so long sought after by evolutionary theorists? Quite possibly. In any event, the new theory of punctuated equilibrium brings the thinking of science remarkably closer to the biblical view. It is notable that the more evidence scientists discover (or fail to discover), the closer scientific theory moves toward the unchanging biblical pattern.

CHAPTER 9
LIFE ON THE LAND

Then God said, "Let the earth bring forth living creatures after their kind: cattle and creeping things and beasts of the earth after their kind"; and it was so.

Genesis 1:24

The first act in the drama of animal life, as we have noted, took place in the sea. The waters teemed with swarms of living creatures, and the fish were the stars of the show. The development of animal life then abated for 50 million years, but behind the curtain of ceased activity, the stage was being set for the invasion of the land.

Before life could exist on the land, there had to be a suitable food source (see figure 9.1). Just as plant life on land probably first developed in marshes and swamps, so the same pattern probably held for animal life. Insects, worms, and snails followed the vegetative advance. They provided a tempting food source for larger marine animals that could crawl out of the water to snatch a few tasty morsels.

The transition of animals from water to land is a difficult one. Major and diverse modifications are required for a fish to change into a four-legged, air-breathing animal that crawls across the surface of the land. Problems of breathing, water retention, reproduction, and locomotion have to be solved. Stronger and more rigid internal skeletal support is required without the medium of water for support. A fish out of water is helpless indeed.

In this chapter we are going to cover the appearance of the amphibians, the reptiles, and their dominant forms—the dinosaurs and the mammals. These are the animals of the land that crawled, walked, and galloped onto the pages of history during the later eras of geologic history.

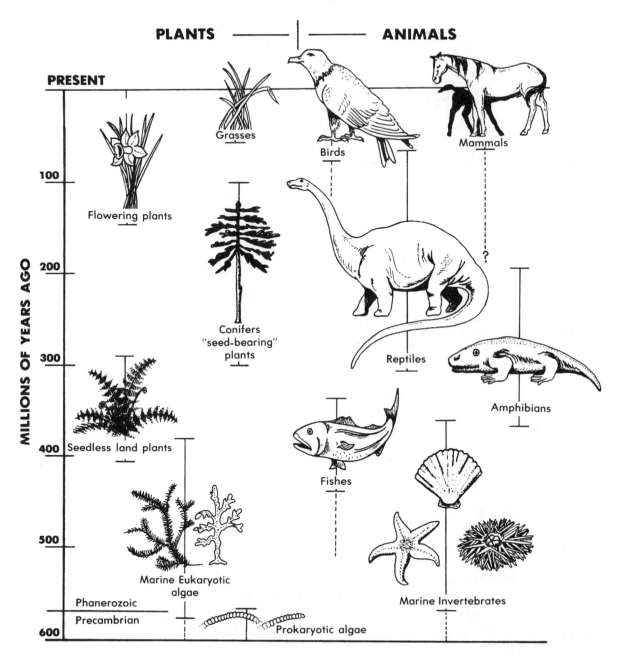

FIGURE 9.1.

Emerging life on the Earth.
Solid lines indicate periods of
relative dominance.

FIGURE 9.2.

The coelacanth, a primitive lobe-finned fossil fish that existed in shallow waters 350 million years ago, is almost identical to its modern form, the latimeria, discovered in the deep waters of the Indian Ocean. (Courtesy Field Museum of Natural History, Chicago.)

AMPHIBIANS

Amphibians such as present-day salamanders and frogs are not fully land animals. They solve the problem of water retention by partially living in water or returning to it frequently. Similarly, they must depend on water to lay their eggs and grow in the early stages. But in their adult stage they differ from fish. Amphibians breathe air and crawl or hop about on land. If, over time, a primitive form of fish were able to change into an amphibian, the problems of air breathing and locomotion would have to be solved.

Scientists have interpreted the fossil record to indicate that amphibian-like fish existed in shallow water environments about 350 million years ago. One such primitive fish is the *coelacanth*, a lobe-finned fish that has fins with bone and strong muscular attachments to its body. It was thought to have become extinct 70 million years ago. But in this century it has been discovered alive and well in the Indian Ocean off the coast of Africa. The present species, called the Latimeria, is larger than its fossil ancestor and lives in the ocean depths rather than the shallow water it is thought to have inhabited in primitive times. The fact that it lives in deep water may dispute its position as a possible missing link from water to land.

There are other fish living today that possess some rather amazing characteristics. Fish that fly for short distances of fifty yards or so are known off the waters of California and Mexico. In fact, these flying fish are the most common bait used by sportsmen fishing for marlin.

There are also fish that actually climb trees. They are known as mudskippers. These small fish live in the muddy estuaries and mangrove swamps in many parts of the tropics. They crawl out of the water and onto the glistening mud to feed on insects. They edge themselves forward with their muscular fins supported by internal bones. They often cling to the aerial roots of mangroves and even clamber up the trunks.

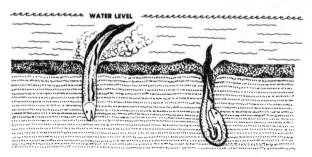

FIGURE 9.3.

The modern West African lungfish adapts to the changing water level in the pond.

The mudskipper manages to stay out of water for brief periods by holding water in its mouth. By swilling the water around on the roof of its mouth it is able to extract oxygen. It is also able to absorb oxygen from the air through its moist skin. However, after a few minutes on land or in the trees, it must return to the sea to wet its skin and gulp a new mouthful of water. While a highly interesting curiosity, the mudskipper does not really breathe air.

A normal fish extracts oxygen from the water by passing it through its gills. However, there are a number of fish alive today that actually breathe air from the atmosphere. One such fish is known as a lungfish and exists in various forms in Africa, Australia, and South America. When the floodplains of rivers dry into sun-baked mud, the lungfish burrows into the mud and hibernates until the next rainy season, perhaps a year away. During this waterless period the lungfish draws air through its burrow hole into its mouth. The air passes into a pair of pouches located in its gut. These function as simple lungs. Thus, by adapting to air breathing, the lungfish is able to exist until the next rains again flood the area.

The lungfish and the lobe-finned fish illustrate ways in which fish might have adapted to land. The lungfish has the capability to breathe air, and lobe-finned fish have a possible potential to crawl on land. Both are found as primitive fossils in the ancient sedimentary record of 350 million years ago. Yet neither is regarded as the direct ancestor of descendants that explored the land. The lungfish could breathe air. The lobe-finned fish could possibly have crawled, but that is not enough. Both capabilities are required to colonize the land. Further, the bones of their skulls are not similar to those of the early

138

amphibians. They do not appear to have been transitional forms.

There is a fossil fish, however, from those ancient times that could qualify as the ancestor of amphibians. It is called the *eusthenopteron*. Its fins resemble the leg-like paddle fins of the *coelacanth*. Further, the bone pattern of its fins is similar to that found in the legs and feet of amphibians and the other land vertebrates. Its skull also has the crucial feature lacking in lungfish and the *coelacanths*. There appears to be a passage linking the roof of the mouth to the nostrils. The *eusthenopteron*, a lobe-finned fish, was very much like an amphibian. It appears to have been preadapted to life on the land. It may have colonized the land and given rise to the first group of amphibians, the *labyrinthodonts* (see figure 9.4).

Today, the amphibians are best represented by frogs and salamanders. The lifestyle of the amphibian itself may be thought of as transitional between water and land. A frog cannot leave the water for long periods or its skin will dry out. It must return to water to lay its eggs because the eggs will hatch only in an aquatic environment.

The development of the tadpole is fascinating to watch; first wiggling about the water with its long whip-like tail; then growing limbs with feet; and, finally, crawling out of the water to croak to the world. The fossil record, a modern comparison of skeletal structure *(morphological similarity)*, and direct observation of individual growth and development designate the amphibian as a transitional form that bridges the gap between water and land.

FIGURE 9.4.

A possible transitional form from fish to amphibian.

FIGURE 9.5.

The final stages in growth from a tadpole to frog. Amphibians represent transitional forms between those that live on water and those that live on land.

FIGURE 9.6.

Primitive amphibians of the group known as Labyrinthodonts. Sketch shows eryops, *above*, and cacops.

The Age of Amphibians, during which amphibians dominated the Earth, lasted from about 350 to 275 million years ago. This took place during the geologic periods known as Mississippian, Pennsylvanian, and early Permian. This was also the age of the great coal-forming swampy vegetation. The fossilized bones of the primitive *labyrinthodont* amphibians are often found in coal mines today.

Some of these creatures must have been terrifying (see figure 9.6). They ranged up to twelve feet long and had jaws lined with cone-shaped teeth. Some resembled fat, stub-nosed alligators. The *labyrinthodont* amphibians slowly declined to extinction about 200 million years ago. Modern amphibians such as salamanders and frogs do not appear in the fossil record until about 100 million years ago. Their relationship to the *labyrinthodonts* is obscure because they differ in major ways.

FIGURE 9.7.

The shelled egg is an important feature in distinguishing a reptile from an amphibian. A reptile such as a crocodile reproduces by means of a protective shelled egg, which contains the necessary nutrients to nurture the embryo to a fully developed form. The egg must have been fertilized within the body of the female reptile before it can develop the protective shell. Thus, both male and female reptiles possess reproductive organs greatly different from those of amphibians.

REPTILES

The next animals to appear on the land were reptiles. The major distinction between amphibians and reptiles is that whereas amphibians require both water and land for existence, reptiles can exist completely in a dry-land environment. The reptile is further distinguished by its scaly, water-retentive armor and a shelled egg. The relatively impermeable skin and the scales of a reptile serve an important function. They conserve water and body fluids within the body of the animal. They prevent it from drying out. The shelled egg not only prevents its contents from drying out, but contains the nutrients necessary to nurture the embryo to an advanced stage of development. An egg encased by a shell allows the embryo to grow and develop in its own self-contained liquid environment. When growth is completed, the small but otherwise fully formed animal can break out of its shell to view its new world.

Freed from having to remain near large bodies of water, the reptiles could occupy land areas denied to the amphibians. The land areas were filled with vegetation and juicy bugs. The environment was ripe for larger animals that could occupy the vast unexploited "ecological niches" that were present. In a short period of geologic time the reptiles appeared in many diverse forms. They underwent an explosive "adaptive radiation." Some are thought to have grown into the dinosaurs.

GIANTS RULE THE EARTH

Today reptiles are represented by snakes, lizards, turtles, and crocodiles. Of these, only the crocodile is a truly ancient form. In their heyday during the Age of Dinosaurs, crocodiles may have reached fifty feet in length.

The Age of Reptiles began about 265 million years ago. Reptiles dominated the land for 200 million years until 62 million years ago when the Age of Mammals began. During the early Age of Reptiles the fossil record indicates that reptiles resembled amphibians with short legs and the elongated shape of an alligator or crocodile. Mammal-like reptiles with longer but still stubby legs appeared later in the fossil record. They were called the *therapsids* (see figure 9.8) and are

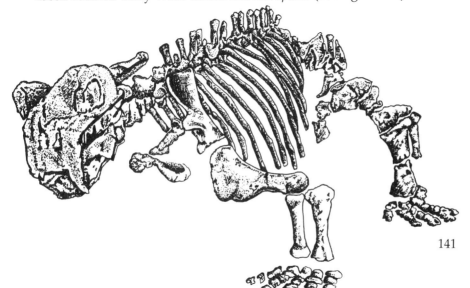

FIGURE 9.8.

The early mammal-like reptiles, called therapsids, are illustrated in the sketch above. Actual size of the skeleton is about 3 feet in length. Note that, unlike true mammals or dinosaurs, the legs extend outward from the body in a sprawling position.

141

thought to have been the ancestors of the mammals.

About 200 million years ago, the Age of the Dinosaurs began. They established a dynasty that ruled the land, the sea, and the air for the next 140 million years. They are present in the fossil record in virtually all shapes and sizes. Some ate vegetation exclusively (*herbivorous*), others were *carnivorous* and preyed on their *herbivorous*

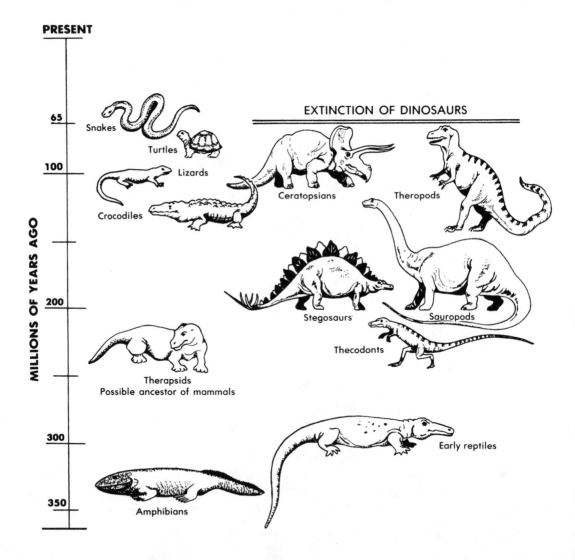

Figure 9.9 Reptiles on the Land

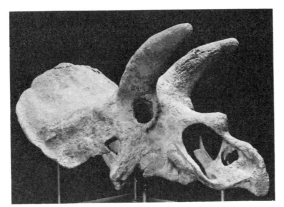

FIGURE 9.10.

Triceratops calicornis. The skull of a ceratopsian dinosaur found in strata dating from the late Cretaceous period near Chalk Butte, Montana. (Courtesy Field Museum of Natural History, Chicago.)

relatives. Larger size was not a permanent advantage. Various waves of extinction wiped out the larger forms, but the smaller reptiles that survived would in turn give rise to new giants.

The name *dinosaur* means "terrible lizard" and some of them were terrible indeed. Although some were about the size of a chicken, others grew to great size, larger than elephants of today. The plant-eating *Brontosaurus* (now called *Apatosaurus*) is thought to have weighed more than thirty tons. It belonged to the small-skulled, long-necked, long-tailed group of dinosaurs known as the *sauropods* (see figure 9.9).

The group known as *theropods* were carnivorous and preyed on their plant-eating relatives. They walked erect on their hind legs. *Tyrannosaurus rex,* the largest of this carnivorous group, was characterized by two stout hind legs for running and short forelimbs for seizing prey. Its short neck and huge head with menacing teeth must have made it the terror of the dinosaur world.

Dinosaurs appeared in weird and extravagant body forms. The *stegosaurs* had large diamond-shaped plates staggered along their backbone. These may have been used for some type of temperature regulation. It appears they had sharp spikes on the end of the tail that could have been deadly weapons against their enemies (see figure 9.11).

Another curious body form that appeared late in the Age of Dinosaurs is exhibited by the horned group known as the *ceratopsians.* Like the *stegosaurs,* their teeth indicate they were vegetarians. One of this group, the tank-like *triceratops,* is shown in Figure 9.10. This huge, horned dinosaur weighed about nine tons and carried three horns on its immense skull. The two, long, spear-shaped horns above its eyes together with the rhinoceros-like horn on its nose

FIGURE 9.11.

In this painting by Charles R. Knight, two specimens of the dinosaur Stegosaurus are shown foraging for food in an area now called southeastern Wyoming. (Courtesy Field Museum of Natural History, Chicago.)

must have been formidable weapons. The great bony frill around the base of its neck probably served for protection. *Triceratops* is thought to have had a relatively large brain, about a kilogram (2.2 lbs.) in weight. In spite of this relative intelligence, huge size, and protective armor, it was not spared in the coming disaster.

WHAT HAPPENED TO THE DINOSAURS?

The fossil record reveals that there have been several major extinctions of life forms over geologic time. None is so dramatic or so widespread as the mass exterminations that took place at the end of the Mesozoic era 63 million years ago. The dinosaur reign that had lasted for 140 million years fell with a resounding crash. The dinosaurs disappeared from the land, seas, and air. Only their fossilized bones and tracks remain as witness to their once-dominant place in geologic history.

Why did they vanish? There are numerous hypotheses and explanations. While none is completely satisfactory, it is worthwhile to review some of the major suggestions. Unsolved mysteries are far more fascinating than solved cases. We can also review some of the things about the dynamic processes of our planet in the investigation.

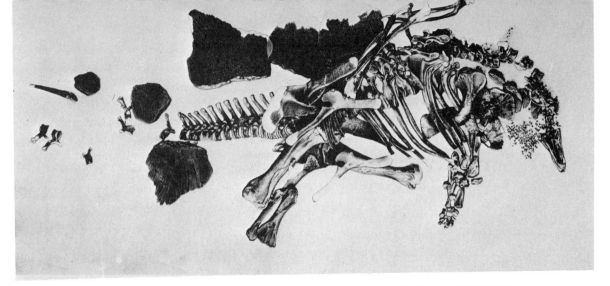

Gradual Climatic Change. The Mesozoic era that began with the Age of Reptiles more than 225 million years ago was a period of benign climate. The Earth's climate was not only relatively warm, but, as the age progressed, it is thought that there were not great temperature extremes of heat and cold. Two hundred million years ago the continents were assembled into one great land mass or megacontinent called Pangaea. But by 65 million years ago the continents had largely separated, and the northern land masses had drifted more toward the polar regions.

The vast shallow seas that existed on the fringes of and in the middle of continents gradually drained. The climate of continents was no longer ameliorated by these seas. Greater temperature extremes became common. The winter seasons became cold and long. Animals such as the dinosaurs that were *ectotherms* were hard pressed to survive.

All reptiles and amphibians are *ectotherms*. Their body temperatures fluctuate to match that of the surrounding air or water. They do not generate heat internally in an effort to maintain a constant body temperature as do *endotherms* (mammals and birds).

Amphibians and reptiles, the *ectotherms*, must derive their heat energy directly or indirectly from the Sun. When the climate is warm and mild, this is an advantage. The reptiles do not need to eat much to stay alive because they don't need to metabolize or convert food into energy to heat their bodies. The Sun does this for them. Consider the difference between a busy squirrel gathering nuts and a torpid lizard sitting on a rock. Reptiles may require only 10% of the food needed by the more active *endothermic* mammals and birds that must maintain a constant body temperature.

But when the climate turns cold, especially for long periods, the

FIGURE 9.12.

The sketch of a Stegosaurus skeleton, as it was discovered in the Jurassic formation, is essentially complete. (Courtesy Smithsonian Institution.)

145

reptiles are doomed. Their bodies either freeze or become so inactive that they cannot move. Reptiles have no method of converting their food into heat energy to stay alive. They must hibernate, seek shelter in a burrow deep underground, or die. But where would a ten-ton dinosaur go to seek shelter from a raging blizzard? They were not able to burrow into a hole like a snake or lizard. At the onset of winter, they perish.

While this climate change undoubtedly occurred and affected the dinosaurs, there are three problems with listing it as the major cause of the dinosaurs' extinction. The first problem is that they were not alone in their downfall 63 million years ago, and any major explanation for their extinction must also explain the extinction of other forms of life at the same time. Vast groups of marine plankton, land plants, and marine invertebrates including some species of clams and oysters were also wiped out. It has been estimated that more than 75% of the previously existing plant and animal life disappeared at about the same time as the dinosaurs.[1] However, the marine invertebrates as well as the ocean-dwelling dinosaurs should have been protected from extremes of temperature by the ocean waters.

The second problem with the climatic causation theory is that the temperature change was thought to have been somewhat gradual. Continents move very slowly, and, if evolutionary theory is correct, life should have adapted and adjusted to these changing conditions. It didn't. Further, there should have been a relatively warm and constant temperature belt around the equator as there is today. The dinosaurs should have survived in these warm pockets as did the crocodiles. They didn't. Some dinosaurs survived longer than others, but they all ultimately perished.

The third problem with listing the gradual climate change as the cause of the dinosaurs' downfall is that there is no evidence to indicate they were on a gradual decline. Toward the end of the Mesozoic era the diversity of dinosaur species did not decrease. In Mongolia the diversity actually increased.[2] Such an increase in the number of varied species is the reverse of what scientists expect from a group that is tending toward extinction.

Although a gradually changing climate may have contributed to the demise of the dinosaurs, their relatively sudden demise together with the extinction of other plants and animals has led scientists to search for a more catastrophic explanation.

Catastrophic Explanations. There are three general catastrophic explanations for the demise of the dinosaurs: magnetic field reversal, volcanic eruptions, and "extraterrestrial forces."

The reversal of the Earth's magnetic field is a possible explanation for the dinosaurs' extinction. The Earth's unique solid inner and fluid outer iron core acts as a giant magnet, generating a magnetic field that reaches far out into space to help shield the Earth from charged particles known as *cosmic rays*.

On a highly irregular time schedule and for reasons unexplained, the magnetic field is known to reverse: the North Pole becomes negative and the South Pole positive. Later the North Pole changes to positive and the South Pole negative, taking perhaps a few thousand years to reverse its direction.[3] About eighty magnetic field reversals are known to have occurred in the last 110 million years.[4]

During the reversal it is possible that the magnetic field briefly collapses, leaving the surface of the Earth vulnerable to harmful cosmic radiation. Lethal cosmic rays could have damaged the genetic machinery of the dinosaurs on an unshielded Earth. Other forms of life might also have been selectively affected.

However, the magnetic field reversal hypothesis is, as yet, not well correlated with the dinosaur and other major mass extinctions that have taken place over geologic time. Furthermore, it is thought that the majority of lethal cosmic rays are absorbed by the Earth's protective atmosphere, rather than shielded by the magnetic field. For the present then, the possible collapse of the Earth's magnetic field can be listed only as one of several speculative possibilities for the extinction of the dinosaurs.

Volcanic eruptions are also a possible explanation. When volcanoes erupt they spew out gigantic clouds not only of water vapor, but of noxious gases such as carbon dioxide and carbon monoxide. The smoggy gases could have caused acid rain, which in turn raised the acidity of the oceans. This could have killed off the marine plankton and disrupted the food chain.

Volcanoes also spew out large quantities of ash and dust. The dust and gas pollution resulting from major volcanic eruptions could have suffocated the dinosaurs. The large animals would have been especially vulnerable. They would have had no place to hide. The clouds of dust and gas could also have brought about a sudden climatic change by blocking out the Sun's rays and disrupting the photosynthesis of plants. The dense volcanic clouds could also have produced the greenhouse effect discussed in Chapter 7. This could possibly have raised the Earth's temperature sufficiently to have caused problems for the dinosaurs.

The third explanation for the culprit that killed the dinosaurs is "extraterrestrial forces." These could have included comets, a supernova explosion, or an asteroid. The most favored theory is that an asteroid (small planet) from our own Solar System struck the Earth with enormous force sending not only shock and tidal waves around the globe, but also sending huge clouds of gas, dust, and asteroid material into the atmosphere. The effects would have been similar to those of catastrophic volcanic eruptions.

While on the surface this theory sounds like science fiction, there is some evidence to support it. Scientists from the University of California at Berkeley have discovered in Italy a unique *iridium*-rich clay layer at the very end of the Mesozoic era. A similar layer of the same age has been found in Denmark. *Iridium*, a very dense metallic element that is related to platinum, is very rare on Earth. It is most often found associated with iron and a large quantity may exist in the Earth's iron-rich core. However, in asteroids and meteorites the concentration of iridium is 1,000 to 10,000 times higher than on the surface of the Earth. The iridium-rich clay layer that marks the boundary of the dinosaur extinction may have been the debris from either a giant meteor or an asteroid.

While the asteroid theory is the first one with at least one concrete piece of evidence to support it—the iridium claymarker—it too has its problems. The chief problem is that if the dense cloud of gas and dust blocked out the Sun, the photosynthesizing vegetation should become extinct first, followed by the dinosaurs which would have nothing to eat. But the fossil evidence indicates that the opposite occurred. There are fossil sites in Montana, Wyoming, and Alberta, Canada, where, according to Leo Hickey, a paleobotanist at the Smithsonian Institution, it looks as if the dinosaurs became extinct tens of thousands of years before a large extinction of many major plant forms occurred.[5] Further, William Clemens of the University of California at Berkeley has also found fossils that contradict the asteroid theory. He has found a site in Montana that indicates the dinosaurs perished before the iridium marker anomaly.[6]

There are numerous other interesting theories that have been proposed by scientists over the years to account for the demise of the dinosaurs. In physicist Paul Hoffman's words, "The list of suspects is a long one, and it is a tribute to what human ingenuity can come up with when confronted with something it can't understand."[7] For the present we must be content with the fact that the dinosaur extinction happened abruptly 63 million years ago. The demise of these great

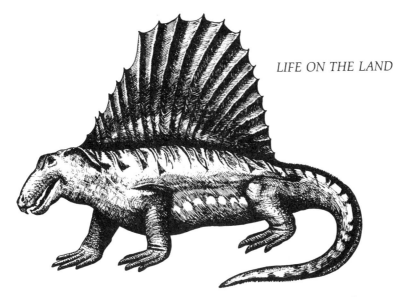

FIGURE 9.13.

A simulated sketch of a *pleycosaur*, a primitive reptile that may have been able to regulate its body temperature. This branch of reptiles may have been ancestors of the mammal-like reptiles known as therapsids.

reptiles left the land, seas, and air empty of large animals. Whatever gradual or sudden catastrophe caused the extinction of these giants, the small burrowing animals survived it. The meek were to inherit the Earth.

THE DIFFERENCE BETWEEN MAMMALS AND REPTILES

With the Earth empty of the long-dominant dinosaurs, the way was now open for the mammals to move to the center stage of history. Mammals differ from reptiles in several important ways. One major difference is in the manner in which they care for their young. Instead of laying a shelled egg like a reptile, mammals internalize the egg. The embryo is nurtured within the body of the female animal where it can be developed and protected. The baby mammal is then born live and nurtured by its mother with the milk produced by the mammary glands from which mammals derive their name.

The other major difference between reptiles and mammals is in the manner in which they maintain their body temperature. Reptiles are said to be cold-blooded, but this term is misleading. Their blood can get very warm indeed. Their blood temperature varies with the surrounding air and exposure to sunshine. They are *ectotherms.* The warm-blooded mammals, on the other hand, maintain a constant body temperature. They are *endotherms.* Mammals are thus able to lead a more active life and adapt to extremes of heat and cold.

This advantage is not without its cost, however, as mammals must eat a great deal more than reptiles to maintain their internal body temperature. The advent of the grasses 60 million years ago was

149

FIGURE 9.14.

The animal shown at the top is a representation of the small therapsid (mammal-like reptile) that survived the initial dinosaur onslaught. It was about a foot long. The therapsid is thought to have given rise to the first tiny rat-like mammal, shown in the lower sketch, which was about 6 inches long.

important for the mammals. Grasses concentrate their energy in seeds as do fruit and nut trees. Seed-eating animals are thus able to obtain and digest greater sources of energy from seed-producing grasses and trees.

Mammals typically have hairy coverings to aid them in maintaining their constant body temperature. Fur or hair is the typical mark of a mammal, as scales are the distinctive mark of a reptile. Mammals also have larger brains in proportion to body size, and thus more capacity for directing intelligent action.

It should be noted here that there is a growing line of thought that the dinosaurs may have been warm-blooded, or at least have had some means of maintaining a relatively constant body temperature. The dorsal, fin-like sail on the back of some forms may have been used as a temperature regulator or solar panel: sail up—radiate or capture heat, sail down—conserve body heat (see figure 9.13).

If the dinosaurs were warm-blooded, as analysis of fossil bones is beginning to hint, it would explain their long period of dominance on the land. On the other hand, environmental analysis tends to favor the cold-booded hypothesis. Vegetative analysis suggests that the Age of Reptiles was associated with a mild and rather constant climate. Further, the extinction of the dinosaurs was concurrent with a change in the Earth's climate to a drier, more variable one with greater extremes of heat and cold. Warm-blooded animals would be decidedly more suited to the climatic change that began to take place 70 million years ago.

The differences between mammals and reptiles—warm blood, hair, and milk-producing glands—do not lend themselves to fossilization. However, there are differences in the patterns of jaws and teeth which have left fossil records. The ability to maintain constant body temperature requires a great deal of food energy. Unlike the torpid reptiles, the more active mammals must eat amply and on a regular basis to maintain their high metabolic rate. Their jaws and teeth, therefore, must be more adapted to cutting, crushing, and grinding than those of reptiles. The analysis of jaws and teeth is therefore the basis of tracing the early evolution of the mammals.

THE ORIGIN OF THE MAMMALS

The fossil record of jaws and teeth has led scientists to the conclusion that mammals arose from the *therapsids* (see figure 9.16).

These mammal-like reptiles appeared very early in the history of reptiles, before the Age of the Dinosaurs. In fact, it is a curiosity of geologic history that mammal-like reptiles of varying size and type dominated the land for close to 90 million years before the Age of the Dinosaurs (see figure 9.9). Why they were supplanted and almost totally extinguished by the dinosaurs is not clearly known. Apparently the *thecodonts*, the ancestors of the dinosaurs, devoured or displaced all but the smallest *therapsids*.

Fossil evidence indicates that the surviving rat-sized *therapsids*

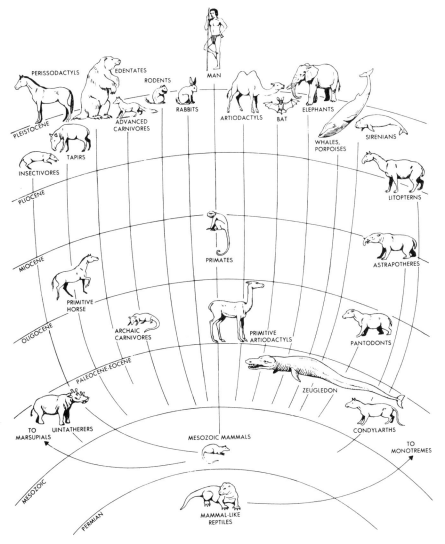

FIGURE 9.15.

Simplified phylogenetic chart of the placental mammals. This illustration also emphasizes the varied adaptations of the groups to different modes of life.

151

(mammal-like reptiles) gave rise to the first tiny primitive mammal at the beginning of the dinosaur reign, 190 million years ago (see figure 9.14). For the next 130 million years, they remained obscure little animals that scurried about the forest in search of food to meet the demands of their high metabolic rate. Theory suggests that to keep from becoming a dinosaur's dinner, they became creatures of the night, foraging for seeds, insects, and worms when the predatory dinosaurs were asleep. How mammals survived the 130-million-year dinosaur dynasty is uncertain, but during this time it is likely they developed increasing intelligence and keen senses of sight, smell, and hearing.

THE AGE OF MAMMALS

Sixty-three million years ago the dinosaurs died out in a final wave of extinction, leaving many unoccupied ecological niches. The grasses appeared and concentrated protein in their seeds which provided nourishment for the high metabolic requirements of mammals. The mammals went forth, multiplied and filled the Earth. Within less than 20 million years, all the basic orders of the class mammalia appeared and are thought to have changed subsequently over time into the familiar animals of today (see figure 9.13). Scientists call this rapid burst of new life forms the explosive adaptive radiation of the mammals.

Some of the mammals that appeared have not survived to the present time. Most changed in size and physical characteristics to adapt to a variable and changing environment. Continents drifted apart and changes in sea level isolated animal groups on different continents. It was a time of variable climates, but the warm-blooded mammals thrived.

About 3 million years ago, the glacial ordeal began. Great cold and sheets of ice crept down from the North. Woolly coats appeared on rhinoceroses and the elephant-like woolly mammoths. It was a time of great migrations and displacement. Although the total number of animals declined, most animal species were able to remain intact as the ice sheets advanced and retreated.

For some land animals, new ecological opportunities were created as ice bridges enabled them to migrate to new continents and new territories. For others, such as the primates, their forest habitats shrank and created pressures for new adaptations. The age of domi-

nance by animals was coming to an end. It was time for the Age of Man.

FIGURE 9.16.

The fossil jawbone of the Jurassic mammal, *Dryolestes vorax*, measures approximately 2.5 centimeters. (Courtesy Smithsonian Institution.)

SOME THOUGHTS TO SHARE ON SCRIPTURE AND EVOLUTION

In Chapter 8 we used the fossil evidence from the Cambrian explosion of life in the sea to test the Darwinian theory of evolution. We found that major changes in life forms—*macro*-evolution—were not documented in the fossil record. Darwin's theory of gradual change was unsupported by 400 million years of sedimentary deposits, which contain not one transitional form.

In this chapter we have examined the amphibians, the reptiles, and the mammals and found that there are some possible transitional forms in the fossil record. Scientists claim that the fossil record contains a well-documented transition from the lobe-finned fish to the amphibian. Amphibians exhibit a lifestyle that is transitional between water and land. This leads to the conclusion that the amphibian itself might be considered a transitional form. Also there are strong indications of transitional forms from the reptiles to very primitive mammals. In contrast, the hypothetical transition from amphibian to reptile is not well documented.

The question arises as to whether evolutionary theory can account for these major transformations in life forms. How really "natural" are these transformations? It is one thing to invoke "natural selection" operating on "genetic variability" to explain how a peppered moth changes from light to dark in color. It is quite another matter to explain how an amphibian changes into a reptile and then into a

153

mammal. Mechanistic evolutionary theory just doesn't seem adequate to explain how minute changes gradually accumulate to produce a totally new life form. How do the in-between stages work? Of what use are they? We can see how the amphibian functions, how the reptile functions, and how the mammal functions. It is the gradual hypothetical changes from one to the other that stretch the imagination.

What then are we to conclude? Has evolution taken place or not? If we consider the word *evolution* to mean that *change has taken place over time,* we can conclude that evolution has indeed occurred. Change over time is demonstrated not only in the fossil record of life, but also in the physical record of changing seas, oceans, mountains, and continents. However, we can make no conclusive statement concerning some of the "changes" that are hypothesized to have taken place—amphibians into reptiles, for instance—because there is no physical evidence for them. Such "changes" may or may not have occurred.

While we can agree that change over time has taken place, the point of disagreement begins when we consider the causes and purposes of the observed changes. Here people split into two broad camps—those who believe in a Creator and those who do not. *Creator* versus *no-creator* is the real issue—*not* creation versus evolution.

Those who believe in a *Creator* believe God has either directly or indirectly created all things. They believe that the vast sweep of historical events from the beginning of time to the advent of man has a purpose—the full preparation of the Earth for the creation of man.

Those who believe in *no-creator* hold that all things are the product of random chance and accidental forces. They see no direction or purpose to the geologic or biologic changes that have taken place on Earth. Stanford University oceanography professor, Tjeerd van Andel says, "Evolution is not progress, only change. As a human, I do not represent progress over an amoeba: I'm simply adjusted to a more complicated environment."[8]

Those who believe in *no-creator* view the changes that have taken place over time as only short-term adjustments to the particular situation at hand.

Those who believe in a *Creator* hold that the changes that have taken place over time are part of God's long-term cohesive plan and see the hand of God in the vast panorama of historical events.

Those who believe in a *Creator* do so because they choose to. It is an act of faith. Those who choose to believe in *no-creator* do so because they choose to. The belief solely in mechanistic processes is also an act of faith. No amount of data or scientific evidence can resolve the issue. It is a matter of personal choice. We will discuss these two belief systems further in Chapter 14. For now I would like to focus on what might be inferred from the Bible about evolution. Here the term *evolution* will be used in its broader sense of change over time.

The Bible teaches that all the present diverse races of the world have descended from the first man and woman, Adam and Eve. They were our common ancestors. We are their descendants. And we are a diverse and varied group of people. All the present races of the world have evolved from Adam and Eve.

Furthermore, I believe Genesis 1 is a step-by-step account of changes that God made in the geologic and biologic forms on the Earth. The scientific record confirms that the events recorded in Genesis did take place in real time in geologic history. However, the question remains, *how* did God do it?

The Bible's major focus is man's relationship to his Creator. It contains the answers to the *who* and the *why* of creation. It is not intended to be a science book which contains the answers to the *how* and *when* of creation. The Bible does not give us any details of the creation process. Neither does it give any direct clues, but perhaps there are inferences we can draw.

The Hebrew verb *bārā*, which means "create," is used very sparingly in the Old Testament. In Genesis 1 it is used only three times: when God *created* "the heavens and the earth [i.e., the Universe]" (1:1); "The great sea monsters and every living creature that moves, with which the waters swarmed [i.e., animal life in the water]" (1:21); and "man" (1:27).[9] As opposed to *fashioning* or *shaping* an object, the word *bārā* emphasizes the initiation of the object. *Bārā* is limited to divine (as opposed to human) activity, and its primary emphasis is on the newness of the created object.[10] It is only God who can initiate the action of causing the result termed in Hebrew *bārā*.

While the Hebrew word *bārā* (create) does not necessarily preclude the use of existing material, it appears to imply more than a simple change in life forms. It implies a more direct creation, an original creation from scratch. Tools and materials may be used as when an artist uses a canvas, paints, and a paintbrush to create a work of art. But the word *bārā* suggests more than a mere change in color to improve a picture. *Bārā* suggests the creation of an original masterpiece.

We have looked at two of the three places where *bārā* (create) is used in Genesis 1. We have found that the creation of the heavens and the earth (the Universe) appears to be, scientifically speaking, a clear step or *original* creation. We have also analyzed the appearance of animal life in the sea and in the air. While there may be disagreement about the origin of birds, we have seen in the last chapter that the origin of animal life in the sea is totally undocumented in the fossil record. This gaping "black hole" in 400 million years of sedimentary deposits leads to the conclusion that this also is a very direct and special intervention by God in His plan of creation.

The third place the word *bārā* is used is in God's creation of human beings. We will explore the scientific evidence for this in the next chapter. The point which must be made here is that a highly visible miracle is *not* required by Scripture in the creation of animal life on the land because of the fact that the word *bārā* is *not* used. In my judgment, Scripture does not therefore preclude the transformation by God of a fish into an amphibian. The fact that the *eusthenopteron* lobe-finned fish appears to have been preadapted to life on the land indicates a long-term cohesive plan. Whether one believes God created in this way or not is a matter of judgment. However, I believe we should allow God to perform His miracles in His way and in His time. He may have chosen to perform these miracles in a seemingly more "natural" way than some had considered, but the prerogative is His.

It is uncertain whether God created amphibians from fish, reptiles from amphibians, or mammals from reptiles. But He may have chosen this route to accomplish His miracle when He said, " 'Let the earth bring forth living creatures after their kind: cattle and creeping things and beasts of the earth after their kind'; and it was so" (Gen. 1:24).

Regardless of the specific processes by which God created animal life on the land, the scientific record of the order of events is again in harmony with Scripture. The creation of animal life on the land followed animal life in the sea. Major new life forms appeared quite suddenly in geologic time and rapidly multiplied into a variety of new life forms. The next significant event in both biblical and scientific history was the creation of man. However, before we can deal with this emotionally charged subject, we must explore the primates as a whole—the biological order in which scientists classify apes, monkeys, and humans.

CHAPTER 10
PRIMATES—THE MONKEY PUZZLE

Be diligent to present yourself approved to God as a workman who does not need to be ashamed, handling accurately the word of truth.

2 Timothy 2:15

The moment one begins to deal with the family tree of humanity, several major problems have to be faced. These problems largely arise because humans and apes are classified together within the same biological order called *Primates*. Thus, an evolutionary relationship is assumed. Because this challenges man's uniqueness, we are dealing with an emotionally charged and highly sensitive subject.

The first problem is that the subject is highly subjective. We are the subjects. We are studying the origin of ourselves. Thus it is very difficult for scientists to be objective. The problem is acutely difficult for a Christian like myself because I understand the Bible to say that we are uniquely created by God in His image and likeness, created separately from other animals.

The second problem is scarcity and incompleteness of specimens. In his recent book, *The Making of Mankind*, Richard Leakey quotes one of the world's leading experts in the field, David Philbeam: "If you brought in a smart scientist from another discipline and showed him the meager evidence we've got, he'd surely say, 'forget it, there isn't enough to go on.'" Leakey then comments, "Neither David nor others involved in the search for mankind can take this advice, of course, but we remain fully aware of the dangers of drawing conclusions from evidence that is so incomplete."[1] In addition, there is lack of agreement among specialists regarding the classification of the few fossil remains we do have.

The third problem is the present a priori assumption within the field of anthropology that we are descended from an ape ancestry. This is the conventional scientific wisdom. All textbooks are written and research conducted from this mindset.

However, recent research data has shed new light on the situation, leading us to the possibility of new interpretations of old evidence. Once it was popular to believe that the Earth was flat. Today it is equally important that we open our minds to some new possibilities. First it is necessary to work our way through some scientific terms and information.

THE PRIMATES

Following the extinction of the dinosaurs 63 million years ago, the Age of Mammals began. Within the class *Mammalia* is the order called *Primates.* The biological classification of primates includes premonkeys, monkeys, apes, and humans.

The earliest primate-like fossils date at about 60 million years ago. Shortly thereafter, two key primate characteristics made their appearance in the fossil record: the opposable thumb, which enables the user to grip branches or food, and stereoscopic vision, in which eyes are placed in the front of the skull rather than to the sides. The possession of stereoscopic vision enables depth perception, which is important in judging distances and heights. This characteristic is vital to survival in the trees of the forest.

The 50-million-year-old fossil pre-monkeys are thought to have been similar to the squirrel-like lemurs of Madagascar and the big-eyed tarsiers of Sumatra and Borneo of today (see figures 10.2). They are known as *prosimians* or the lower primates. The suborder *Anthropoidea* or higher primates consists of monkeys and apes.

Monkeys are considered quadrupeds (four-footed) because they run or scamper very efficiently on their four limbs. The arms of apes, however, are designed more efficiently for swinging. Instead of walking or running along branches as do monkeys, apes swing, hang, or often sit on them.

Apes, particularly chimpanzees and gorillas, are knuckle-walkers when traveling on the ground. They rest their forward weight on the backs of their hands, specifically the middle joints of their fingers. Their posture is said to be semi-erect, and they sometimes stand erect when reaching for fruit or looking over tall grass.

Primitive monkeys and apes appeared in the fossil record more than 25 million years ago, and a progressive increase in size occurred. Primitive apes abounded in the forests until roughly 8 million years ago. At this point, the fossil record vanishes. Modern

FIGURE 10.1.

The pileated gibbon, a Southeast Asian ape, uses its long arms and fingers to swing through trees. Orangutans are also brachiators. (Courtesy Zoological Society of San Diego.)

gorillas, orangutans, and chimpanzees simply appear on the modern scene. According to current scientific interpretation, the fossil record of apes for the past 8 million years has not been discovered.

Evolutionary theory holds that humans did not evolve directly from a monkey, but developed from an ape-like line of ancestry. Recent advances in molecular biology, especially the comparison of DNA composition, indicate a very close biochemical relationship between apes and humans. Anatomical similarities and some social behavior patterns tend to confirm this close relationship.

However, similarity does not necessarily prove a common ancestor. A close relationship can also be used to prove a common designer. Similarity of design may be used as circumstantial evidence for a common ancestor, a common designer, or both.

Evidence that humans are actually descended from an ape or protoape must ultimately depend on fossils that show a transition from ape to man. What is the evidence in the fossil record?

THE SEARCH FOR THE MISSING LINK

Ever since Darwin's theory of evolution became the conventional scientific wisdom, paleoanthropologists (those who study human ancestors) have searched for a missing link between monkeys, apes, and man. They have placed great reliance on jaws and teeth as the premise of their hypotheses for two reasons. First of all, jaws and

FIGURE 10.2.

The lemur of Madagascar, *left*, and the big-eyed tarsier of Borneo, *right*, are thought to be similar to possible primate ancestors.

159

FIGURE 10.3.

A discussion of the Piltdown skull. This group portrait shows the principals in the controversy. Sir Arthur Keith, seated in the center in a laboratory coat, reconstructed a complete skull from some fossil pieces. Standing to his left is Charles Dawson, who found the fossils.

their teeth are far less subject to consumption by scavenger animals and decay than bones of the body. Thus, jaws and teeth are basically what have been preserved in the fossil record and what the paleoanthropologists have to work with.

Secondly, there is a distinct difference between the jaws of apes and the jaws of humans (see figure 10.12). Ape jaws are basically a rectangular U shape, and the human jaw is shaped more like a gently curved horseshoe. Because of this distinction, it was long thought by evolutionists that the famous *Piltdown Man* was the transitional form between apes and men. The Piltdown Man was "discovered" in 1912. The fossil had an ape-like jaw and a human-like skull. It was the pride of British anthropology, because the fossil was found in England and therefore indicated that the first pre-man was an Englishman. The Piltdown Man has since been proven to be exactly what it looked like—the jaw of an ape and the skull of a man.

Although evidence had accumulated that the Piltdown Man did not fit properly into the theoretical transition from ape to man, it was hailed as the missing link until the early 1950s when the clever hoax was exposed. It is considered among the ten greatest forgeries by which man has been duped. Some unknown person with a good bit of scientific knowledge had taken the jaw of an ape and the skull of a man and cleverly doctored them to fit the scientific expectation of what the missing link should look like. Subsequent scientists had let prejudice interfere with their scientific judgment. The unfortunate result was that two generations of students were taught that science had fossil evidence proving that man had descended from apes.

Although jaws and teeth continue to be important factors in the search for man's family tree, it is now thought that the major evolutionary advance that led to humans may have been walking upright.

OUT OF THE FOREST AND ONTO THE PLAIN

The lush tropical forests that covered Asia and Africa began to shrink about 14 million years ago. As the climate gradually gave way to grassland, savannas, and plains, the habitat of tree-dwelling animals was greatly reduced. Thus, faced with a shrinking supply of food, the tree-dwelling apes felt great pressure to seek a new food source and way of life on the plains.

Ramapithecus. The first potential primate fossils that hint at adaptation to life on the plains come from Pakistan, East Africa, Turkey, and China. The place they were first discovered was in the Punjab in northern India. The species is called *Ramapithecus* ("Rama" for a deified hero worshipped by Hindus and "pithecus" for ape).

Ramapithecus ("Rama ape") is thought to have made the transition from a tree-swinging ape to a partial life on the ground. Its teeth are similar to those of eaters of grass seeds, which indicates that it may have sought food sources on the plains rather than in the trees.

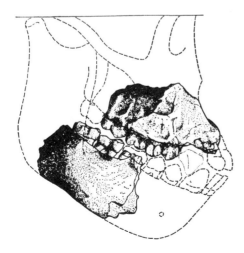

FIGURE 10.4.

Hypothetical appearance of the face of *Ramapithecus* based on existing fragments of *kenyapithecus wickeri* (Leakey, 1962). Dashed lines are conjectural.

FIGURE 10.5.

Richard Leakey examines a skull of *Australopithecus* on the spot of its discovery near Lake Rudolf, Kenya. (Courtesy Meave Epps Leakey, © National Geographic Society.)

The fossils of *Ramapithecus* indicate that it lived during the period between 14 and 9 million years ago. This creature is known only from a few fragments of jaws and teeth. From these remains it is not possible to know whether it walked erect. Nor do we know whether it became extinct, evolved into apes or into man. There simply are no fossils of apes or *hominids* (upright walkers) from 8 million to 4 million years ago. This period is termed the great black hole of human paleontology. To quote one of the world's leading paleoanthropologists, Donald Johanson, "There are no in-between types known. There are, in fact, *no ape fossils from anywhere* after about eight million (years ago)"[2] (italics Johanson's). He also comments, ". . . science has not known, and does not know today, just how or when the all-important transition from ape to hominid took place."[3]

Nevertheless, until mid-1982 when David Philbeam discovered unknown parts of its facial skeleton, *Ramapithecus* was considered by some paleoanthropologists to be the first critical link in the chain leading from a common ancestor of ape and man to man. There is no other likely fossil candidate for this position. To quote Elwyn Simons, who leads the Duke University Center for the Study of Primate Biology and History, "*Ramapithecus* is ideally structured to be an ancestor of *hominids*. If he isn't, we don't have anything else that is."[4]

HOMINIDS

A *hominid* is defined by anthropologists as a member of the family of humans. The major characteristic of the family (*Hominidae*) is upright walking—walking on two feet only (bipedal locomotion). Hominids are further characterized by erect posture. Apes are not hominids (they do not walk upright as their primary means of locomotion, and they do not stand completely erect).

The only presently living hominids are humans, but there are hominids in the fossil record that are thought to be human ancestors or at least very closely related. According to anthropology textbook author, William Haviland, "*Ramapithecus* is believed by some scientists definitely to be a hominid."[5] This assertion is based solely on the analysis of jaw fragments and a few teeth. The connection between dentition that indicates seed-eating and being "definitely hominid" has not been accepted by all scientists. Most paleoanthropologists have simply believed *Ramapithecus* may have been ancestral to the hominid they call *Australopithecus*.

Australopithecus is the term used to designate a genus of prehumans—hominid ancestors or close relatives of humans which appear in the fossil record several million years ago. The term *Australopithecus* is often abbreviated by the letter *A* and presently includes three species, *A. africanus*, *A. robustus*, and *A. afarensis*.

It should be noted that the suffix *pithecus* means "ape." Yet because it is a hominid, an *Australopithecus* is not an ape; it is classified as a member of the human family. But it is not a human being in the modern sense either. In effect the term *Australopithecus* is used to describe a "man-like ape" or "near-man"—the transitional form—the missing link between apes and humans.

Australopithecus africanus. Following the demise of the Piltdown Man in 1953, scientists recognized that the *Australopithecus africanus* might represent the transition from ape to human. *Australo* means "southern," *pithecus* means "ape" and *africanus* refers to the continent of Africa where it was discovered by Raymond Dart in 1924. In lay terms, *Australopithecus africanus* thus means "Southern Ape from Africa."

The most numerous and best fossils of *A. africanus* come from scattered locations in the rift valleys of East Africa, the most famous being the Leakeys' renowned site at Olduvai Gorge in Tanzania. The skeleton of *A. africanus* is about the size of a modern chimpanzee, and the brain cavity size is also the same (440 cubic centimeters).[6]

From comparative analysis of hip and limb bones and the opening in which the spine enters the skull, scientists have concluded that the posture of *A. africanus* was upright. For this reason *A. africanus* qualifies as a *hominid*, an upright walker. It is not a true ape, but not a human either—a sort of near-man. This composite of hominid and ape-like characteristics suggests that *A. africanus* is the closest fossil available to a missing link.

Australopithecus robustus. A larger and more robust type of *australopithecine* was later discovered in East Africa. It was not only larger (almost as big as a small gorilla), but it appeared to have large molars for grinding coarse vegetation. It has been given the name *Australopithecus robustus*. The majority opinion holds that *A. robustus* evolved out of *A. africanus* and came to an evolutionary dead end. However, the line of *Australopithecus africanus* was thought to have continued on another branch of the tree to give rise to man.

In 1972, Time-Life Books published *The Emergence of Man*. The missing link lineup appeared to be fairly complete in their simulated reproductions. The *australopithecine* figures in the illustrations look

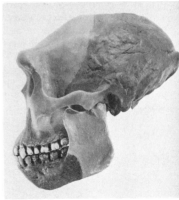

FIGURE 10.6.

A reconstruction drawing of the head of a young *A. africanus, top,* based on the Taungs skull discovered in Bechaunaland. Skull of *Pithecauthropus robustus, below,* as restored by Dr. Franz Weidenreich. (Courtesy American Museum of Natural History.)

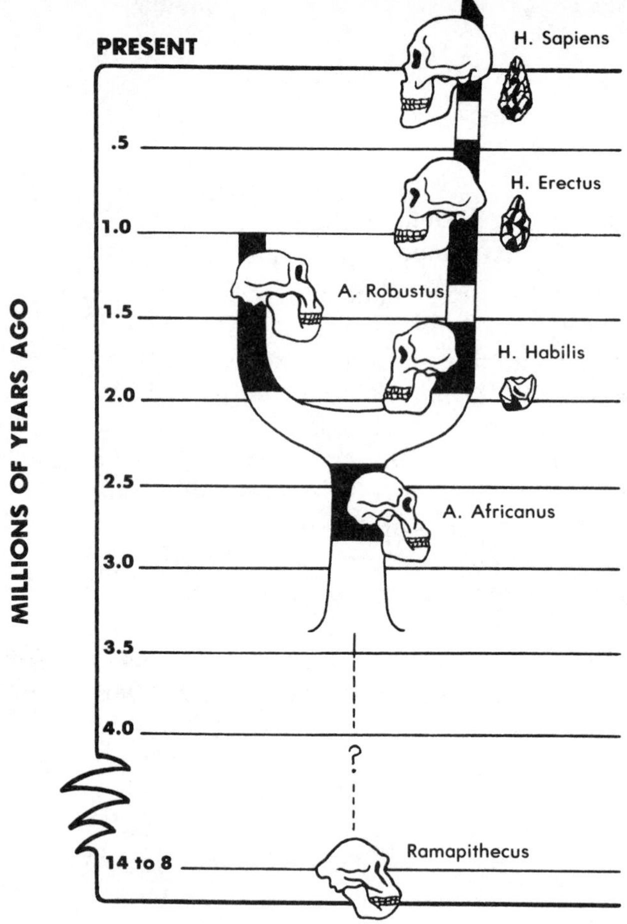

PRESENT

MILLIONS OF YEARS AGO

.5
1.0
1.5
2.0
2.5
3.0
3.5
4.0
14 to 8

H. Sapiens
H. Erectus
A. Robustus
H. Habilis
A. Africanus
?
Ramapithecus

FIGURE 10.7.

The most widely held family tree of human beings by paleo-anthropologists during the 1960s and 1970s. There were other hypothetical family trees during this period, but they also placed *A. africanus* as the fossil ancestor of humans. Dark areas represent range of known fossil specimens, light areas the most significant fossil gaps. The addition of Ramapithecus is based on Johanson's contention that it foreshadowed hominids.

rather like humans. It is interesting to contrast these with the more ape-like reproductions published in 1978 in William Haviland's textbook, *Anthropology*.

During the 1960s and 1970s, paleoanthropologists developed several possible family trees of human beings. The most widely accepted family tree is illustrated in Figure 10.7. Note that the most widely held scientific opinion placed *A. africanus* as the ancestor of both *A. robustus* and *H. habilis*.

Homo habilis. In 1964, the famous paleoanthropologist Louis B. Leakey identified the next candidate for human ancestry in East Africa. Because it begins to resemble humans and probably used primitive tools, he classified this hominid as Homo (man) with the full name of *Homo habilis* (handy man). A far better skull specimen was later found by Louis's son, Richard Leakey. *Homo habilis* is now accepted by scientists as possibly being in the ancestral line to modern man. Its brain cavity size is intermediate between that of apes and humans (800 cu. cm.). It is thought to occupy the time slot of roughly 1.8 million years ago.

164

Homo erectus. About 1.5 million years ago *Homo erectus* appeared in the fossil record. Skeletal remains have been interpreted to indicate that he resembled modern man from the neck down and stood upright. Thus he was given the name *Homo erectus* or *Upright man.* His eyebrow ridges are protruding and heavy, his upper jaw heavy and thrust forward, and he lacked a chin. He made hand-held tools and weapons of skillfully shaped chipped stone with which he is thought to have attacked and killed giant baboons.

Where did *Homo erectus* come from? Current evolutionary theory holds that he arose from *Homo habilis.* Donald Johanson injects a sobering note of warning to this conventional wisdom: "What we don't know is just how or when—and perhaps, even *if*—he emerged out of *Homo habilis.*"[7]

Homo erectus was a world traveler. He is thought to have originated in East Africa and thence expanded into Asia (Peking Man), Java (Java Man), and Europe. Although his brain cavity size is between that of apes and humans, and in some cases approaches that of modern man, his physical appearance would not make him a welcome guest at a dinner party.

Australopithecus afarensis. In 1974, Donald Johanson discovered the partial skeleton of "Lucy" in the Afar Triangle of Ethiopia. The name *Lucy* was chosen because the Beatles' song "Lucy in the Sky with Diamonds" was playing on the tape player in camp during the preliminary analysis of this exciting discovery.

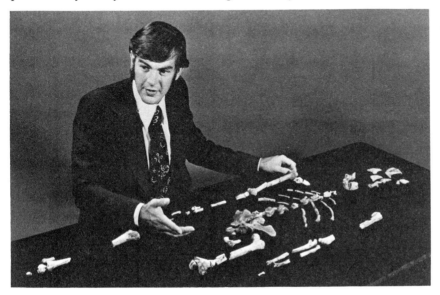

FIGURE 10.8.

Dr. Donald Johanson discovered "Lucy" in Ethiopia in 1974. His analysis of the fossilized remains placed Lucy in the new species *Australopithecus afarensis* (Afar ape-man). Her leg bones indicate she walked erect like modern humans, but her jaw and skull fragments are more ape-like. (Courtesy Cleveland Museum of Natural History.)

FIGURE 10.9.

"Lucy" was a female approximately four feet tall and twenty years old who lived three million years ago in present-day Ethiopia. The skeleton is 40% complete. (Courtesy Cleveland Museum of Natural History.)

Lucy is a highly unique find not only because of her great age (between 3.0 and 3.5 million years), but also because of her completeness. All specimens in the hypothetical human family tree from *Ramapithecus* through *Homo erectus* were pieced together from fragments: a bone here, a skull fragment there, a few teeth nearby. Lucy is unique in that her bones and the pieces of her skull were found in the same location and represent about 40% of a complete skeleton (see figure 10.9).

Johanson and his associate, Tim White, believe that Lucy and her related family were apes that walked erect and had other human-like characteristics. The name *Australopithecus afarensis* (Southern Ape from Afar) has been chosen for this hominid.

Lucy was about three and one-half feet tall, and her skull resembles a small female gorilla.[8] That she walked erect is indicated from her pelvic bones, which are distinctly different from those of a modern chimpanzee. Upright walking at this early date is confirmed by discoveries made by a team headed by Mary Leakey (wife of Louis Leakey and mother of Richard Leakey). In 1977, Mary Leakey's team at Laetoli (1000 miles south of the Afar Triangle) found fossil footprints cast in volcanic ash, which allowed for reliable dating. Believed to be footprints of *Australopithecus afarensis,* they established that upright-walking creatures existed in East Africa at least 3.7 million years ago.

The hominid *A. afarensis,* represented by Lucy, appears to cover the time period from roughly 3.5 to 3.0 million years ago. In June 1982, J. Desmond Clark and Timothy D. White of the University of California at Berkeley announced that their fifteen-member expedition had found the upper part of a thigh bone and frontal skull fragments that date at 4 million years ago. The fragments were found forty-five miles south of the site of the Lucy discovery. While Clark and White were rightly cautious in their comments regarding the significance of their finds, *Time* magazine carried this sub-headline: "A 4-million-year-old human ancestor is unearthed in Ethiopia" (*Time*, June 21, 1982). From part of a thigh bone and a few skull fragments reporters concluded that a human ancestor had been found.

Because the four-foot-high *A. afarensis* apparently walked only on two legs, it became the world's first-known hominid. No tools are associated with the fossil skeletons, and it is uncertain what Lucy ate or how she survived. There is no concrete record of where she came from or what her family evolved into, but, at present, some an-

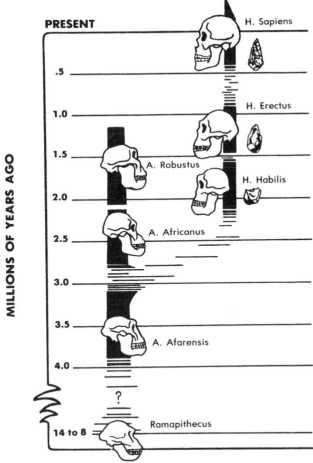

MILLIONS OF YEARS AGO

PRESENT

H. Sapiens

.5

1.0

H. Erectus

1.5

A. Robustus

2.0

H. Habilis

A. Africanus

2.5

3.0

3.5

A. Afarensis

4.0

?

14 to 8

Ramapithecus

FIGURE 10.10.

The new hypothetical family tree of human beings as revised in the 1980s. Black lines represent range of fossil specimens. *A. africanus* is now placed outside the direct line to the Homo specimens. Note also the direct line from *A. afarensis* (represented by Lucy) to *A. africanus* and *A. robustus,* and the rather tentative branching to the Homo line.

thropologists consider Lucy a possible candidate for the first ancestral human.

Donald Johanson has drawn a new family tree of human ancestors (see figure 10.10). I have taken the liberty of adding to this sketch *Ramapithecus*, which Johanson says "foreshadows hominids."[9] It is especially noteworthy that Johanson places *A. africanus* outside the hypothetical family tree leading to man. This removal of *A. africanus* from the hypothetical human family line is now widely accepted within the scientific community.

Richard Leakey in his 1982 book, *Human Origins,* presented his choice of the most likely relationships between the fossil hominids.[10] Leakey's chart is reconstructed to conform to the format used by Johanson in Figure 10.11. Note that Leakey places all of the australopithecine hominids including *A. afarensis* (Lucy) outside the hypothetical line leading to man.

If one accepts Leakey's hominid lineup, then not only does the *A. africanus* disappear as a missing link, but also *A. afarensis* disappears

167

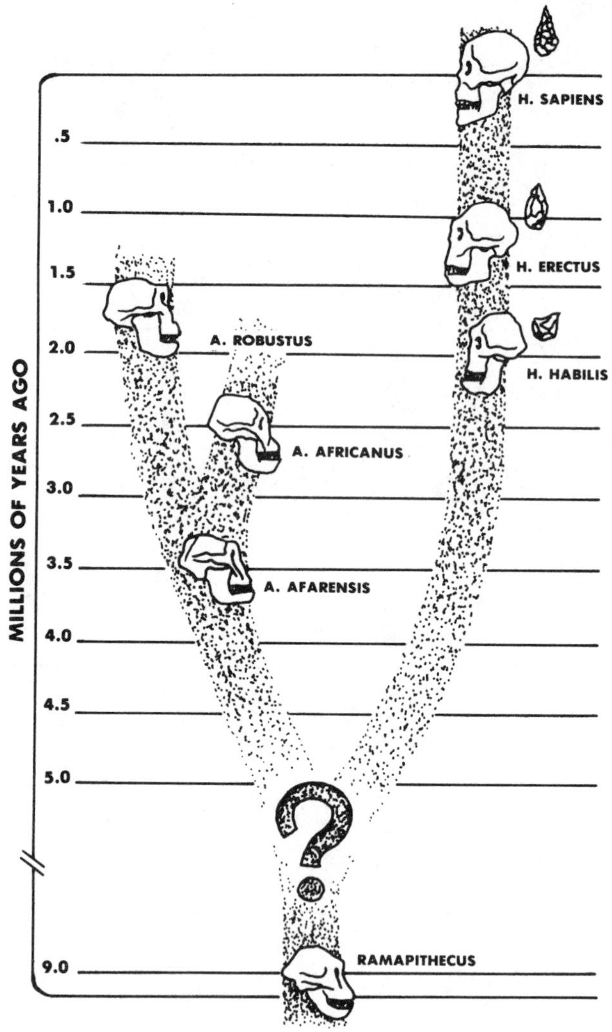

FIGURE 10.11.

The most likely hypothetical family tree of human beings according to Richard Leakey. This lineup of fossil creatures was drawn prior to the recent evidence indicating that *Ramapithecus* is the ancestor of the orangutan. Note also that *Australopithecus afarensis* (Lucy) is charted as the ancestor of the later australopithecines instead of in the line leading to humans.

as a probable human ancestor. However, both Johanson and Leakey as of mid-1982 indicate that *Ramapithecus* is a potential missing link in the hypothetical chain leading from ape to humans.

Some vitally important new fossil evidence has recently been discovered on *Ramapithecus*. Until mid-1982, the only fossil parts of the *Ramapithecus* skeleton that had been discovered were jaws and teeth, which indicated seed-eating. An expedition led by David Philbeam, probably the world's leading expert on fossil apes, returned from Pakistan with fossils that included formerly unknown parts of the facial skeleton of *Ramapithecus*. According to Philbeam and Susan Lipson, an associate anthropologist at Harvard University, these new fossil specimens indicate that *Ramapithecus* is not the ancestor of man, but rather the ancestor of the orangutan.[11]

168

With *Ramapithecus*, *A. africanus*, and possibly *A. afarensis* acquiring doubtful reputations as missing link candidates, I feel that lay people are justified in taking a new look at the monkey puzzle.

A NEW LOOK AT THE MONKEY PUZZLE

In 1982, I attended a lecture at the University of California at Santa Barbara and listened to Vincent Sarich describe his work in molecular genetics. He and Alan Wilson have studied the DNA structure of modern humans and apes and found strikingly close similarities.

They have also developed a kind of molecular clock. According to their studies, they hypothesize that the line between apes and humans split about 4.5 to 5 million years ago. Before the recent discovery by David Philbeam indicating that *Ramapithecus* is most likely the ancestor of the orangutan, the prevailing opinion of paleoanthropologists held that the split must have occurred between 10 and 20 million years ago. With *Ramapithecus* out of the picture, the molecular clock's more recent date begins to look more accurate.

John Gribbin and Jeremy Cherfas have grasped the importance of the work of Sarich and Wilson and present a cogent discussion of it in their book *The Monkey Puzzle*.[12] Gribbin and Cherfas hold the position that humans descended from a common ancestor with the apes, but they maintain that, based on the molecular genetic studies of Sarich and Wilson, the human family tree should be drastically revised. Their theory does not contradict the fossil evidence. They intrepret the fossil evidence somewhat differently than others, and their interpretation solves some enigmas that have puzzled anthropologists.

BACK TO THE TREES

Let us review the evidence presented in this chapter. However, this time let us look at the evidence in a new way. Instead of looking for missing links to fill in the human family tree, let us look for missing links in the ape's family tree.

Recall the statement that there are no ape fossils from anywhere after 8 million years ago. The fossil record vanishes. Donald Johanson has stated, "modern gorillas, orangutans, and chimpanzees spring out of nowhere, as it were. They are here today; they have no yesterday."[13] Or have we missed seeing them? Have we been so eager to find support for the theory that humans descended from monkeys that we have actually been listing upright-walking fossil apes as our ancestors? Have we been stealing our "would-be" ancestors from the apes?

It has been assumed that the apes came down from the trees, began to walk upright, and developed into humans. But if apes can come down from trees and adapt to upright walking, they can certainly climb back up into the trees where they would be much safer from lions and saber-toothed cats. Furthermore, the trees were not only safer, but contained desirable food to eat. The search for a free lunch would provide a powerful incentive to return to a life in the trees. But this is evolutionary speculation. What about the fossil record?

One of the problems that has puzzled anthropologists is that the fossils of *A. robustus* overlap in time with *Homo habilis*. Moreover, the fossil finds of *A. africanus* come close to this time overlap. All three hominids may have coexisted during some period in ancient history just as chimpanzees, gorillas, and humans coexist today.

Perhaps we have been interpreting the fossils incorrectly. Maybe the missing record of the fossil apes has been there all along. Perhaps our preconceived conventional wisdom has prevented us from seeing the early hominid creatures as fossil apes.

Look back for a minute at Figure 10.6. Study the reconstruction of the australopithecine hominid. What do you see? Can you visualize the ancestor of a man, *or* the ancestor of a chimpanzee and a gorilla?

The possibilities that Gribbin and Cherfas suggest in their book *The Monkey Puzzle* are:

- *Australopithecus africanus* is the fossil ancestor of the chimpanzee.
- *Australopithecus robustus* is the fossil ancestor of the gorilla.
- *Ramapithecus* is the fossil ancestor of the orangutan.

This suggestion by Gribbin and Cherfas, which may be called the "missing links for apes" hypothesis, does not violate the charts of human ancestry drawn by either Johanson or Leakey (see figures 10.10 and 10.11).

Not only is their hypothesis consistent with the fossil record, it is also consistent with the time periods proposed by Sarich and Wilson in their dating by the genetic molecular clock. Moreover, David Philbeam's new fossil evidence that *Ramapithecus* is most likely the ancestor of the orangutan is clearly supportive of this "missing links for apes" hypothesis.

This new hypothesis could prove to be a major blow to the popular belief that scientists have the fossil evidence to prove humans are descended from apes. From 1912 through the early 1950s, the Piltdown Man was the missing link. But he was a hoax. From 1953 to 1982, the two missing links were *Ramapithecus* and *Australopithecus africanus*. We now have indications that they are only the ancestors of the orangutan and possibly the chimpanzee and the gorilla. Missing links have been found, to be sure, but they appear to be links in the chain leading to modern apes, not to humans.

But let's give the paleoanthropologists credit for not calling the australopithecines human beings. They called them hominids or near-man. Listing them in man's direct ancestry as the missing link may prove to be their major error.

Furthermore, Johanson removed *Australopithecus africanus* from the main trunk of his postulated family tree when he replaced it with Lucy. And Lucy—*Australopithecus afarensis*—might still be a possible candidate for both the ancestor of human beings and the chimpanzee. Johanson says that Lucy's pelvic bones are closer to the human line than to that of apes. However, his impression of Lucy's reconstructed skull indicates otherwise: "Rather, (forgetting its hominid teeth), it looked very much like a small female gorilla."[14] When we examine a photograph of those teeth (see figure 10.12), the jaw structure of *A. afarensis* (Lucy) appears to be much closer to that of a

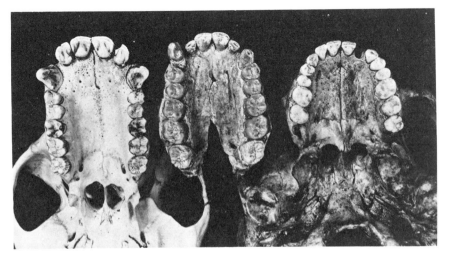

FIGURE 10.12.

The upper jaws and teeth of *Australopithecus afarensis* (Afar ape), *center*, are more similar to those of a chimpanzee, *left*, than to those of a human, *right*. This comparison is true for the entire skull. The pelvic bones of the Afar ape-man more closely resemble those of humans. (Courtesy Cleveland Museum of Natural History.)

modern chimpanzee than that of a modern human.

The molecular clock places the hypothetical divergence of humans from chimpanzees at 4.5 to 5 million years ago. If this is true, then Lucy, between 3 and 3.5 million years old, could be the ancestor of chimps and gorillas or of humans, but *not* of both lines. And if Lucy is the ancestor of humans, then what fossil species is common to both apes and man? There is no other candidate now that *Ramapithecus* has been eliminated.

Are there modern equivalents of Lucy? Not exactly, but there is evidence that *A. afarensis* (Lucy) may be the ancestor or close relative of the rare pygmy chimpanzee that lives today in the forests of Zaire in Africa. Comparisons by Andrienne Zihlman of the University of California at Santa Cruz between Lucy and the pygmy chimp, show that they are almost identical in cranial capacity, height, and overall body size.[15]

Further, Jeremy Dahl of the Yerkes Regional Primate Research Center of Emory University in Atlanta has frequently observed pygmy chimps walking on two feet and standing upright.[16] Since Lucy's major tie to the human line is based on bipedality and upright posture, it could be that she rightly belongs in the ancestry of the pygmy chimpanzee she so closely resembles morphologically.

Was Lucy a true hominid? There is currently a dispute in anthropological circles as to whether Lucy was in fact a true hominid (walked upright as her primary means of locomotion). Scientists from the State University of New York at Stony Brook believe that Lucy's anatomical features indicate she was an adept climber and walked upright more like a toddler than a human older child or adult.[17] Some features, specifically her short hindlimbs and curved toes, are indicative of a posture and gait reminiscent of bipedal chimpanzees.[18]

In summary, it appears that there are too many unsettled questions to claim with any degree of scientific certainty that Lucy is the ancestor of the human race. In fact, based on the evidence uncovered to date, it appears that *A. afarensis* (as represented by Lucy) is the missing link in the chain leading to modern chimpanzees.

Where does this potential new "missing links for apes" hypothesis leave us in the search for human ancestors? There are two major possibilities:

- Both humans and apes are descended from a common ancestor.
- Humans are uniquely created and therefore do not appear in the ancient fossil record.

FIGURE 10.13.

A number of animals exhibit tool-using behavior. A chimpanzee is shown here brandishing a stick as a weapon. Chimpanzees also use sticks to dig for termites, and baboons use sticks to immobilize scorpions. (From *In the Shadow of Man* by Jane Van Llawick-Goodall. Copyright © by Hugo and Jane Van Llawick-Goodall. Reprinted by permission of Houghton Mifflin.)

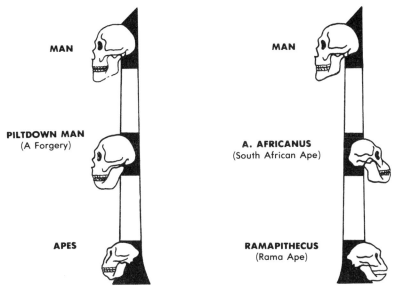

MAN

PILTDOWN MAN
(A Forgery)

APES

MAN

A. AFRICANUS
(South African Ape)

RAMAPITHECUS
(Rama Ape)

1912—1953
PILTDOWN HOAX

1953—1982
HOMINID HOAX

FIGURE 10.14.

The Piltdown Hoax and the Hominid Hoax. In their eagerness to link human ancestry to apes, anthropologists have committed major errors in interpretation. The Piltdown Man was the missing link from 1912 until 1953 when the clever forgery was finally unmasked. It now appears that the public has been misled by the Hominid Hoax. Upright-walking fossil apes formerly listed as the ancestors of human beings most probably belong in the ape's family tree.

The lack of present fossil evidence supports the latter possibility. David Philbeam has indicated that *Ramapithecus* should be removed from the human family tree and assigned to that of the orangutan. Both Johanson and Leakey have eliminated *A. africanus* from the missing link lineup. And Leakey has charted *A. afarensis* (Lucy) as not belonging in human ancestry. In light of the current fossil evidence, it appears that the key question remaining is whether these fossil creatures became extinct or are the long-lost missing links in the ape's family tree.

Where does this leave *Homo habilis* and *Homo erectus*? Scientists have spent a great deal of time documenting the chimpanzee's use of tools and have even reported the crude manufacture of tools. Chimpanzees have been observed in the wild in the process of killing young baboons to eat. This evidence has been used in the past to indicate that the behavior of chimpanzees is so close to that of human beings that we must share a common ancestor. But this same evidence can also be used to indicate that *Homo habilis* and *Homo erectus* were hominids that became extinct. If paleoanthropologists can list australopithecines as extinct beings, they can surely consider the possibility that *Homo habilis* and *Homo erectus* met the same fate. At least we should keep an open mind on this question until further evidence is uncovered.

173

THE HOMINID HOAX

Both science and the public have been duped in the past with the Piltdown Hoax. It now appears we have been duped, albeit unintentionally, with a kind of hominid hoax.

Since the Piltdown discovery in 1912, we have graduated four generations of students with the impression that science had the fossil evidence to prove we are descended from apes. It is time that students be taught with honesty and candor. We must not be guilty of a cover-up of the vast holes in our records and end up with an

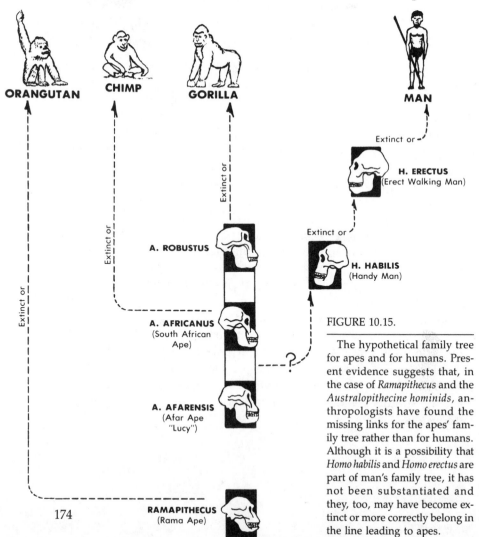

ORANGUTAN **CHIMP** **GORILLA** **MAN**

Extinct or

H. ERECTUS
(Erect Walking Man)

Extinct or

A. ROBUSTUS

Extinct or

H. HABILIS
(Handy Man)

Extinct or

A. AFRICANUS
(South African Ape)

?

FIGURE 10.15.

A. AFARENSIS
(Afar Ape "Lucy")

The hypothetical family tree for apes and for humans. Present evidence suggests that, in the case of *Ramapithecus* and the *Australopithecine hominids*, anthropologists have found the missing links for the apes' family tree rather than for humans. Although it is a possibility that *Homo habilis* and *Homo erectus* are part of man's family tree, it has not been substantiated and they, too, may have become extinct or more correctly belong in the line leading to apes.

174 **RAMAPITHECUS**
(Rama Ape)

anthropological Watergate. Students should be clearly presented with the discredited missing link record of the past seventy years and be made aware of the lack of present evidence. Let them draw their own conclusions about their roots.

Richard Leakey presents the following comments on the objectivity of his science: "When considering our origins it is clear that we have often been less than objective." He then continues:

Science is often seen as a search for answers that, given sufficient time, must surely be forthcoming, but because of the nature of the evidence—or rather, lack of it—this may not be the case in paleoanthropology. David Philbeam concludes, "It's my conviction that there may be many aspects of human evolution that will always elude us. We should be straightforward and honest about that. So far the spotlight has always swung to those who appear to come up with answers. It's salutary to consider that perhaps in the future the prizes should go to those people who are able to differentiate between those questions that have answers and those that do not."[19]

CHAPTER 11
THE EMERGENCE OF MAN

Then God said, "Let Us make man in Our image, according to Our likeness; and let them rule over the fish of the sea and over the birds of the sky and over the cattle and over all the earth, and over every creeping thing that creeps on the earth." And God created man in His own image, in the image of God He created him; male and female He created them.

Genesis 1:26–27

What is man? What is a human being? At what point did the first human beings appear in the historical fossil record? The scientific answer to this question depends on how one defines "human being."

Anthropologists use the term *Homo* to describe the generic name of various species of erect, large-brained primates. The magic number for brain size (cranial capacity) to be classified as Homo is set at 800 cubic centimeters and is the extreme low end of the cranial capacity for humans. The average cranial capacity of human beings is 1350 cubic centimeters, while that of the early hominids and modern chimpanzees is 440 cubic centimeters. Brain cavity size, however, does not really define a human being.

What about tools? The use of tools is another attribute of human beings, but it is not unique to *Homo*. Intricate use and primitive manufacture of tools is a quality that chimpanzees possess. Termite fishing by chimps is a well-documented and elaborate process. Woodpecker finches use cactus spines to probe holes in trees for insects. Off the coast of central California, sea otters use stones to crush and break open clams. Beavers build intricate dams in rivers and barn swallows carry mud to build cone-shaped nests in eaves. The tools of modern man are far more complex, but where is the line to be drawn? Anthropologists draw this line for humans at the point where *consistent* toolmaking is the *primary* adaptation to the environment. While this is a useful distinction, it is difficult to measure in the paleoanthropological record.

What about language? Our language gives us a unique form of communication, but other animals such as bees, termites, ants, and birds also have incredible powers of communication. Recordings have been made of whales singing. Intricate forms of communication are common to many animals.

What about complex social behavior patterns? Again, this is not unique to human beings. The activity of cows at calving season provides an interesting example. The first calves are a delight to behold. They are also hard to find because their mothers select a secret place, far from the area of their usual social group, to give birth. The cow hides her calf and keeps it separate from the herd for several days. She stays very close to it and sometimes forgoes food and water to insure its protection. She also seems to be insuring a close maternal bond. Her calf is hers and is to respond and nurse from her only. When the calf is strong enough and the mother-calf bond is solid, they rejoin the herd.

The interesting part begins at this time. Instead of associating with her usual group, the mother cow seeks out other new mothers and forms a co-op nursery. She joins with a group of about five new mothers, and the newborn calves form a kind of playground group that butt and play together. The calves appear to play a kind of sequential game which alternates between tag and follow-the-leader.

When the games are over, the calves tire and bed down in a close-knit group, a kind of bedtime nursery. One cow is left to guard this nursery from coyotes while the other cows take the long trip to water or to other feeding grounds. Some means of communication must exist to establish this nursery system and to decide which cow stays to guard the nursery. A complex and useful social pattern is followed that is very similar to one followed in our human society. Does this prove that the cow is our ancestor or that we are closely related? Or does it tell us that we must focus on other than complex social behavior patterns to define a human being?

Brain size, tool use, language, and complex social behavior patterns are all indicative of intelligence and may be used to qualify a being as a *homo sapiens*—"man of wisdom." But there is obviously something more unique about modern man. Richard Leakey says, "Humans are more than just intelligent. Our sense of justice, our need for aesthetic pleasure, our imaginative flights, and our penetrating self-awareness, all combine to create an indefinable spirit which I believe is the 'soul.'"[1]

Humans alone possess a "soul," a "spirit," and have the quality of self-conscious reason. These are distinctively human gifts. From them come the desire and ability to know about ourselves, artistic awareness of beauty, the power of conceptual thinking, the capability to grasp the difference between right and wrong, and the knowledge of and the possibility of a relationship with the Creator.

While the unique qualities of humanness are difficult to measure in the fossil record, let us look at Neanderthal man, Cro-Magnon man, and civilized man and study the artifacts and signs they have left behind. Then we can reach our own conclusions about the point at which human beings began.

NEANDERTHAL MAN

Our classic picture of Neanderthal man is that of the brutish cave man with a club, a kind of dimwitted creature who occupied Europe during the Ice Ages. He was indeed different from us, but not so different as his public image. He seems to have been the victim of a bad press.

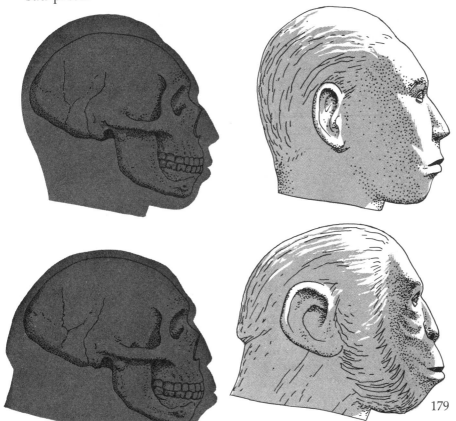

FIGURE 11.1.

The guesswork involved in reconstructions based on Neanderthal skulls is illustrated in the sketch at left. The fleshy parts of the face could fit the structure of the skull in quite different ways.

179

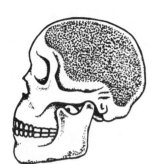

MODERN HUMAN

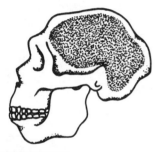

NEANDERTHAL

FIGURE 11.2.

A comparison of the modern human skull with the "classic" Neanderthal skull. The latter is less rounded and lacks a predominant chin.

A new look at Neanderthal has tended to correct this image. Richard Leakey cites an anatomical reconstruction of European Neanderthal performed by William Strauss and A.J.E. Cave. They comment on Neanderthal as follows: "If he could be reincarnated and placed in a New York subway—provided he were bathed, shaved and dressed in modern clothing—it is doubtful whether he would attract any more attention than some of its other denizens."[2]

Furthermore, our classic picture of Neanderthal has been modified by discoveries that indicate there were more "generalized" (slightly more modern) types living concurrently in areas of the world other than Europe, particularly in the Near East. Differences in skull structure appear in the fossil record as they do today among various races of modern man in various geographic regions of the world. There was also apparently some intermixture as there is among present races of the world. There is a recent trend in anthropology to refer to the period from 100,000 years ago to 40,000 years ago as the "Neanderthal phase" in human history rather than draw a sharp line between classic Neanderthal and the more modern Cro-Magnon man who succeeded him.

Nevertheless, there are differences between Neanderthal man and the more modern man who replaced him more than 35,000 years ago. Neanderthal man is classified as *Homo sapiens neanderthalensis*, whereas the subspecies to which we belong is called *Homo sapiens sapiens* (man of wisdom). The difference in skull morphology is seen in Figure 11.2.

Basically, the classic Neanderthal has a much flatter skull on top with the impression of a bun or knot on the back. He lacks the well-defined, rather flat forehead of modern man, and he has massive prominent brow ridges. The jaws are thrust forward. His chin appears to be receding when compared with modern man's.

Neanderthal's body is thought to have been stocky and somewhat bulky. His limb bones were slightly bowed. An appearance of great strength is deduced from the points where muscles would have attached to his bones. His stature was similar to ours (average height was 5 feet 8 inches).

We have no way of knowing with certainty if Neanderthal man could talk. His brain cavity size was not only equal to but exceeded that of modern man. However, he reportedly lacked the frontal lobe, the speech center of our modern brain. Nevertheless, reconstruction of the Neanderthal larynx and brain has led anthropologists to believe he may have had some sort of spoken language.

The Neanderthal people appear in the fossil record 100,000 years ago during a relatively warm (interglacial) period. By 70,000 years ago, Europe was again in the grip of the Ice Age, and the most numerous classic remains are known from cave sites during this period. Neanderthal used fire for cooking and undoubtedly for warmth to survive the glacial cold.

Instead of merely shaping a single natural stone into a useful object, Neanderthal may be said to have actually manufactured stone tools. This was apparently accomplished by striking several precisely shaped flakes from a single piece of flint. The resulting flakes of flint were then processed into a variety of tools and weapons of advanced design including awls, knives, scrapers, spear points, and hand axes. Tools made from bone have also been found associated with the remains of Neanderthal man.

The Shanidar cave is located in the Zargos Mountains of Northern Iraq near the headwaters of the Tigris and Euphrates rivers. At this site, some 60,000 years ago, a very interesting event is thought to have occurred: a ritual burial with flowers.

Ralph Solecki of Columbia University spent twenty years excavating the cave at Shanidar. He found the remains of several classic Neanderthal individuals that had been carefully laid in a crypt scooped out among rocks and covered with earth. This was not too startling because archeological evidence of ritual burial is found in other Neanderthal sites. What is unusual is that one of the individuals, an adult male, designated by Solecki as "Shanidar IV," had been buried with flowers.

Pollen analysis of the soil indicates that eight different varieties of brightly colored wildflowers were used in this burial. Evidence from soil analysis also indicates that the flowers may have been woven into green branches from a pine-like shrub. The flowers appear not to have been randomly scattered, but rather carefully arranged around the body of Shanidar IV.[3]

There is additional evidence of those qualities associated with humanity at the Shanidar cave. The analysis of undeveloped bone structure indicates that another man, known as Shanidar I, was a severe cripple from birth. His right arm was entirely useless and may have been amputated just above the elbow. Extensive bone scar tissue indicates that he was blind in his left eye. He was apparently cared for by his people until his death at age forty, a very old age by Neanderthal standards. This is the first sign of compassion and tenderness in the archeological record.

FIGURE 11.3.

Upper Paleolithic tools, typically made by chipping the shape from a narrow flint blade, include a barked blade, *top,* a shouldered point, *middle,* and a long, leaf-shaped point, *bottom.* (From "Ice-age Hunters of the Ukraine," by Richard G. Klein. Copyright © 1974 *Scientific American.*)

FIGURE 11.4.

The cutaway artist's reconstruction of the El Juyo cave in Spain reveals the internal structure of a prehistoric shrine. Animal bones, unusual stones, and decorative columns lead archaeologists to conclude that the hunter-gatherers who lived here had a highly developed religious ritual. (M. E. Challinor for *Science 82.*)

Neanderthal man vanished from the archeological record about 40,000 years ago (he disappeared in Europe 35,000 years ago, and 40,000 years ago in the Near East). His place was taken by Cro-Magnon man.

CRO-MAGNON MAN

Between 35,000 and 40,000 years ago, Cro-Magnon man appeared throughout the Near East, Russia, Europe and somewhat later in North America. Cro-Magnon man is classified *Homo sapiens sapiens* (man of wisdom). He is thought by anthropologists to be the ancestor of all the modern races of the world and is therefore given the same biological classification as modern man. His physical appearance was very similar to that of modern man and was different from Neanderthal man in the same ways that modern man differs from Neanderthal man.

Cro-Magnon man was somewhat larger than modern man; many of the males were six feet tall or more. He also surpassed modern man in his average brain size. He had a high forehead as we do and his chin did not recede. If he were dressed in modern clothing, you would probably feel very comfortable sitting next to him on the bus.

Cro-Magnon man is best known for his artistic ability as seen in his magnificently beautiful cave paintings in France and Spain (see figure 11.5). These paintings are not simple representations. They are masterpieces of dynamic form and color. Cro-Magnon man painted vivid life-like pictures of cattle, bison, rhinoceros, horses, and mammoths. These were the animals he hunted on the fringes of the ice as it advanced and retreated.

Significantly lacking in Cro-Magnon art are human forms. The few representations of the human form that do occur are conspicuous by the lack of rich and dynamic detail afforded the animals. Richard Leakey comments: "Nowhere is there a portrait of a human face equivalent in detail to one of the giant bulls at Lascaux. It is almost as if there was a taboo against the representation of the human form."[4]

In a few caves Cro-Magnon man left an important and evocative symbol of his presence: the imprint of his hand. These imprints, together with abstract designs and symbols, imply that Cro-Magnon possessed an awareness of being and creative communication. His animal art was magnificent. There is even evidence of some sort of religious sanctuary and of rituals being performed. Why his few representations of human forms were so scant and impoverished is an interesting problem for students of human development.

The Cro-Magnon Mystery. Where did Cro-Magnon man come from and what happened to the Neanderthal man? This is an unresolved problem in paleoanthropology, the study of ancient man. There is no general consensus on the subject. Neanderthal man as represented by his classic form simply disappeared 40,000 years ago

FIGURE 11.5.

The famous color paintings from caves in France and Spain indicate the artistic ability of Cro-Magnon man.

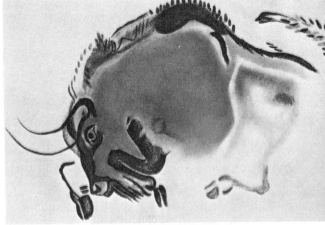

in the Near East and 35,000 years ago in Europe. He was replaced by the modern and more culturally advanced Cro-Magnon man.

Some scholars hold that Neanderthal man (as represented by the more generalized form) gradually changed over time into Cro-Magnon man. Others hold that a population of Cro-Magnon arose in another geographical area (perhaps Africa or the Near East) and then invaded and displaced Neanderthal. Cro-Magnon may have interbred with Neanderthal. He may also have killed Neanderthal, although there is no evidence of a massacre. But is there evidence for a transition from Neanderthal to Cro-Magnon?

In his book *The Making of Mankind*, Richard Leakey describes the human remains found in three ancient caves located in northern Israel. The first cave is called Mugharet et Tabun (Cave of the Oven). It is situated on the slopes of Mount Carmel overlooking the Mediterranean Sea. In this cave have been found two skeletons of classic Neanderthal man that date at about 45,000 years ago.

A few hundred yards from this Neanderthal cave lies Mugharet es Skhul (Cave of the Goat Kids). In this cave the remains of ten individuals have been found that are difficult to classify. They appear to be somewhat of a mixture between Neanderthal and Cro-Magnon. Further inland from Mount Carmel near Nazareth lies another cave (Jebel Qafzeh) which contained the remains of eleven "modern-looking, though rather robust," individuals. Their tool kit was that typical of Neanderthal man. Both caves date at 40,000 years ago. Many scholars interpret the individuals found in these caves as intermediate forms between Neanderthal and Cro-Magnon. Others interpret the fossils as lacking in definitive Neanderthal characteristics with the implication that they are not transitional forms. If this latter view is correct, it appears that these may be the earliest remains of Cro-Magnon Man.

CIVILIZED MAN

For 25,000 years Cro-Magnon man pursued the game animals of Europe in the shadow of the glaciers. Then, about 12,000 years ago (10,000 B.C.), the glaciers began to retreat. The climate of North America and Europe became warmer and more temperate. The Ice Age ended, and the flowers and grasses extended their range northward. The agricultural revolution and a settled way of life was at hand.

The first step in the transition from a nomadic hunter existence was the domestication of animals. The wild dog was the first animal domesticated, although we are not certain where this occurred. Sheep are thought to have been domesticated about 9,000 B.C. in what is now northern Iraq (ancient Mesopotamia). Man was still nomadic, however, as he had to constantly move his sheep and cattle to fresh pasture. Civilization depends on a settled community and had to await cultivated agriculture.

The Jordan Valley in Palestine is unique in the history of man, for it is here, in the ancient oasis of Jericho and similar sites in Israel and Jordan, that settlements began to take a permanent shape and that cultivated agriculture is first known to have developed. In the burst of vegetation that followed the close of the Ice Ages, wild wheat appeared in the Middle East. The ancient people of Jericho and similar villages harvested this wild wheat with sickles made of flint pieces embedded in horn or bone.

Two unique developments (J. Bronowski calls them "genetic accidents") are then thought to have happened. The first "gift of nature" was the cross between wild wheat and native goat grass to produce a hybrid wheat called *emmer.* Emmer produced a much plumper head of grain for the harvest. Although probably cultivated, its seeds scattered in the wind the way other wild grasses do today.

The second "genetic accident" was truly a marvel. Emmer crossed with another type of wild goat grass and produced a still larger hybrid: bread wheat. The seeds of bread wheat do not scatter in the wind. They must be removed from the stalk by man and planted to spread and propagate. Man and wheat came together in Jericho to found the world's first and oldest known city. A settled way of life had become possible. Civilization could begin.

THE GARDEN OF EDEN

Current records indicate that civilization began along the Tigris-Euphrates river complex and in the oasis of Jericho in the Jordan Valley. It was there that man and water and bread wheat came together to begin the agricultural revolution. With the scientific record placing the beginning of human civilization in the same place as the biblical record places it, the question of the reality of the Garden of Eden instantly confronts even the secular scholar. Science and Scripture have met again, this time at the origin of man himself.

The search for the Garden of Eden starts with its geographical

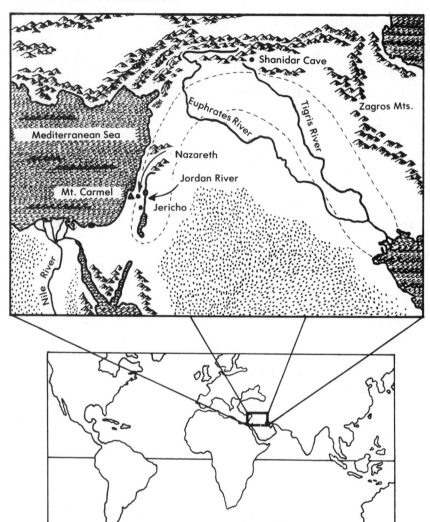

FIGURE 11.6.

The cradle of civilization is located in ancient Mesopotamia along the Tigris-Euphrates river complex and extending in a crescent shape through modern Syria, Israel, and Jordan. The Fertile Crescent is truly the birthplace of humankind.

location. The only clue given in the Bible is that four rivers flow out of this Garden, and two of these can be positively identified: the Tigris River and the Euphrates River. I believe the Garden of Eden was situated somewhere within the northern Fertile Crescent (modern Iraq, Syria, Israel, and Jordan).

It is highly significant that evidence of so many crucial events in the origins of human beings have occurred in this region (see figure 11.6). It is indeed the Cradle of Civilization. The Shanidar cave located near the headwaters of both the Tigris and Euphrates rivers has yielded the first evidence of compassion and altruism—the care of a crippled man. Furthermore, the first evidence of a ritual burial with flowers is found in the Shanidar cave. There are signs of humanity here.

Then, there are the curious human remains in the Mount Carmel caves and the cave near Nazareth. If these remains are transitional between Neanderthal and Cro-Magnon, then this is a location for the emerging stock of Cro-Magnon. If these remains are lacking in close Neanderthal affinity, this is a location for the earliest known Cro-Magnon man. Because anthropologists regard Cro-Magnon man as the ancestor of all the modern peoples in the world today, Israel might be the homeland of the entire present human race.

Current evidence indicates that Israel may lay claim to the beginnings of cultivated agriculture. Archeologists long thought that agriculture began along the fertile Tigris-Euphrates river complex. Logic dictated that they extend their search to the upper hill country at the foot of the Zargos mountains, and their search was rewarded with signs of primitive ancient cultivation and harvest. But the earliest agricultural cultivation discovered so far took place in the ancient oasis of Jericho. It was here about 8,000 B.C. that the series of "genetic accidents" resulted in bread wheat. It was in Jericho that man is first known to have tilled the ground, to have earned his bread by the sweat of his brow.

The first animal husbandry, the first agriculture, the first towns, and the beginnings of civilization occurred in ancient Israel and Mesopotamia, not in Egypt or other parts of Africa, not in Mexico, or South America, or India, or China, or the Bronx. Bronowski states, "The largest single step in the ascent of man is the change from nomad to village agriculture."[5] This momentous step took place in the same geographic area that the Bible describes as the center of human origin and development—another striking testimony to the harmony between science and Scripture.

ADAM AND EVE?

Both science and the Bible are in harmony as to the geographic location for the "Garden of Eden." But how do Adam and Eve fit in, and when did our ancestors first appear in scientific history? We will attempt to correlate scientific and biblical time in the next chapter, but the calendar date for God's creation of Adam and Eve will remain unresolved. The Bible simply doesn't tell us when this event took

Did Eve Really Exist?

J. A. Miller reported in the August 13, 1983, issue of *Science News* (vol. 124: 7, p. 101) that "Biologists studying DNA differences in individuals around the world, have now traced human lineage back to a common female ancestor." Allan C. Wilson of the University of California at Berkeley is quoted as claiming that "We all go back to one mother living 350,000 years ago." Another group of scientists at Stanford University claim a common ancestor appeared in history at a more recent date, ranging from 50,000 to 100,000 years ago. Luigi L. Cavalli-Sforza of Stanford states that this more recent time period is closer to those dates derived from fossil examination and other genetic approaches.

While much additional work remains to be accomplished in refining, calibrating, and reconciling DNA dating, the latest evidence from biology suggests all of us share a common mother in our distant ancestral past. The Bible calls this common female ancestor Eve. In its quest for truth, science has uncovered another signpost pointing to the Word of God.

place. Furthermore, archeologists have not discovered definite evidence that might settle the question. We can only speculate as to when Adam and Eve might have appeared in scientific history. The evidence is insufficient to resolve this mystery. However, some possibilities can be eliminated. Perhaps it will help to bracket the problem into a relatively short period of geologic time.

Let's start by reviewing what we have learned about Primates—the biological order in which science classifies humans. The legitimacy of the discoveries identified as missing links between apes and humans has not been sustained by subsequent scientific evidence. From 1912 through the early 1950s science confidently displayed Piltdown Man as the missing link between apes and man. Following the exposure of this clever forgery, paleoanthropologists promptly pushed *Ramapithecus* and the *Australopithecine hominids* into the gap. The latest evidence indicates that these creatures may be the missing links in the apes' family tree—not man's. The missing ancestors for the orangutang, the chimpanzee, and the gorilla may have at last been found. The current evidence certainly does not justify including these fossil creatures in the ancestry of the human race.

I believe we can also dismiss *Homo habilis* and *Homo erectus* as likely candidates for Adam and Eve. For one thing science is not certain whether they led to *Homo sapiens* at all. They may have become extinct. Furthermore, the present fossil evidence does not indicate they possessed those traits that we consider uniquely human.

What about Neanderthal man? The archeological record shows indications of humanity during his period in history. We have evidence from the Shanidar cave in northern Iraq of compassion in the care of a crippled man. We have evidence of a ritual burial with flowers. These signs of humanity, together with the location of the Shanidar cave at the headwaters of the Tigris and Euphrates rivers, would indicate that Neanderthal man should not be excluded in the search for modern man's ancestors.

Should we look for Adam and Eve in the mysterious appearance 40,000 years ago of Cro-Magnon man? He created the world's first great art, and anthropologists believe him to be the common ancestor of all the modern races. There are those intriguing fossil remains in the caves on Mount Carmel and near Nazareth. There is that rapid spread of the Cro-Magnon population throughout the world. The present evidence indicates that the Near East, specifically Israel, is the most likely point of origination.

Something very profound in the social and economic development of humankind happened between 7,000 and 8,000 B.C. The hunter-gatherer culture and the art of Cro-Magnon man disappeared. The beginning of agriculture occurred. Towns and cities appeared. Gone from the mainstream of civilization was the dominance of the socio-economic practice of *sharing* as is typical of hunter-gatherer societies. In its place was substituted the concept of *possession* of property and goods. Man not only began to till the fields, he now protected his crops from nomadic tribes and ambitious neighbors.

Walls appeared around the town of Jericho around 7,000 B.C. Some scholars believe the walls were there to keep sediment out of the fields. But they could have been for defense and protection from unfriendly nomads. The dramatic change in art suggests the latter. Cro-Magnon art focused on animals. The first art from the new age of agriculture shows human beings, often with weapons and in warfare. Scenes of battle become common. There is an obsession with conflict. The biblical description of the evil of man and resulting conflicts begin to fit this picture.

It is therefore not possible to determine whether Adam and Eve were the ancestors of Neanderthal man or Cro-Magnon man. Evidence of characteristics associated with human beings appear as early as Neanderthal man. To date it is impossible to identify such characteristics any earlier. God's timing of events is often mysterious.

A NOTE TO THE READER

The primary focus of this book is to concentrate on scientific *evidence* rather than *theory* in order to explore the harmony between science and Scripture. However, the reader should be aware that popular and scientific literature is filled with imaginative and speculative hypotheses that attempt to explain how evolutionary forces could have produced a human being from an ancestral ape. The major failure of these hypotheses is that they totally fail to account for man's unique qualities of reason, creativity, humor, altruism, or for his knowledge of God. To claim that the "struggle for survival" could have produced the ability to appreciate the symphonies of Beethoven is utter nonsense. Readers who wish to explore the total failure of evolutionary theory to account for the unique qualities of man should consult the excellent book *God Is,* by British scientist Alan Hayward (see Suggestions for Further Reading).

We should be content to be grateful for the eternal mystery and majesty of His creation.

Questions of timing remain, but in our review of what science has to say about our origins, the historical reality of Genesis is verified with new clarity. All the significant developments in the history of the human race take place in the same geographic location the Bible identifies for the creation of Adam and Eve. Perhaps of more importance is the fact that in scientific discovery, as in the Bible, the advent of man takes place at the end of the vast sequence of cosmic and geologic history. All events in both science and the Bible lead to preparation of the Earth and life upon it for man. Science is once again in harmony with Scripture.

CHAPTER 12

AGES AND DAYS

For a thousand years in Thy sight
Are like yesterday when it passes by,
Or as a watch in the night.
Psalm 90:4

One of the most difficult matters to deal with in understanding the relationship between science and Scripture is the matter of time. Many people have felt that the scientific evidence of cosmic and geologic time is in conflict with a literal understanding of what the Bible says about the time involved in creation. Once again, however, if we approach the scientific evidence and what Scripture says with an open mind and fresh insights, we can begin a resolution of this problem. Scientific evidence does not contradict Scripture.

A PERSPECTIVE ON TIME

Millions and billions of years of time are difficult to comprehend when our current life spans are less than one hundred years long. Many people have trouble grasping the enormous periods of time involved in the history of the Universe and the planet Earth.

Sometimes Christians opt for a quite recently created Earth and Universe, a so-called "young earth." However, astronomers have discovered galaxies of stars that are two, three, four *billion* light years away! That by itself should indicate the kinds of time periods involved. Moreover, since God is eternal, a 15- or 20-billion-year-old creation is no more far-fetched than a four-thousand-year-old one.

To place key events and ages into a time frame we can more easily comprehend, let 5 billion years represent one year in discussing the history of the Universe and Earth. The history of the Universe would then be three years in length.

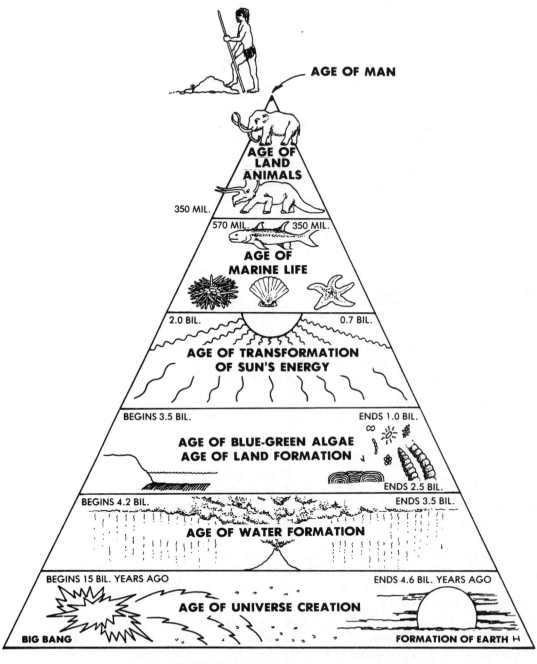

AGE OF MAN

AGE OF LAND ANIMALS

350 MIL.

570 MIL.   350 MIL.

AGE OF MARINE LIFE

2.0 BIL.   0.7 BIL.

AGE OF TRANSFORMATION OF SUN'S ENERGY

BEGINS 3.5 BIL.   ENDS 1.0 BIL.

AGE OF BLUE-GREEN ALGAE
AGE OF LAND FORMATION

ENDS 2.5 BIL.

BEGINS 4.2 BIL.   ENDS 3.5 BIL.

AGE OF WATER FORMATION

BEGINS 15 BIL. YEARS AGO   ENDS 4.6 BIL. YEARS AGO

AGE OF UNIVERSE CREATION

BIG BANG   FORMATION OF EARTH

FIGURE 12.1.

The six days of God's creation corresponding to the six major eras in the history of the Earth. The beginning of the Universe is estimated to be between 10 and 20 billion years ago. The use of 15 billion years in this figure is arbitrary. The numbers on the left indicate when the age begins. The numbers on the right indicate when the process or life form ends or ceases to be a dominant factor.

192

Age of Universe Creation. The creation of the Universe from the Big Bang to the formation of planet Earth would occupy two entire years on our relative time scale. The subsequent events in the history of the Earth would take place over the final period of one calendar year.

Age of Water Formation. The final year would start 4.6 billion years ago when the Earth condensed from its nebular cloud of gas and dust particles. During January of this last year nothing of significance would happen. About the beginning of February the Earth would start to outgas its primordial atmosphere of water vapor and carbon dioxide. With the arrival of March, the water vapor would begin condensing to form the Earth's first liquid water. By the end of March, the Earth would be covered by a shallow sea.

Age of Land Formation. The first continental cratons would begin to appear at the end of March. By the middle of June the era of great vertical movement in the Earth's crust would be essentially complete. Thereafter the Earth's crust would be divided into large continental cratons and interconnected deep ocean basins.

Age of Vegetation. The age of blue-green algae would also begin at the end of March. It would dominate life until the arrival of October when more advanced forms of algae would appear.

Age of Transformation of the Sun's Energy. Photosynthesis of the blue-green algae would also begin at the end of March. It would not have an appreciable effect on the atmosphere until July 20. It would take from July 20 until October for enough free oxygen to accumulate to form the Earth's ozone screen. The Sun's energy would become increasingly beneficial to advanced forms of life.

Age of Marine Life. About the middle of November the Cambrian explosion of marine life would take place. Primitive fish would dominate the oceans by the end of the month.

Age of Life on the Land and Man. The Age of Amphibians would begin on December 4, and reptiles would appear on December 10. The dinosaurs would rule the Earth from December 15 until Christmas. About the end of Christmas Day, mammals would begin their explosive adaptive radiation. In less than a week familiar cattle, horses, dogs, and elephants would be present.

Cro-Magnon man would not appear on the calendar until six minutes before midnight on New Year's Eve! The beginning of agriculture and civilization—the appearance of modern man as we know him—would occur about one minute before midnight. About twelve seconds before midnight Christ would be born. The Industrial Revolution would last for about the final one second in this relative time history of the planet Earth.

This perspective on time is a little breathtaking. Our watches ticking off seconds, minutes, hours, and days seem like nothing in the vast sweep of cosmic time. It causes one to wonder what time is like for God. In reality, time itself is one of God's created relationships of the physical world.

Until the early part of this century people thought they lived in a three dimensional world. Length, width, and height were the familiar dimensions that could be measured. Then Einstein discovered that time is relative to motion, and the fourth dimension of time was added to man's knowledge of his world. It is interesting to imagine what time might be like for a being who can transcend time and space. According to Einstein's theory of relativity, the faster one travels, the slower the clock runs. If one could travel at the speed of light, there would be no movement of time as we understand the concept. In effect, there would be no past or future. Everything would take place *right now.*

We are beings that live in a particular space called the planet Earth. We measure time according to the orientation and motion of our planet in relationship to the Sun. One year from now the Sun will appear in our sky in the same position it is in today. This regularity of planetary motion forms the basis of our calendar year. It is how time is measured in the normal course of events.

SCIENTIFIC DATING METHODS

To measure the age of the Universe, the Earth, and to date the events that took place over geologic time, scientists use a variety of methods. The methods based on the inorganic "radioactive clock," radiocarbon dating, and racemization (amino acid) dating are described in detail in the Appendix.

Absolute dates for rocks formed from a molten state (igneous rocks) are obtained primarily through radioactive dating techniques. Radioactive elements are unstable. That is, their atomic nuclei spontaneously break up or disintegrate to form a more stable element from a parent radioactive or unstable element. The transformation from uranium to lead is the most familiar example. Samples of radioactive elements decay at known rates into stable elements. Thus, if one can calculate the size of the original material and know the amount of the residual material, if the sample is uncontaminated and if the assumption is made that the rate of decay has been the same over the lifetime of the sample, it is possible to determine the date at which the original material was formed with a fair degree of accuracy.

When a rock is remelted or new molten material wells up from the mantle to cool, a new clock starts or is reset. This is a very useful phenomena in dating new or remelted igneous rocks. It is by using this method that scientists are able to date the continental cratons that formed during the great age of land and continent formation and have determined that it took place between 3.5 and 2.5 billion years ago. In the United States, the craton is thought to exist under the soil and sediments of the continent's heartland. In eastern Canada, the craton is exposed to the surface to form the Canadian Shield.

The eruption of a volcano often spewed out large quantities of ash and dust that settled over the landscape. It may have left a deposit several inches or more in thickness. These deposits often contained radioactive nuclides that today tell geologists how many years ago the volcano erupted. The volcanic marker was sometimes covered over later by sedimentary deposits. The age of these sedimentary deposits can therefore be determined by determining the age of the volcanic deposit. Thus, the volcanic markers give important clues to the ages of fossils lying above or below them.

Fossils became abundant 570 million years ago with the advent of the Cambrian explosion of marine animal life. From this time forward to the present, the dating of sedimentary formations becomes much more reliable. The crust of the Earth contains sedimentary deposits literally miles thick. Many of these deposits contain fossils. Some of the fossil animals and plants lived only during certain geologic periods and serve as key indicators of the age of the formations in which they are found. For example, if geologists find dinosaur bones in a sedimentary deposit, they can assume the formation is more than 62 million years old, for our present knowledge indicates the dinosaurs became extinct 63 million years ago.

The record of ancient life is often worldwide in scope. Geologists in Europe can frequently correlate fossils with those found in America. Somewhere in the sedimentary deposits of the world there is likely to be a volcanic or igneous intrusion marker that will supply a radioactive date for calibration of the indicator fossils. To experienced geologists, reading the layers of sedimentary rocks is like reading the pages of a book. Geologists use indicator fossils and radioactive markers to tell them where they are in geologic history.

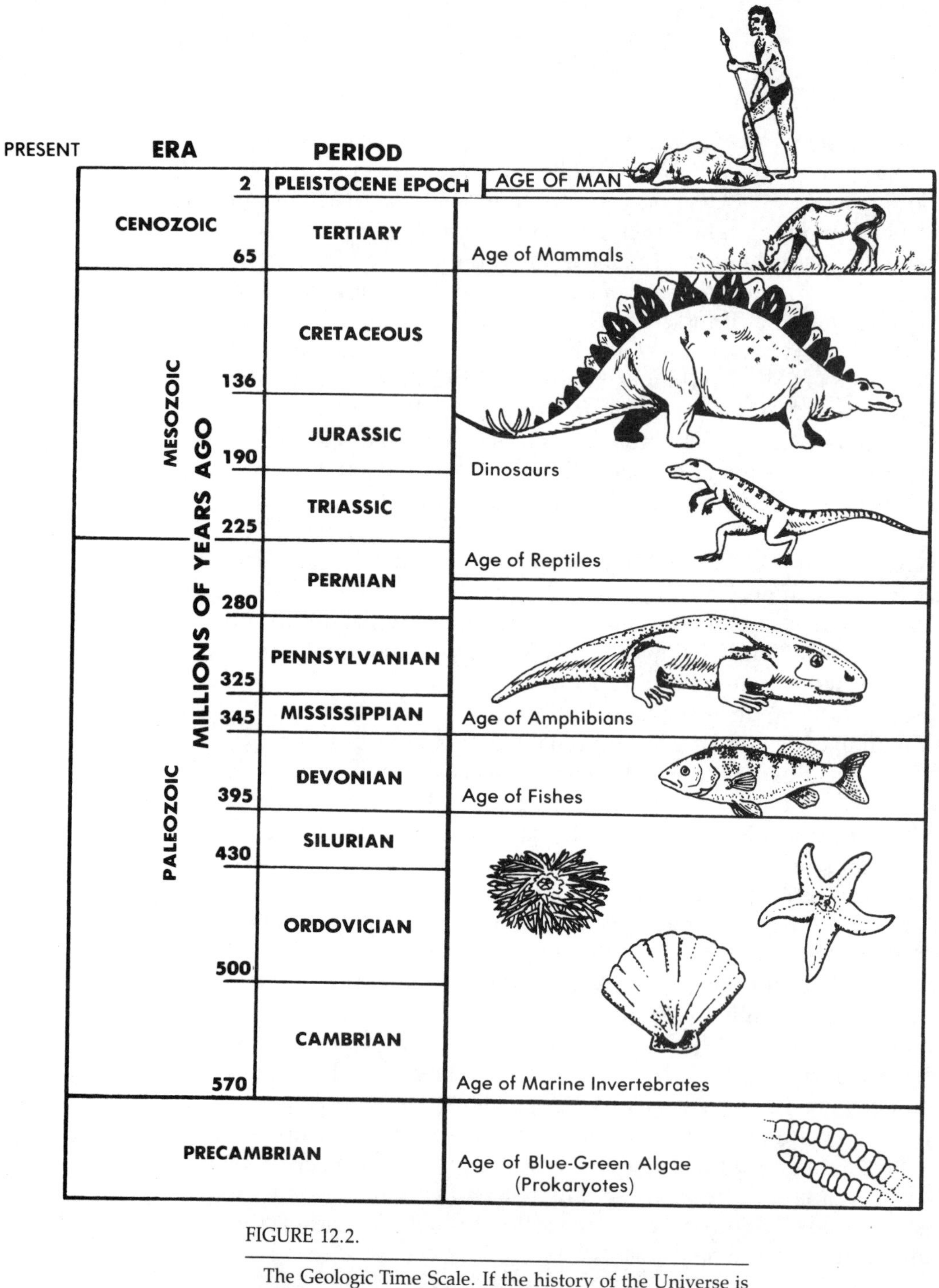

PRESENT	ERA	PERIOD	
2		PLEISTOCENE EPOCH	AGE OF MAN
	CENOZOIC	TERTIARY	Age of Mammals
65			
	MESOZOIC	CRETACEOUS	Dinosaurs
136		JURASSIC	
190		TRIASSIC	
225			Age of Reptiles
	PALEOZOIC	PERMIAN	
280		PENNSYLVANIAN	
325		MISSISSIPPIAN	Age of Amphibians
345		DEVONIAN	Age of Fishes
395		SILURIAN	
430		ORDOVICIAN	
500		CAMBRIAN	
570			Age of Marine Invertebrates
	PRECAMBRIAN		Age of Blue-Green Algae (Prokaryotes)

(MILLIONS OF YEARS AGO)

FIGURE 12.2.

The Geologic Time Scale. If the history of the Universe is conceived as taking place in a three-year time frame, the portion of that history from the Cambrian period through the present would be represented by the last six weeks of the last year.

THE GEOLOGIC AGES

Geologists have constructed a time scale divided into eras and periods (see figure 12.1). The primary basis for the delineation of eras and periods is the type of fossil life characteristic of the respective chapters in geologic history. In the same way that historians refer to the "Age of Greece" or the "Age of Rome," geologists refer to the "Age of Fishes" (the *Devonian period*) or the "Age of Reptiles and Dinosaurs" (the *Mesozoic era*).

Some people have been critical of the scientific dating methods discussed above. Sometimes the dating of events changes with more careful research before settling down to some generally agreed upon age.[1] While it is certainly true that the dating of specific events and of fossils themselves is often dependent upon the dating of the geological beds above and below them, the great majority of reported geologic ages are fairly well calibrated and consistent with the vast sweep of geologic history. An expert watchmaker, an artist, or a silversmith will often stamp a date on his work. It speaks of the pride of an expert craftsman. In a similar way, the creation bears the marks of its Maker, with special records in the Earth's crust to allow us a helpful look into the secrets and the wonders of the handiwork of God.

THE SIX DAYS OF CREATION

In the light of substantial evidence that the Earth is indeed billions of years old, the question naturally arises as to why the opening pages of Scripture seem to indicate that the creation occurred in a short span of time. If we believe that Genesis 1 and the scientific account of creation are describing the same historical events, we must deal with the fact that some biblical scholars choose to regard the six days of Genesis as literal twenty-four-hour periods of creation.

While a literal twenty-four-hour day interpretation does not violate the Hebrew language, there is both biblical and traditional support that the "days" in Genesis 1 refer to ages of creation. Biblical support for this view centers on the fact that the Scriptures use known periods of time as metaphors for long, almost incomprehensible time spans. For example, King David wrote, "For a thousand years in Thy sight/Are like yesterday when it passes by,/Or as a watch in the night" (Psa. 90:4). And centuries later, the Apostle Peter observed that, "with the Lord one day is as a thousand years, and a thousand years as one day" (2 Pet. 3:8). In the fifth century Saint Augustine reached the conclusion that the Earth was very old. He came to this opinion solely from studying the text of Scripture.[2] This was long before modern geologists found evidence of the ancient history of the Earth.

There are other plausible reasons for suggesting that the six days may be interpreted as six ages or eras of creation.

1. The poetic nature of ancient writing. The ancient Hebrews wrote much of what they had to say in poetic language. If we assume that the writer of Genesis is praising God for His creation as well as teaching, what more poetic and beautiful language could he have used to separate the significant steps of creation than: "And there was evening and there was morning, one day" (Gen. 1:5)?

2. The literary framework of ancient writing. Dr. Ronald Youngblood, specialist in Semitic languages writes, "Ancient Near Eastern literature, particularly from Mesopotamia and Canaan, provides numerous examples of the use of seven days as a literary framework to circumscribe the completion of a significant or catastrophic event. The pattern in these works runs uniformly as follows: 'One day, a second day, so and so happens; a third day, a fourth day, such and such occurs; a fifth day, a sixth day, so and so takes place, then, on the seventh day, the story comes to its exciting conclusion.'"[3]

   It should be noted that some translations of the Bible read "The first day," "The second day," and so on, which would seem to imply that one continuous seven-day week is being described. However, the original Hebrew meaning is "One day," "a second day," "a third day," and so on. The use of the definite article *the* is not used until the sixth day when God created man. Thus, the days (or periods of time) in Genesis 1 may be separated by vast and indefinite time periods. As Youngblood points out, "The omission of the definite article *the* from all but the sixth day allows for the possibility of random or literary order as well as rigidly chronological order."[4]

3. The six days of Genesis 1 could well have been six days of revelation. This explanation would indicate that God told the

story of His creation to Moses in a six-day period and Moses told or wrote the creation story in that format. Similarly, the six days may represent six points in time when God spoke "Let there be . . ." and consequently initiated a whole new phase of creation at each of these points in time—the light, the animals, man himself.

It is my belief that there is sufficient biblical authority to interpret the six days of Genesis as six major eras or time periods of creation. I believe that Moses was originally speaking to pre-scientific Hebrew people in a time frame they could comprehend. He used a literary structural framework with which they were familiar. He used poetic language which was not only beautiful but easy to remember. Genesis was written for our modern era as well, and we should make the linguistic and cultural transition.

CHAPTER 13
THE GENESIS CONNECTION

Thus the heavens and the earth were completed, and all their hosts.
Genesis 2:1

The idea that science and Genesis 1 are similar and compatible is not a revolutionary thought. The compatibility of the scientific version of the creation of the Universe and the creation command "Let there be light" is well outlined in Dr. Robert Jastrow's book *God and the Astronomers*. Similarly, Dr. Alan Hayward's book *God Is* points out the dignity of the Genesis creation account as the critical missing force in the hypothesis of evolution.

What has been lacking is a comparison of the entire creation account of Genesis 1 with the latest scientific evidence. Many people have felt that the two were in harmony. This chapter will directly compare the discoveries of modern science with the biblical account of creation. This comparison, however, cannot be between *scientific theory*, which interprets evidence, and Scripture, but between scientific evidence itself and Scripture. Most scientific *theory*, rightly or wrongly, limits itself to the concept of a *closed* Universe—one that excludes the possibility of supernatural or divine causes. Therefore, when comparing modern science and the biblical account of creation, we must exclude scientific *theory* by its own definition. What we will look at is the *scientific evidence*, the *actual events* in the scientific history of our origins. Do the scientific observations and discoveries confirm or deny biblical creation? Let's look at the *evidence*.

We have found that modern science and Genesis are in complete harmony in affirming that there was a beginning to the Universe. The direct simplicity of the opening words of the Bible "In the beginning . . ." are as applicable today as they were 3,000 years ago. The biblical words "The earth was formless and void, and darkness was over the surface of the deep" is an apt description of what modern science has to tell us about conditions that may have existed prior to the birth of the Universe. Following this introduction or stage setting, Genesis then presents eight creation commands grouped into six basic time periods or days of creation. Let us follow the flow of scientific history using the format of the biblical account of God's creation.

FIRST DAY OR ERA OF CREATION

Let there be light (Gen. 1:3).

The Universe began in an explosion of dazzling brilliance termed the Big Bang. The Universe was filled with light. All energy, matter, natural forces, and natural laws were created at this time. Energy was transformed into matter and then into galaxies, stars, and planets including Earth.

The Universe came into being about 15 billion years ago, and its creation ceased to dominate events from our perspective about 4.6 billion years ago when the Earth was formed. The *Age of Universe Creation* can be thought of as dominating history from about 15 billion to 4.6 billion years ago. Following its initial solidification, the Earth emerged as a naked body of rock which looked like the moon. The planet lacked both air and water.

SECOND DAY OR ERA OF CREATION

Let there be an expanse in the midst of the waters, and let it separate the waters from the waters (Gen. 1:6).

The Earth outgassed through volcanic processes a dense atmosphere of water vapor and noxious gases. The crust of the Earth cooled and most of the water vapor condensed to form a shallow sea blanketing the Earth. The shallow sea composed of liquid water was separated by the expanse in the lower sky from the remaining atmospheric clouds of water vapor and gases.

The *Age of Water Formation* occupied the time period from 4.2 to 3.5 billion years ago. Although minor additions may occur from time to time, the Earth's supply of water was essentially formed during this period. At the end of this time, oceans covered the entire globe with the possible exception of a few volcanic peaks or islands piercing the surface of the waters.

THIRD DAY OR ERA OF CREATION

> Let the waters below the heavens be gathered into one place, and let the dry land appear (Gen. 1:9).

The shallow seas were gathered into deep interconnected ocean basins, and the light granitic rocks welled up from below to form huge platform-like continents. This era of great vertical separation of the Earth's crust, the *Age of Land Formation,* occurred during the period from 3.5 to 2.5 billion years ago. Recycling of the land continues to the present in the basically lateral movement of plate tectonics.

> Let the earth sprout vegetation, plants yielding seed, and fruit trees bearing fruit after their kind, with seed in them, on the earth (Gen. 1:11).

Blue-green algae appeared and dominated life on the planet Earth. The *Age of Blue-green Algae* lasted from 3.5 to 1.0 billion years ago. Red, green, and brown algae then appeared followed by land plants with spores, then seed plants, and finally flowering plants (the Big Bloom) 130 million years ago.

One of the most startling correlations between modern science and Scripture is that the dominant ages of land formation and vegetation (as represented by blue-green algae) coincide with God's third day of creation. The *Age of Land Formation* and the *Age of Blue-Green Algae* both occur during the same period in geologic history. It is noteworthy that in accord with God's creation commands, these events also take place during the same time period, that is, God's biblical third day of creation.

FOURTH DAY OR ERA OF CREATION

> Let there be lights in the expanse of the heavens to separate the day from the night, and let them be for signs, and for seasons, and for days and years; and let them be for lights in the expanse of the heavens to give light on the earth (Gen 1:14–15).

Photosynthesis of the first vegetation (the blue-green algae) together with chemical processes cleaned the atmosphere of noxious gases, created free oxygen and erected the ozone screen. The *Age of Transformation of the Sun's Energy* began about 2 billion years ago when free oxygen began to accumulate in the atmosphere and waters of the Earth. By at least 700 million years ago, light from the Sun reaching the Earth had been transformed from lethal ultraviolet rays into a beneficial energy source for advanced life.

FIFTH DAY OR ERA OF CREATION

Let the waters teem with swarms of living creatures, and let birds fly above the earth in the open expanse of the heavens (Gen. 1:20).

The curtain in the drama of animal life rose to reveal the waters of the Earth teeming with swarms of living creatures over 500 million years ago. All the major marine invertebrate phyla were present, and the fishes appeared relatively soon thereafter. Flying insects appeared during the Devonian age which began 400 million years ago. Current fossil evidence shows that birds occurred much later in geologic history.

The *Age of Marine Life* during which marine invertebrates and fish dominated history began with the Cambrian explosion 570 million years ago. It ended 350 million years ago when the Age of Fishes closed the Devonian Period (see figure 12.1). It was time for life on the land.

SIXTH DAY OR ERA OF CREATION

Let the earth bring forth living creatures after their kind: cattle and creeping things and beasts of the earth after their kind (Gen. 1:24).

Amphibians crawled on the land, followed by reptiles and small primitive mammals. Giant dinosaurs ruled the Earth. Following their extinction, all the major forms of mammals appeared and spread throughout the Earth.

The *Age of Land Animals* began 350 million years ago. The dominance of animal life ended with the arrival of man.

Let Us make man in Our image, according to Our likeness (Gen. 1:26).

We currently live in the *Age of Man*. One's understanding of when this era began depends on one's choice as to whether Neanderthal (100,000 years ago), Cro-Magnon (40,000 years ago), or Civilized man

(10,000 years ago) is considered to be the first human being. The present archeological evidence indicates that all critical cultural events (from the first signs of ritual burial 60,000 years ago to the beginnings of agriculture 10,000 years ago) occurred in the same geographical area the Bible identifies as the birthplace of mankind.

THE HARMONY OF GENESIS AND SCIENTIFIC HISTORY

Three rather startling yet obvious facts emerge from the foregoing comparison.

1. *The order of events in Genesis 1 and the scientific record are in substantially the same sequence.* Books on historical geology are generally written around a chronological sequence of events. However, they often diverge from a chronological order to a topical order. Topics such as the development of the Earth's water, air, land, and major life forms are most often written in complete chapters. It is truly remarkable that Genesis 1 is written in virtually the same chronological order as geology textbooks which address the history of the Earth.

There are two places in Genesis where topics are carried through to completion after their origin and most dominant effects have been introduced. The topic of vegetation appears in the biblical account of events where science also says it begins. However, the Bible rapidly carries the topic of vegetation through to more recent times. Scripture also tells of God's creation of the birds in the same verse as life in the sea. This may be a topical rather than chronological treatment. God is filling the spaces, the water and the air, which He had created earlier. Life in the air (winged insects and birds) is grouped with life in the sea.

It also might be argued that the Sun is out of sequence in Genesis compared with scientific history. There is no disagreement among cosmologists that the Sun came into existence at the same time as the Earth. However, there is also no disagreement among scientists that the first vegetative life existed for more than 2 billion years before the light from the Sun became beneficial to animal life. The first vegetative life had to be created before the Sun's energy could be beneficial.

The history of the Universe, the planet Earth, and life upon the Earth is presented graphically in Figure 13.1. As mentioned earlier there are eight creation commands in Genesis grouped into six basic time periods or days of creation. Both the periods of land formation and the first vegetation coincide in time, both in Genesis and in scientific history. The same may also be said for the appearance of land animals followed by man.

The ages or eras of creation in the Genesis record appear to be in harmony with scientific history. From a scientific viewpoint, each era of creation is a necessary precedent to the following one. Each era forms a solid foundation upon which to build the following one. The biblical ages of creation are not only in logical developmental order, they are in the order confirmed by actual scientific history.

It is only recently that scientists have been able to place all the major events in the Earth's history in sequential order. It was only in the mid-1800s that scientists first discovered that animal life in the oceans began before animal life on the land. It is only within the last twenty-five years that scientists have affirmed that the Universe began with light and that seas appeared before continents.

Not only is there harmony between Genesis 1 and science as to the sequence of creation events, but those of us who have at times questioned God's Word must understand that the written biblical account predates the modern scientific account by more than 3500 years.

2. *All major explosive adaptive radiations correlate with Scripture's creation commands.* One major modification has been made in Darwin's theory of evolution. The fossil evidence accumulated over the last one hundred years has shown that the development of life did not progress in the gradual uniform way that Darwin envisioned. Instead, the evidence has shown that various forms of life have remained basically the same for very long periods of geologic time. Then in very short spurts of geologic time dramatic changes and transformations have taken place. The term *punctuated equilibrium* is used to describe this giant stairstep view of the history of life. These rapid evolutionary bursts are called "explosive adaptive radiations."

The fact is, all major explosive adaptive radiations occur at the same points in scientific history that there is a creation command in Genesis! Furthermore, all the major dramatic transformations in life forms not only occur at the same point, but also in substantially the same way as the creation steps in Genesis. "Let the waters teem with swarms of living creatures" is a good example. It describes what science textbooks call the Cambrian explosion of marine life.

The concept of punctuated equilibrium has brought scientific thinking much closer to the unchanging biblical pattern. The major point of disagreement between science and Genesis is no longer the fact of dramatic transformations, but the *cause* of the dramatic transformations that the evidence shows to have taken place. Science is still searching for rational explanations or natural causes of these events.

3. *Each creation command in Genesis correlates with a scientific puzzle or gap.* There are many questions scientists have not yet answered, including questions of the cause behind certain events in the history of the Cosmos. A startling but obvious fact is that each of the creation commands in Genesis gives an explanation for one of these scientific puzzles or gaps.

- What brought this Universe into existence in the first place? Where did the unimaginable power come from that brought the heavens and the Earth into being? All energy, materials, forces, and laws of science and nature were determined in the initial creation. Further, according to evolutionary theory, all subsequent events in the history of the Earth are based upon the materials and forces and natural laws that were determined at the time of the creation event. Regardless of what secrets of nature science unlocks, they *all* owe their ultimate scientific explanation to an initial creation event that is shrouded in complete mystery. The ultimate *first cause* that determined subsequent events transcends the bounds of science.

  The Bible contains the straightforward answer to this primary dilemma of science. After affirming that there was a beginning (the Universe is not eternal), the Bible says creation began with God's command: "Let there be light" (Gen. 1:3).

- What caused the first continents to arise from the flat surface of the Earth which was covered by a blanket of water? Gravity by itself does not explain the lateral separation of the Earth's crust between light lands and heavy ocean basins. Although a general picture of the forces and mechanisms involved has been formulated, a precise theory awaits further evidence.

  The Bible answers this scientific problem by God's command: "Let the waters below the heavens be gathered into one place, and let the dry land appear" (Gen. 1:9).

- How did the first living organisms arise without reference to some presently unknown selective or directive force? How did they or their successors acquire the capability of photosynthesis—the ability to transform the Sun's energy to a beneficial source of life?

  The Bible contains the solution to these problems with God's commands: "Let the earth sprout vegetation" (Gen. 1:11), and "Let there be lights in the expanse of the heavens . . . to give light on the earth" (Gen. 1:14–15).

- What caused the sudden Cambrian explosion of life in the oceans? How did single cells change into multicelled, complex animals with tissues and organs? Where is the fossil record of this dramatic transformation?

  The Bible straightforwardly states: "Then God said, 'Let the waters teem with swarms of living creatures'" (Gen. 1:20).

- What caused the "explosive adaptive radiation" of the mammals? The extinction of the dinosaurs might have contributed to it, but there is no definite explanation for their extinction. The climatic change? Cosmic bombardment from outer space? One possible answer leads only to another question.

  After creating life to occupy the sea and the air, God issues his next creation command: "Let the earth bring forth living creatures after their kind: cattle and creeping things and beasts of the earth after their kind" (Gen. 1:24).

There are many mysteries connected with the origin of man. We don't know why the powerfully built, large-brained Neanderthal man vanished from history. We don't know where Cro-Magnon man came from and why he spread so rapidly throughout the Earth. Furthermore, we are puzzled as to why all the most significant events in mankind's early development take place in the area identified with the biblical Garden of Eden—the Fertile Crescent. Moreover, ever since Darwin proposed his theory of evolution, anthropologists have been on a quest to find the missing link between apes and humans. It is beginning to appear likely that the missing link between ape and human will not be found. In fact, we might even begin to ask: Does it exist?

THE BIG QUESTION

While the puzzles listed above will probably continue to attract the attention of scholars, the real question of why humans are here at all is the most profound question of all. Let's step back from examining the trees for a minute and look at the forest—the big picture.

If one considers the vast harmonious panorama of cosmic, geologic, and biologic history, we can imagine a million alternate directions in which cosmic, geologic, or biologic forces could have fashioned life—if indeed the cosmic parameters existed in the correct form to fashion life in any form whatsoever. If one accepts mechanistic evolutionary processes at face value, there is simply no reason or likely probability for our Universe, our planet, or ourselves to exist at all. Yet we are here wanting answers to the questions of how did we come to be here? And why?

We do find answers to these questions in the Bible. The first chapter of Genesis states that God created the heavens and the earth. He began His creation with light, followed by His creation of water, land, vegetation, beneficial sunlight, animals of the sea and air, and animals to occupy the land. As a final step, He created man to enjoy and care for His other creations.

The most beautiful words in the Bible are "And God created man in His own image, in the image of God He created him; male and female He created them" (Gen. 1:27). This verse affirms that we are not material objects created by random processes and chance events. It affirms that we are sacred human beings, created by God; and as the New Testament attests, we are here to enter into a joyful and loving relationship with our Creator.

There is no conflict between the events recorded by modern science and Genesis. In fact, Genesis contains the answers to the key mysteries which remain unsolved by science.

The thought was put forward long ago that what is called evolution might properly be considered God's process of creation. What needs to be considered in the light of recent scientific evidence is that the cosmic, geologic, and biologic events recorded by modern science may have actually occurred in response to the specific creation commands of God Himself as recorded in Genesis 1.

HOW DID MOSES KNOW?

This chapter has presented evidence that the six major eras in the scientific history of the Earth correspond to God's six days of creation.

We have also compared God's creation commands or steps with scientific history and found that:

- The order of events in Genesis 1 and the scientific record are in substantially the same sequence.
- All major explosive adaptive radiations correlate with Scripture's creation commands.
- Each creation command in Genesis correlates with a scientific puzzle or gap.

Scientists are now furnishing substantial evidence that the biblical account of Genesis 1 is an accurate historical account of creation. At the very least, one is drawn to the conclusion that there is no conflict between the evidence provided by modern science and Genesis 1.

The question then arises: How did Moses, the author of Genesis, know?

Most creation stories that date from ancient times are filled with tales of animal or anthropomorphic gods that fight or strive to bring the Earth and humans into existence. Most of them sound like fanciful myths or fairy tales to our modern ears. One has to be struck by the simple straightforward dignity of Genesis.

In addition to the straightforward dignity of Genesis, I am amazed by the fact that there is an orderly sequence of events at all. Man sees a rhythmic cycle of seasons—winter, spring, summer, fall. Why not assume that man and animals and land and water have always existed as they are today? Why this explanation of a beginning? Why this orderly sequence of events?

But perhaps Moses is simply a keen observer of nature. Therefore, he would probably put vegetation before animals because he could perceive that vegetation is the base of the food chain for animals. But how did Moses know that:

- the heavens and the Earth were not eternal? There was a beginning.
- the Universe began with light?
- the Earth was first covered by water?
- the land rose out of the waters while the waters were gathered into deep ocean basins?
- life in the waters preceded life on the land?

How did Moses know what science has only discovered in the last hundred years? How did Moses know these things 3,500 years ago? Could science be furnishing evidence that the Bible is the revealed Word of God?

CHAPTER 14
HIS WAY, HIS TIME

"O Lord, it is Thou who didst make the heaven and the earth and the sea, and all that is in them.

Acts 4:24

When I was a small boy of about ten, long before I wanted to be a geologist, my father and mother took me on a trip to see the wonders of the Grand Canyon. I stood at the edge of a cliff and marveled at the colors of the rocks as I tried to focus my mind on the vast distance to the river below.

That evening we attended a lecture by a park ranger. He told us how the rocks were originally deposited by water and wind over eons of time. He told how the land then rose, and how the Colorado River had slowly cut its path through the rocks to form this Grand Canyon.

An elderly gentleman in the back stood up and said, "Young man, you are wrong. God made this canyon!"

The ranger was taken aback for a moment. Then he replied, "Sir, you are right. God did make this canyon. In *His way* and in *His time*."

What a sensible way to resolve the apparent conflict between science and Scripture. "God made this canyon in His way and in His time."

The Word of God. The word of science. They do not appear to be in conflict at all. But there is a war being waged in the classroom at present. It is known as the Creation-Evolution controversy, and it is being heatedly fought in the courts and in the press, as well as on the high school and college campuses.

Underneath all the rhetoric, the cause of the conflict is very simple: *Both sides are using science to teach religion!* While it may be relatively easy to recognize the elements of religion in creationism, the fact that there are stong religious elements in evolutionism may come as a

211

FIGURE 14.1.

The Grand Canyon. The Colorado River has cut this magnificent canyon more than one mile below the plateau rim. The rocks exposed at the bottom are thought to have been formed more than 1 billion years ago.

new idea to those steeped in its tradition. But those who advance the theory of evolution have stretched beyond its goal of discovering an order and composition in nature into the realm of a philosophical belief system called evolutionism.

The belief in evolutionism has two central articles of faith. First, there is the scenario of our origins which generally runs as follows:

- The Universe (all matter, energy, space, and time) originated from random fluctuations in nothing or from some other Universe or world with an as-yet-undetermined origin.

- Owing to the vast numbers of stars and planets in the Universe, vast numbers of solar systems have evolved.

- Over a period of approximately 4 million years, some of these planets have continually possessed a life-inhabitable environment (the proper temperature for water to exist as a liquid).

- Forms of life are bound to arise spontaneously from chemical elements on these planets.

- Life forms quite naturally evolve toward more complex forms.

212

- Intelligent life has important survival value and therefore quite naturally occurs under the doctrine of natural selection (given enough time and enough statistically probable accidents).

The second article of faith of evolutionism holds that reality includes only that which can be scientifically observed, quantified, tested, and measured, and the experiments to prove this reality must be repeatable.

A careful examination of the first article of faith of evolutionism exposes the lack of hard evidence to support these statements of our origin. Indeed, the latest scientific evidence supports the opposite view. In the recent book, *Are We Alone?*, physicist James Trefil examines the evidence for a similar scenario and states: "If I were a religious man, I would say that everything we have learned about life in the past twenty years shows that we are unique, and therefore special in God's sight."[1]

In addition to lacking hard evidence for the origin model of evolutionism, there is an even greater problem with its dogma. Given our present state of knowledge, the two central articles of faith of evolutionism are contradictory. Its second article of faith cannot be applied to its first. The origin of the Universe is non-repeatable. The major changes leading to intelligent life are largely non-repeatable, and even those that can conceivably be reproduced require initial starting materials, energy, and a creator (ourselves). Further, there are presently no other Universes, habitable planets, or intelligent life to study.

It therefore seems obvious that evolutionism is not only unscientific on all counts but must be classified as a system of faith. Those such as Carl Sagan who boldly proclaim that "evolution is a fact, not a theory"[2] would be well advised to carefully define their terms before making such dogmatic pronouncements.

In an effort to begin a meaningful dialogue on the present controversy, I have written two letters, one to the young-Earth creationists and the other to teachers of science.

To the Young-Earth Creationist:

Thank you for your unwavering commitment to Holy Scripture.

What time frame did God use in His magnificent plan of creation? I have presented in this book what seems correct to me, but I honestly don't know for certain. We know that God often performs sudden miracles. We also know that most transformations we attribute to

213

God are slow, constant processes. I feel we may properly view our Creator as having a long-term cohesive plan that is carried out with harmony, patience, and order.

My appeal to you is to stop insisting that the Earth is only 6,000 to 10,000 years old. I believe you have defined God and His concept of time too narrowly. Expand your horizons, pray for insight, and believe the Word of God: "But do not let this one fact escape your notice, beloved, that with the Lord one day is as a thousand years, and a thousand years is as one day" (2 Pet. 3:8).

I too am a believer in the inerrancy of Scripture. Those of us who hold this belief have a special obligation and responsibility. It is very important that we be clear about what the Bible *explicitly does say* and what it *does not say.* The Bible is very clear throughout on the central point: *God created the heavens and the earth and everything in it.*

However, the Bible does not give a date in time for the initial creation event nor for any subsequent event of creation. The use of the word *day* in Genesis may be a twenty-four-hour day, or it may be an eon of time. The days or periods of time may be a continuous week, or they may be separated by vast periods of time. We simply do not know.

I believe Jesus is speaking to our current unwarranted fixation with time in the same spirit in which He addressed His curious disciples of old when He says, "It is not for you to know times or epochs which the Father has fixed by His own authority" (Acts 1:7).

What does make a difference in our relationship with the Lord is that we personally bow to Him as our Creator. Time after time in the New Testament, the apostles witness to this fact. It is this witness that we are called to give. "And when they heard this they lifted their voices to God with one accord and said 'O Lord, it is Thou who didst make the heaven and the earth and the sea, and all that is in them'" (Acts 4:24).

To Science Teachers, Parents, and Students:

It is our curiosity, a facet of the intelligence that sets us apart as human, that drives us to investigate such natural phenomena as the Grand Canyon. We stand in awe and want to explore, to discover, and to explain for ourselves God's magnificent creation.

As we explore this world, we find it to be very rationally created. There are natural laws and processes in the Universe. Scientists such as Francis Bacon and Isaac Newton took great pleasure in searching out these laws, well aware of their Creator. They understood the

Judeo-Christian view of the world and acknowledged God's presence in their lives. Their desire to comprehend His creation was a driving force in their work. They held an *open system* view of the world.

The *open system* allows for a personal and rational God who created the world with beauty and harmony and universal laws that can be relied upon to give continuing order. We can therefore expect to find natural and, for the most part, uniform cause-and-effect relationships. However, the cosmic machine is not all there is to reality. The Universe is *open*. God exists *outside* of the system He has created. God can and does intervene in the apparent uniformity of natural causes. Francis Schaeffer states that "things go on in a cause-and-effect sequence, but at a point of time the direction may be changed by God or by people. Consequently, there is a place for God, but there is also a proper place for man."[3]

But something has changed in the last century. We have become so intrigued with the success of our research and technology that we now overlook the Creator of all that we are so feverishly studying and utilizing. Instead, we stand in awe of science and those who claim to understand it. We treasure their discoveries, which improve our physical lives, and ignore the God who stands behind it all. Once God has been omitted, we have fallen directly into the trap that Francis Schaeffer calls the *closed system.*

The *closed system* is a philosophic view of the Universe that strictly limits itself to what scientists can directly perceive, observe, quantify, and reduce to mathematical formulas. It holds to the concept of uniformity of natural causes, but only within a *closed* cosmic machine. Nothing can exist *outside* of this box—this *closed* system of "natural" cause and effect.

But does the evidence prove we live in a closed system? Certainly not! The creation of the Universe appears to be *outside* of the closed system. It is a point of singularity. A step of creation! And there may be many other steps of singularity or creation that come from *outside* a closed system.

I would like to request that if we teach evolution *by random chance,* we also do the following:

- State that we are teaching *only* the closed system view of the world. We should state the prejudices of this belief system at the beginning and throughout the course.
- When we teach the origin of life, it is not fair to start with all of the materials, energy, and natural laws in place. We should tell our students that science simply does not know the ultimate origin of the

materials, energy, and natural laws in the Universe. The origin of the Universe is a complete mystery to scientists. Perhaps the ancient Hebrew prophet Moses has a case after all.

- We should teach that the Universe began with light. We should not be timid about using the word *light* to describe this magnificent creation event just because the Bible describes creation with the same word.
- Let's present the gaps in the fossil record. We must clearly point out where there is lack of hard evidence for scientific theory.
- Let us look at what the *actual evidence* is for *evolution by pure chance*. Note that I am not saying *evolution*. I am talking about *evolution by pure chance*. Many people believe that a close biologic or morphologic relationship is also equal evidence for a common designer. To prove that *evolution by pure chance* is a viable theory, we must do three separate things:
  1. Provide evidence that our highly unique Universe was created out of nothing *by pure chance*.
  2. Document step by historical step the fossil record from organic life to microbe to man.
  3. Prove that pure chance is sufficient to account for all major transformations in life forms.

Of course this cannot be done. We can't even prove one of the three.

Why am I being so tough on this issue? Because we have been teaching—in the guise of objective science—the belief that the Universe is a *closed* system. We should admit to the possibility of the presence of God and an *open* system.

The major problem with our current teaching of evolution is that it is being taught solely from the philosophic viewpoint of a closed system, a system which excludes God. If we teach our children that all that exists is a cosmic machine and it is governed by pure chance, then how do we answer their questions about the meaning and purpose of human life?

If all we teach is the *closed* system view of the world, our children tend to picture themselves and others as mere objects—cogs in the cosmic machine—the end-products of genetics plus environment. In the final analysis a human being becomes nothing more than a highly sophisticated computer, an object to be manipulated and re-programmed at will.

The alternative is to accept the *open* system view of the world. This system not only allows for an outside power in the forming of the Universe, it offers us a whole new perspective for our lives. Our minds are freed from the bondage of the closed cosmic machine to contemplate the God who created the universe—the God who made us—the power whom we can come to know and rely on in our personal daily lives. Thus, we can find meaning and significance in our lives.

The Genesis record of God's creation makes sense. It fits. It is in harmony with the scientific evidence. Science once again becomes a discipline that enlarges our vision of God.

Does it require faith to believe in the Bible? Of course it does. Does it require faith to believe we are here as a result of cryptic evolutionary processes? In view of the evidence, or rather lack of evidence, such a belief system requires a great leap of faith.

The goal of science is to discover what order there is in nature. In the history of the Universe, Earth, and man, some will perceive this order and harmony as being caused by a series of "improbable accidents." Others will see the "hand of God" in the vast panorama of cosmic history. But this choice is not one that the discipline of science can make for us. Let us present scientific evidence as honestly and fairly as possible, but let's be honest about the limits of science.

The choice between Creator or no-creator, God or random chance, depends on one's belief system, one's religion. Let us stop teaching the religion of "random chance" in the public schools. Let us present scientific evidence in a way that allows our students to make the religious choice between Creator and no-creator, Creator and random chance.

Where did I come from? Why am I here? The Word of God has answered this question for me. I pray that it will do the same for you.

APPENDIX
SCIENTIFIC DATING METHODS

AGE OF THE UNIVERSE

Cosmologists believe the Universe is between 12 and 20 billion years old. When astronomers use their giant telescopes to take pictures of distant galaxies and stars, it is possible to take pictures of what the Universe looked like in the past. This was because the light generated from a remote galaxy would take millions and even billions of years to travel to a telescope here on Earth.

To determine how far away a light-emitting galaxy is in the first place, astronomers evaluate the brightness of the star or galaxies of stars. It is roughly the same method used by the driver of a car on a moonless night to judge the distance of an approaching car. The farther away the approaching car is, the dimmer will be its headlights. As the car comes closer, the headlights become brighter. The same is true for galaxies. The closer they are, the brighter is their light. Those that are far out in space are very dim indeed.

To measure the speed and distance of galaxies far out in space, astronomers use what is known as the "red shift" effect. As a galaxy moves away from Earth its color becomes redder in the same way that a receding automobile horn or train whistle becomes deeper in tone as it moves farther and farther away. Visible light is basically a train of waves in space. As a lighted object moves away from a viewer, its light waves appear stretched out or lengthened by the receding motion.

Our eye perceives the length of light waves in the form of color. We perceive short light waves as blue (an advancing object) and longer light waves as red (a receding object). In a process called spectrographic analysis, scientists are able to compare the colored spectrum of light from a distant galaxy with the color spectrum from a source that is not moving relative to the Earth. They are then able to determine the degree of red shift in a receding galaxy's color spec-

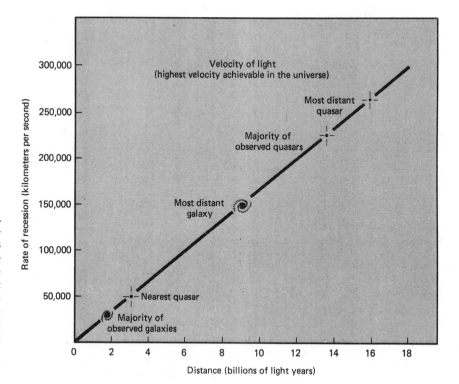

FIGURE A1.1.

The increasing rate of recession of galaxies and quasars with increasing distance. The velocity of light provides an upper limit for the distance (about 18 billion light years) that an object can be from us, and hence for an assumed time (about 18 billion years) since the Universe began.

trum and calculate its speed and distance.

The most distant objects we can observe in deep space are *quasars* (quasi-stellar objects). These are not huge galaxies but rather small star-like objects that are abnormally bright. They are thought to represent an early phase of the Universe when matter was in a different state and much closer together than at present. The most distant *quasar* that has been observed is possibly as far away as 16 billion light years. It should be noted that not all astronomers are in agreement that the objects called quasars are being correctly interpreted. Quasars may be simply strange events in the nuclei of galaxies or other unexplained phenomena. However, if the observations are indeed retreating star-like objects and their measurement is correct, we can deduce that the Universe is at least 16 billion years old and probably somewhat older.

Radioactive decay rates are also used to determine an approximate age for the Universe. The radioactive isotope used is the rare rhenium 187 which decays to stable osmium 187. Independent studies of the concentrations of these isotopes in meteorites at the Law-

RED ←———————— Visible spectrum ————————→ VIOLET

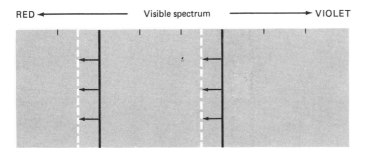

FIGURE A1.2.

A rapidly receding light source will cause emission lines of an element to shift from their normal positions to new positions (dashed) that are always toward the red end of the spectrum.

rence Livermore Laboratory in California and at the University of Chicago indicate an age of 18 billion years for the origin of the elements.[1] These studies thus indicate a minimum age for the Universe of 18 billion years.

It should be noted that we are speaking of the "visible universe." Preston Cloud points out that the "visible universe" is "that region of space where everything is flying outward at less than the speed of light and thus can, in theory, be observed. Whether anything lies beyond such limits can neither be affirmed nor denied."[2]

The farthest galaxies observable through our present telescopes are around 6 billion light years away from us. At least we assume this to be the case. It should be remembered that what we are really looking at is not the galaxies themselves but rather the light generated by these galaxies 6 billion years ago. At the present time, we don't even know if these galaxies exist. For that matter, an observer on a galaxy 6 billion light years away, could not see us because our own star, the Sun, did not come into existence until about 5 billion years ago. Six billion years would be required for the light from our Sun to reach a galaxy that was 6 billion light years away.

RADIOACTIVE DATING

Before the advent of radioactive dating methods, geologists used to try to estimate the age of the Earth by attempting to calculate the time required for the enormous quantity of sedimentary rocks to be deposited by water and wind. Today scientists have a more precise timepiece known as the "radioactive clock." It allows the geologist to pinpoint with a fair degree of accuracy the age of rock formations in which certain radioactive elements exist.

In order to understand how the radioactive clock, or "atomic clock," keeps time, we need to know something about the structure

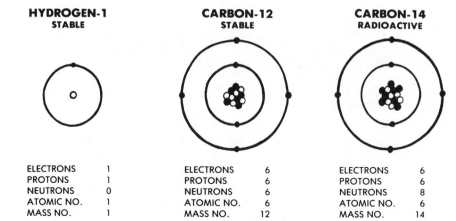

HYDROGEN-1 STABLE		**CARBON-12** STABLE		**CARBON-14** RADIOACTIVE	
ELECTRONS	1	ELECTRONS	6	ELECTRONS	6
PROTONS	1	PROTONS	6	PROTONS	6
NEUTRONS	0	NEUTRONS	6	NEUTRONS	8
ATOMIC NO.	1	ATOMIC NO.	6	ATOMIC NO.	6
MASS NO.	1	MASS NO.	12	MASS NO.	14

FIGURE A1.3.

The structure of atoms

of atoms (see figure A1.3). The nucleus in the center of an atom is composed of particles that carry a positive electrical charge known as protons and electrically neutral particles known as neutrons. Orbiting about the nucleus are negatively charged particles known as electrons which are equal in number to the positively charged protons.

A *nuclide* is a single kind or type of atom with a particular *atomic number* and *mass number.* The *atomic number* is the number of protons in its nucleus (or the number of electrons in its shell—both numbers are always the same). The *mass number* is the sum of the number of protons plus the number of neutrons in the nucleus. The *atomic number* determines the *element* to which the atom belongs. Thus, in Figure A1.3, both carbon 12 and carbon 14 have the same atomic number of 6. However, these *nuclides* have different *mass numbers*, 12 and 14 respectively, because carbon 14 has two more neutrons than carbon 12. They are said to be different *isotopes* of the element carbon.

How does the radioactive time clock work? Certain kinds of nuclides are radioactive. They are unstable. That is, their atomic nuclei spontaneously break up or decay to form more stable nuclides of other elements. The unstable radioactive nuclides are known as the "parent" material. The stable nuclides into which they decay is known as the "daughter" material.

A given quantity of parent radioactive material decays into stable daughter material at a known and constant rate. Two points are important here. The first point is that it is not the individual atom that decays at a constant rate, but rather the mass of radioactive

FIGURE A1.4.

The hourglass and the radio-active clock. This analogy is useful in visualizing the transformation of parent to daughter material. However, in the example of an hourglass, the sand runs steadily at a uniform rate; half the sand has been transferred when half the time has elapsed. After the next half-hour all the sand will have been transferred to the bottom of the glass. In this case the sand passes through the hourglass at a linear or constant rate. In the case of radioactive nuclides, the decay occurs at a geometric rate. Half of the material will be transferred very early in the total life of the specimen. For example, if the half-life of the material is 5,000 years, then one-half of the original radioactive nuclides will remain after the first 5,000 years have elapsed. During the second 5,000 years, one half of the remaining parent material will be transformed. At the end of 10,000 years, one quarter of the original parent material will remain. This in turn will yield up one half of its remaining material in the next 5,000 years, and so on, until only an undetectable amount of parent material remains.

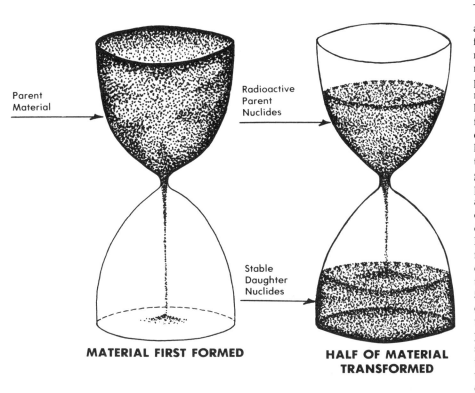

Parent Material

Radioactive Parent Nuclides

Stable Daughter Nuclides

MATERIAL FIRST FORMED

HALF OF MATERIAL TRANSFORMED

RADIOACTIVE SPECIMEN

1.0

0.5

Relative Number of Atoms

1/2

1/4

1/8

1/16

1/32

0 1 2 3 4 5

HALF-LIFE

TIME ⟶

HOURGLASS

1.0

0.5

Relative Number of Sand Grains

0 1 2 3 4

TIME ⟶

nuclides as a whole that is transformed at a constant rate. This is very similar to the way in which life insurance companies calculate that the average lifetime for the population as a whole is 73.6 years. Some people will die in their early youth and others will die at age 80 or 90. However, the average over the population as a whole will be about 73.6 years. In a similar manner, it is the average of the nuclides in our sample that matters, not the decay of the individual atoms. The second point is that different radioactive isotopes decay at different rates. Some take billions of years as in the example of rhenium 187 used to estimate the vast age of the universe. Others such as carbon 14 decay at relatively fast rates. Their lifetime is relatively short and carbon 14 is used to calculate dates up to only about 40,000 years ago.

In understanding how the radioactive clock tells geologic time, the analogy of an hourglass may be useful. (see figure A1.4) The hourglass represents a closed system. That is, the decay rate cannot be altered by physical or chemical reactions. This is generally true of radioactive clocks but sometimes the system will be upset by escape or leaching out of the daughter material or some other source of contamination.

Scientists have been able to calculate specific rates of decay for various radioactive nuclides. The decay rate of a substance is usually stated in terms of its half-life. This is the time it takes for half of the atoms of the parent to decay (become stabilized). After the first half-life, there is one-half of the radioactive element remaining; after the second half-life one quarter is left, and so on. Those most commonly used are listed in Table A1.1. They are often used as checks on one another to calibrate for possible sources of error or contamination.

Given the known rate of decay of a specific isotope, it is possible to estimate geologic age from an uncontaminated sample. This age is figured by finding the ratio between the amount of nuclides that has disintegrated (daughter) and that which has not (parent).

Minerals first crystallize upon cooling from a molten state in a newly formed rock of igneous (volcanic type) origin. At this point they normally contain no atoms of related daughter material, only parent radioactive material. The intial daughter-parent ratio is zero. The indicated age is also zero. As time passes, the daughter to parent ratio gradually increases. By factoring in the known decay rate, the radiometric age expressed in years before the present can be calculated.

Radiocarbon Dating. There is a chronological tool known as *radiocarbon* or *carbon 14* dating used by archeologists to date more recent events that is useful up to 40,000 years ago and in some special cases for longer periods. It is useful for dating fossils that contain organic (biologically produced) carbon such as shells, bones, and dead wood.

Nitrogen is the most abundant gas in the atmosphere, and it consists of stable nuclides, principally nitrogen 14. Cosmic rays are high energy particles from unknown sources in space that occasionally strike the nitrogen 14 nuclides to substitute a neutron for a proton in its nucleus. As a result, nitrogen 14 is converted into carbon 14. The relatively small quantities of carbon 14 nuclides combine with oxygen to form carbon dioxide. These molecules mix with the more stable carbon dioxide formed from nuclides of carbon 12 and carbon 13 and

THE CHIEF METHODS
OF RADIOMETRIC-AGE DETERMINATION

Parent nuclide	Half-life (years)	Daughter nuclide	Minerals & rocks commonly dated
Uranium-238	4,510 million	Lead-206	Zircon Uraninite Pitchblende
Uranium-235	713 million	Lead-207	Zircon Uraninite Pitchblende
Potassium-40	1,300 million	Argon-40	Muscovite Biotite Hornblende Glauconite Sanidine Whole volcanic rock
Rubidium-87	47,000 million	Strontium-87	Muscovite Biotite Lepidolite Microcline Glauconite Whole metamorphic rock

Table A1.1.

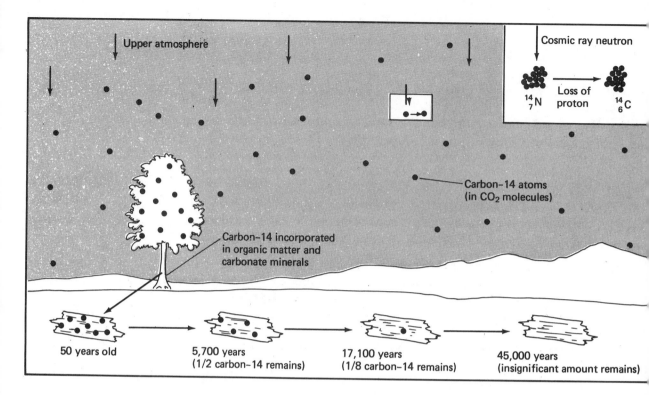

Upper atmosphere

Cosmic ray neutron

$^{14}_{7}N$ → Loss of proton → $^{14}_{6}C$

Carbon-14 atoms
(in CO_2 molecules)

Carbon-14 incorporated
in organic matter and
carbonate minerals

| 50 years old | 5,700 years (1/2 carbon–14 remains) | 17,100 years (1/8 carbon–14 remains) | 45,000 years (insignificant amount remains) |

FIGURE A1.5.

The carbon-14 cycle. Radioactive carbon-14 is produced from atmospheric nitrogen by cosmic rays (inset). It then enters into CO_2 molecules and becomes incorporated into carbon-bearing sediments and organic remains. The amount of remaining carbon-14 is used to date such materials.

enter the carbon dioxide cycle of the atmosphere. Some of the radioactive carbon 14 is absorbed into growing plants and animals.

Since carbon 14 is radioactive, it subsequently converts a neutron back into a proton and again becomes the stable nuclide nitrogen 14. It does this spontaneously and with great regularity. Carbon 14 has a half-life of only 5,730 years.

It should be noted that unlike the other radioactive methods described, the radiocarbon clock does not utilize the measurement of parent (C-14) and daughter (N-14) material. This is because the nitrogen 14 almost immediately escapes to the soil and atmosphere, so the daughter material cannot be accurately measured. Carbon 14 dating involves the measurement of the radioactivity itself, not the end-products. While age dating by this method may sometimes be imprecise due to unknown rates of carbon 14 formation in the past or contamination by other "dead" organic matter, it is nonetheless considered a useful dating tool.

Amino-Acid or Racemization Dating. While carbon 14 dating is generally useful only in dating organic material no older than 40,000 years, *amino-acid* dating is useful in dating older specimens. In Chapter 6 we pointed out that amino acids can exist in both right- and left-handed forms. One of the great mysteries in molecular biology is that living systems contain only left-handed molecules. However, once death occurs, these left-handed molecules slowly change into right-handed ones.

This curious process is called *racemization* and occurs at a known rate. By comparing the quantity of left-handed molecules with the quantity of right-handed molecules in a sample, it is possible to determine how many years have passed since death occurred. The drawback to using this method is that heat is known to speed up the process, and therefore samples subjected to unknown sources of heat in the past would give erroneous dates. Nevertheless, *racemization* is generally useful in dating organic specimens that are from 40,000 to several hundred thousand years old.

AGE OF THE EARTH

The oldest unequivocally dated Earth rocks are located in south-west Greenland. They have radiometric age of 3.76 billion years. Reports from Russia and South Africa have indicated rocks as old as 4 billion years. Yet the Earth is thought to have originally condensed from the nebular cloud of gas and dust 4.6 billion years ago. Scientists have dated some moon rocks at ages approaching 4.6 billion and all meteorites also yield this date. Sophisticated comparative residual lead isotope analysis from deep sea cores on Earth also indicates an age of 4.6 billion years. But why are the oldest dated rocks on the Earth itself only 3.76 to 4 billion years old?

In Chapter 4 we discussed the great melting and subsequent cooling of the Earth. It is only when a rock cools and crystallizes from its melt that it is, in effect, born. In its molten state it has not come into being as a solid rock. Its age begins and the clock in its radioactive nuclides only starts when its minerals solidify and crystallize. Since the oldest dated rocks on the Earth are approximately 3.8 billion years old, it is assumed that the Earth's crust did not finish cooling (and water condense from the great outgassing) until that time.

NOTES

CHAPTER 1

1. Robert Jastrow, *Until the Sun Dies* (New York: Warner Books, 1977), p. 11.

2. Preston Cloud, *Cosmos, Earth and Man: A Short History of the Universe* (New Haven, Conn.: Yale University Press, 1978), p. 25.

3. Paul Davies, *The Runaway Universe* (New York: Harper and Row, 1980), p. 27.

4. Jastrow, *Until the Sun Dies*, p. 2.

CHAPTER 2

1. Davies, *The Runaway Universe*, p. 184.

2. R. T. Rood and James S. Trefil, *Are We Alone?* (New York: Scribner's, 1981), p. 29.

3. Alan Lightman, "To The Dizzy Edge," *Science 82* (October 1982): p. 24.

CHAPTER 3

1. Jastrow, *Until the Sun Dies*, p. 4.

2. W. Lee Stokes, *Essentials of Earth History*, 4th ed. (Englewood Cliffs, N.J.: Prentice-Hall, 1982), p. 140.

3. D. L. Eicher and A. L. McAlester, *History of the Earth* (Englewood Cliffs, N.J.: Prentice-Hall, 1980), p. 8.

4. Encyclopedia Britannica, *Energy, the Fuel of Life* (New York: Bantam/Britannica Books, 1979), p. 38.

CHAPTER 4

1. Stokes, *Essentials of Earth History*, 4th ed., p. 183.

2. Ronald Youngblood, *How It All Began: A Bible Commentary for Laymen on Genesis 1–11* (Ventura, Calif.: Regal Books, 1980), pp. 29–30.

CHAPTER 6

1. P. Huyghe, "New Recipe for Cosmic Soup," *Science Digest* (May 1983), p. 44.

2. Ibid.

3. C. Folsome, *The Origin of Life* (San Francisco: W. H. Freeman, 1979), p. 84.

4. Jastrow, *Until the Sun Dies*, p. 49.

5. Stokes, *Essentials of Earth History*, 4th ed., p. 186.

6. Ibid.

7. T. Dobzhansky, et al., *Evolution* (San Francisco: W. H. Freeman, 1977), pp. 358–359.

8. Jastrow, *Until the Sun Dies,* pp. 51–52.

CHAPTER 7

1. Rood and Trefil, *Are We Alone?,* p. 67.

CHAPTER 8

1. Dobzhansky, *Evolution,* p. 397.

CHAPTER 9

1. D. A. Russell, "The Mass Extinctions of the Late Mesozoic," *Scientific American* 246 (January 1982): p. 65.

2. Ibid., p. 63.

3. F. Press and R. Siever, *Earth,* 2nd ed. (San Francisco: W. H. Freeman, 1978), p. 441.

4. Stokes, *Essentials of Earth History,* 4th ed., p. 208.

5. P. Hoffman, "Asteroid on Trial," *Science Digest* (June 1982): p. 62.

6. Ibid.

7. Ibid., p. 59.

8. J. Boykin, "Enclave of the Castaways: A Stanford Visit to the Galapagos Islands" *Stanford Magazine* (Winter '82): p. 20.

9. Youngblood, *How It All Began,* p. 23.

10. R. Laird Harris, Gleason L. Archer, and Bruce K. Waltke, *Theological Word Book of the Old Testament,* Vol. 1 (Chicago: Moody Press, 1980), p. 127.

CHAPTER 10

1. Richard E. Leakey, *The Making of Mankind* (New York: E. P. Dutton, 1981), p. 43.

2. Donald C. Johanson and M. A. Edey, *Lucy: The Beginnings of Humankind* (New York: Simon and Schuster, 1981), p. 363.

3. Ibid., p. 375.

4. David E. Hunter and P. Whitten, *Anthropology,* 2nd ed. (Boston: Little, Brown, 1975), p. 21.

5. William A. Haviland, *Anthropology 2,* 2nd ed. (New York: Holt, Rinehart, and Winston, 1978), p. 111.

6. Cloud, *Cosmos, Earth and Man,* pp. 260–262.

7. Johanson, *Lucy: The Beginnings of Humankind,* p. 375.

8. Ibid., p. 351.

9. Ibid., p. 364.

10. Richard E. Leakey, *Human Origins* (New York: E. P. Dutton, 1982), p. 50.

11. S. Lipson and D. Philbeam, "Ramapithecus and Hominoid Evolution," *Journal of Human Evolution* (Sept. 1982): pp. 545–548.

12. John Gribbin and Jeremy Cherfas, *The Monkey Puzzle: Reshaping the Evolutionary Tree* (New York: Pantheon, 1982).

13. Johanson, *Lucy: The Beginnings of Humankind,* p. 363.

14. Ibid., p. 351.

15. P. Raeburn, "An Uncommon Chimp," *Science 83* (June 1983): p. 44.

16. Ibid., p. 42.

17. K. McKean, "Facing Up to Man's Past," *Discover* (July 1983): p. 26.

18. R. Lewin, "Were Lucy's Feet Made for Walking?," *Science* 220 (May 13, 1983): pp. 700–701.

19. Leakey, *The Making of Mankind*, p. 53.

CHAPTER 11

1. Leakey, *The Making of Mankind*, p. 20.

2. Ibid., p. 148.

3. Ralph S. Solecki, "Neanderthal Is Not an Epithet But a Worthy Ancestor," from Hunter, *Anthropology*, 2nd ed., p. 27.

4. Leakey, *The Making of Mankind*, p. 179.

5. Jacob Bronowski, *The Ascent of Man* (Boston: Little, Brown 1973), p. 64.

CHAPTER 12

1. R. Lewin, "Fossil Lucy Grows Younger Again," *Science* 219 (Jan. 7, 1983): pp. 43–44. Article cites both faunal collections of fossils and datings of volcanic tuffs. When first discovered, the date for Lucy was set at approximately 3 million years old. In early 1982 the age was increased to 3.5 million years old. In the article cited here the date is changed back to between 2.9 and 3.1 million, a decrease in age of 500,000 years.

2. Alan Hayward, *God Is* (Nashville: Thomas Nelson, 1978), p. 196.

3. Youngblood, *How It All Began*, p. 33.

4. Ibid., p. 27.

CHAPTER 14

1. Rood and Trefil, *Are We Alone?*, p. 252.

2. Carl Sagan, *Cosmos* (New York, Random House, 1980), p. 27.

3. Francis Schaeffer, *How Should We Then Live? The Rise and Decline of Western Thought and Culture* (Old Tappan, N.J.: Fleming H. Revell, 1976), p. 14.

APPENDIX

1. Cloud, *Cosmos, Earth and Man*, p. 33.

2. Ibid., p. 33.

GLOSSARY

Acid rain Rain made abnormally acid by pollutants, particularly oxides of sulphur and nitrogen.

Adaptation The process whereby a species selects from a variable gene pool to produce a population capable of efficient interaction with the environment.

Adaptive radiation The pattern in which different organisms develop from a basic form to fill diversified ecological niches.

ADP (adenosine/diphosphate) A doubly phosphorylated organic compound that when further phosphorylated forms ATP.

ATP (adenosine triphosphate) A triply phosphorylated organic compound that stores chemical energy for cell activities.

Amino acid Any of a large group of nitrogenous organic compounds, some of which serve as structural units in proteins.

Angiosperms (flowering plants) Members of the advanced group of plants that carry seeds in an enclosed ovary and have floral reproductive structures.

Anthropoidea A suborder of primate mammals including humans, apes, and monkeys.

Anticline An arch-shape fold of rock layers.

Aquifers A permeable formation that stores and transmits groundwater in quantity adequate to supply wells.

Asteroids Small minor planets that orbit the Sun chiefly between Mars and Jupiter.

Asthenosphere The hot plastic (semisolid) layer in the mantle of the Earth below the rigid lithosphere.

Atmospheric photolysis The process whereby water vapor in the upper atmosphere is split into chemical elements of hydrogen and oxygen. The energy for this reaction is supplied by ultraviolet radiation from the sun.

Atomic number The number of protons in the nucleus of an atom.

Atomic weight The average weight of an element relative to a standard weight of 12 for carbon.

Australopithecine A member of the genus, Australopithecus.

Australopithecus (southern ape) A genus of extinct small-brained hominids that are thought to have walked on two legs as their normal means of location.

Australopithecus afarensis The scientific name given to a group of hominids over three million years old, found at Hadar in Ethiopia and at Laetoli in Tanzania. The name translates as "southern age from Afar" (the Afar Triangle in Ethiopia). Most well-known specimen is "Lucy."

Australopithecus africanus The scientific name for the glacile (slightly built) australopithecine.

Australopithecus robustus The scientific name given to the robust (heavily built) australopithecine found in Africa.

Autotroph An organism that can create its constituents from inorganic substances. The best examples are green photosynthetic plants.

Basalt A fine-grained, dark, heavy, igneous rock composed primarily of dense iron and magnesium compounds. Basalts occur principally in lava flows and constitute over 90% of volcanic rocks.

BIF (banded iron formations) Cherts with alternating iron-rich and iron-poor laminae, each layer commonly a centimeter or less in thickness, that constitute the bulk of the world's iron ore reserves. They are all of Precambrian age, the majority around 2 billion years old.

Big Bang theory The theory that the presently expanding Universe (including not only all energy and matter, but also space and time) was created at a finite instant in the past in a cataclysmic explosion which flooded the Universe with radiant energy (light).

Big Bloom The appearance, rapid spread, and diversification of angiosperms (flowering plants) that took place about 130 million years ago.

Big Crunch A theory suggesting the end to the present Universe will occur as all matter is pulled back together by gravitational attraction and compressed into a universal sea of fiery hot elementary particles.

Binary fission A form of asexual reproduction in which one cell divides into two essentially equal parts.

Biologic processes Processes involving living as opposed to non-living matter (including reproduction, photosynthesis, growth, development, etc.)

Bipedal Walking on two legs as the normal means of locomotion.

Black hole An object in space with a gravitational field so strong that no light can escape.

Brachiopods One of a phylum or class (Brachiopoda) of nearly extinct molluscoid marine animals having a bivalve shell and a pair of brachial appendages at the sides of the mouth.

Cambrian The first period of the Paleozoic.

Cambrian explosion The relatively sudden appearance of widely varied marine animal forms during the Cambrian period that began 570 million years ago.

Carbonaceous Containing carbon. In geology, this term is used primarily to describe a sedimentary rock containing significant organic material.

Carnivorous Flesh-eating. Used to describe an animal or organism that kills and feeds on other animals.

Cataclysmic explosion A sudden and violent disturbance of the Earth's surface.

Catalysis Acceleration of a chemical reaction by the addition of a substance that is not itself permanently changed by the reaction.

Cenozoic era The latest era of geologic time which includes the tertiary and quatenary periods and is characterized by mammals.

Ceratopsians A horned group of dinosaurs which appeared late in the age of dinosaurs.

Chemical reaction Chemical change in which the atoms or molecules of substances rearranged.

Chert (silicon dioxide) A sedimentary form of extremely fine-grained or amorphous silica found in beds and concretions; commonly a chemical sediment.

Closed system A philosophic view of the Universe that presupposes reality is limited solely to what can be scientifically observed, quantified, and reduced to mathematical formulas. (See open system.)

Coacervate A cluster of macro-molecules surrounded by a shell of liquid in which the individual molecules are rigidly oriented relative to the colloidal particles.

Coelacanth A large-bodied, hollow-spined fish of the crossopterygian group.

Colloidial droplets Large droplets in stable suspension in a solution.

Concentration gap Basically the problem of achieving concentrated solutions from dilute solutions under prebiotic (pre-life) conditions.

Continental drift The relative movement of the continents over the Earth's surface.

Continuous creation theory The theory that the Universe had no beginning in space and time, but rather existed in a steady state condition with new matter being continuously created.

Cosmis rays Very high-speed, subatomic, charged particles (primarily protons) emitted by the Sun and other stars.

Craton An ancient stable area of the continental crust that has been relatively unaffected by deformation for prolonged periods of geologic time.

Cro-Magnon Man A name commonly used for a member of the prehistoric species Homo sapiens sapiens who lived in the area of modern Europe.

Cyanobacteria A form of bacteria sometimes confused with blue-green algae because of the similarity between the cell wall formations.

DNA (deoxyribonucleic acid) A molecule composed of alternating units of nucleotides in the shape of a double helix. DNA carries the genetic code.

Dolomite rock A type of limestone composed of over 15% magnesium carbonate. It occurs either as a primary precipitate from seawater (an evaporite) or from the alteration of calcite rock by magnesium-charged solutions (dolomitization).

Ecological niche The lifestyle of an organism or species in a particular habitat.

Ectotherm An organism whose temperature is determined primarily by the temperature of its environment.

Electromagnetic force Commonly thought of as the force operating between electrically charged particles. However, in addition to being important in the structure of atoms and molecules, the electromagnetic force, by means of massless particles called photons (particles of light), transmits radiation across the spectrum at wavelengths from gamma and x-rays through ultraviolet, visible light, infrared, and radio waves.

Electron A small elementary particle with a negative charge that normally circles the nucleus of an atom.

Endotherm An organism whose temperature is regulated by its own metabolism.

Enzyme A specialized protein compound that controls or mediates a chemical reaction in a living organism.

Eukaryotes Organisms whose cells have true nuclei. Eukaryotes include higher plants and animals and many single-celled organisms.

Evolution by random chance The belief that statistical probability alone is sufficient to account for the physical Universe and all life, including humans.

Evolutionary radiation Rapid divergence of ancestral organisms into new adaptive types.

Explosive adaptive radiation A rapid branching out of basic life forms into a variety of related forms that adapt to varying ecological niches.

Extraterrestrial forces Forces from outside the planet Earth and its atmosphere.

Fault block mountains A mountain range consisting of an elongated body of rock that was elevated between parallel normal faults.

Felid A member of the cat family.

Ferric oxide A red compound of iron and oxygen (Fe_2O_3).

Formaldehyde A colorless pungent gas (CH_2O).

Fossils Remains of past life. Fossils include skeletal remains, impressions in the form of casts or molds, trace fossils, coprolites (fossilized feces) and chemical fossils.

Fossil fuels Fuels such as coal, oil, and gas that have been formed by the alteration and decomposition of substances from previous geologic time.

Free oxygen Oxygen that is not combined with any other elements.

Fungi Kingdom containing organisms with eukaryotic cells and characteristics similar to plants with the important exception that fungi lack chlorophyll (many feed on dead organic matter). Examples are yeasts, molds, and mushrooms.

Galaxy A portion of space in which clusters, stars, dust, and gas are bound together by gravitational attraction.

Gene A unit of inheritance that codes for a specific protein. (See DNA).

Genetic potential The concept that life forms contain within their gene pool the capacity to produce offspring with differing characteristics.

Gluons A massless, neutral particle that binds together the ultimate particles of matter such as quarks.

Granite Light-colored igneous rock, mainly quartz and feldspar, formed when certain types of magma solidify underground.

Gravitational heating Heating caused by the force of friction, as occurred during the Earth's early history when heavier particles moved toward the center of the Earth and slid past the lighter particles moving toward the crust.

Greenhouse effect The heating of the atmosphere by the absorption of infrared energy re-emitted from the Earth's surface.

Half-life The average time required for one-half of a given sample of particles or nuclei to decay.

Herbivorous To eat or live on vegetation.

Hominid Popular form of Hominidae, the family to which humans belong. Hominids generally include bipedal fossil primates such as Australopithecus and Homo.

Hominidae The family that includes all Homo and Australopithecus species but exludes the apes.

Hominoid A member of the superfamiy or group (Hominoidea) of the primate order. Includes both apes and man.

Homo The genus in which humans belong. Anthropologists also include *erectus* and generally *habilis* in this genus.

Homo erectus A hominid that lived from about one and one half million years ago to about 300,000 years ago.

Homo habilis A hominid that lived about two million years ago, at the same time as the australopithecines.

Homo sapiens Biologically modern man. This species includes two subspecies: *Homo sapiens neanderthalensis* (Neanderthal man), and *Homo sapiens sapiens* (fully modern man).

Homo sapiens sapiens The subspecies to which modern humans belong. Includes Cro-Magnon humans who appeared 40,000 to 35,000 years ago because they were anatomically identical to modern humans.

Hydrocarbons An organic chemical compound made up of carbon and hydrogen atoms arranged in chains or rings.

Hydrogen fusion The combining of the nuclei of hydrogen to yield the nuclei of helium with the mass deficit in the reaction appearing as energy.

Hydrologic cycle The cyclical movement of water from the oceans to the atmosphere, through rain to the surface, through runoff and groundwater to streams, and then back to the oceans.

Igneous Formed by rapid or slow solidification from a molten state.

Impermeable Having characteristics that greatly

retard or prevent fluids from moving through.

Inorganic Not having the organized anatomical structure of animal or vegetable life. An inorganic compound is a chemical compound not based on carbon.

Interstellar Between or among the stars.

Invertebrate Animals without a backbone.

Ionized The state of an atom or group of atoms that have gained or lost electrons and thus acquired a net electric charge.

Isotope One of several forms of one element, all having the same number of protons in the nucleus, but differing in their number of neutrons and thus in atomic weight. Isotopes of the same element differ from each other in their atomic weight, not in their chemical properties.

Kelvin An absolute temperature scale whose zero point is $-273.15°$ C.

Krebs cycle A sequence of reactions in respiration: acetyl coenzyme A is oxidized by the removal of hydrogen atoms and high-energy electrons, which are transferred to electron carriers. Oxygen also combines with carbon to form CO_2 during these reactions.

Labyrinthodont Pertaining to a peculiar tooth structure characterized by deep infolding of the enamel. Labyrinthodonts were early, large, now extinct amphibians having massive skulls and teeth with "labyrinth" structure in cross-section. All possessed a tail and a strong rib cage.

Leptons In current thinking, leptons are considered one of two (quarks are the other) classes of indivisible particles that comprise the ultimate building blocks of matter. The electron, the neutrino, and the muon are comprised of leptons.

Lithosphere The solid, outer shell of the Earth, including the crust and the uppermost portion of the mantle.

Limestone A sedimentary rock mainly of calcium carbonate ($CaCO_3$); often formed from the skeletons of marine life.

Macro-evolution Large-scale evolutionary changes, such as the hypothetical long-term evolution of a single-celled organism into a multi-celled, multi-organed animal. (See micro-evolution.)

Magma Molten rock material generated within the Earth, from which igneous rock results by cooling and crystallization.

Mantle The thick layer of Earth between the crust and the core.

Magnetic field reversal A change in the polarity of the Earth's magnetic field, the south pole becoming the north magnetic pole, or vice versa.

Mechanistic Pertaining to the belief that all phenomena and events can be explained solely by the laws of science.

Melanic Being abnormally dark-colored. Refers to the dark variant of a species.

Mesosphere A large solid portion of the Earth's interior. Comprises the bulk of the mantle and lies below the hot plastic asthenosphere and above the outer core.

Mesozoic era The third era of geologic time and characterized by the predominance of reptilian forms.

Meta Altered or changed.

Metabolism The sum of the chemical reaction within a cell (or a whole organism), including the energy-releasing breakdown of molecules and the synthesis of complex molecules and new protoplasm.

Metamorphic rock A rock changed in composition or texture through pressure, heat (without melting) or chemistry.

Metaphyte Any plant in which more than one kind of cell makes up the organs and tissues.

Metazoan Any animal made up of more than one kind of cell. Often used as a term for the multicellular marine animals that appeared in a short space of geologic time during the Cambrian period 500 to 570 million years ago.

Meteorite A mass of mineral or rock matter that reaches the Earth's surface from space.

Micro-evolution Small-scale evolutionary changes, such as that of the peppered moths changing from light forms to dark forms over a few generations. (See Macro-evolution.)

Microspheres (Microscopic spherical chemical systems that are similar in a primitive way to living cells.

Missing links A popular (not scientific) term for hypothetical, transitional, or intermediate forms between apes and humans.

Molecular genetics The study of inheritance at the molecular level.

Monomers Molecular subunits which can be chemically linked to form a polymer.

Morphology Study of the structure or form of an organism.

Mutation An inherited change resulting from modification of the hereditary material in the reproductive cells.

Natural selection The explanation which Charles Darwin proposed for the process of evolution. Its basic premise is that those plants or animals best adapted to their environment tend to survive and consequently to pass on more of their genes to the next generation.

Naturalistic causes Pertaining to the belief that all events and phenomena may be attributed solely to natural laws of science.

Neanderthal man A stockily built type of *Homo sapien* that lived in Europe and parts of Asia between about 100,000 years ago and 35,000 years ago.

Nebula A cloud of gas, dust and particles in space.

Neutrino An uncharged (electrically neutral) particle emitted in the process of beta decay. Currently thought to travel at the speed of light and to be massless.

Nucleic acid Any of several organic acids characteristic of the nucleus of living cells. DNA (deoxyribonucleic acid) is the best-known example.

Nucleotide A section or building block of a DNA or RNA molecule; consists of a phosphate group, a pentose sugar, and a purine or pyrimidine.

Nuclear force The force of interaction that binds the protons and neutrons into the atomic nucleus holding the nucleus together. Also known as the strong force.

Nuclear fusion Combining of light elements to form heavy elements with a resultant release of energy due to a mass deficit.

Nuclide A single kind of atom with a particular atomic number and mass number.

Ooze A soupy sedimentary deposit at the bottom of a body of water; more specifically used to describe those deposits laid down on the bottom of deep oceans that contain the shells of small marine organisms.

Open system As used in this book, this term describes a philosophic view of the Universe that presupposes there is more to reality than what can be proven by the strict application of the scientific method. (See closed system.)

Organic compound A chemical compound in which hydrogen or nitrogen is directly united with carbon.

Oscillating Universe A theory that the Universe eternally oscillates between expansion (starting with a Big Bang) and contraction (resulting in a Big Crunch).

Outgassing The large-scale emission of volatile substances (water vapor, carbon dioxide, etc.) from the interior of a planet to the surface through volcanic activity.

Ozone screen The shielding barrier that helps protect the Earth from the Sun's lethal radiation. The highly concentrated layer of ozone (a molecule containing three atoms of oxygen, O_3) that exists 15.5–20 miles (25–32 km) above the surface of the Earth.

Paleoanthropologist One who is engaged in the multidisciplinary study of human ancestors.

Paleobotany The study of fossil plants.

Paleozoic era The geologic era that includes the Cambrian, Ordovician, Silurian, Devonian, Mississippian, Pennsylvanian, and Permian periods, and is characterized by the appearance of marine invertebrates, fish, land plants, and primitive reptiles.

Pangaea Name for the great theoretical proto-continent from which all present continents have broken off by the mechanisms of sea-floor spreading and continental drift.

Panthalassa The world ocean that surrounded the ancient continent of Pangaea.

Peptide A bonded compound of two or more amino acids. Linked peptides form polypeptides which, in turn, join to form proteins.

Phanerozoic Relating to that part of geological history when larger, more visible forms of life existed; generally refers to the Paleozoic, Mesozoic, and Cenozoic eras taken together.

Photons Particles of light; the massless particles that transmit electromagnetic radiation. (See electromagnetic force.)

Photosynthesis Synthesis of sugar from carbon dioxide and water by living organisms using light from the sun as energy. Oxygen is given off as a by-product.

Phylum (plural: phyla) A major taxonomic division of animals or plants ranking below a kingdom and above a class.

Plankton Floating organisms, usually microscopic, that exist in fresh or salt water.

Plasmas Highly ionized gases composed of approximately equal numbers of positive ions and electrons.

Plate tectonics The theory that the Earth's rigid, outer shell is divided into large structural pieces or plates which move relative to one another to produce earthquake belts, mountain chains, and other major geologic features.

Polymer A large molecule consisting of a chain of small molecules bonded together by repeated linking reactions.

Polypeptide See Protein.

Positron The positively charged antiparticle of the electron.

Prebiotic Before life.

Precambrian era The oldest geologic era of the Earth's history denoting the time prior to 570 million years ago, and characterized by the apperance of primitive forms of life.

Primates The order of mammals that includes lemurs, lorises, bushbabies, monkeys, apes, and man; generally characterized by large brains, prehensile hands, and five digits on hands and feet.

Primordial atmosphere Atmosphere thought to have existed in the early stages of the Earth; thought to have contained little or no free oxygen and much carbon dioxide.

Primordial soup A popular term to denote a soupy mixture of organic chemical compounds from which biologic life may have been constructed.

Prokaryote A cellular organism that lacks a true cell nucleus. Examples are blue-green algae and bacteria.

Prosimian A suborder of widely distributed primates characterized by small size and primitive brain development; includes the lemurs, lorises, and tarsiers.

Protein A long polypeptide chain composed of amino acids. A molecule containing many amino acid units linked together is called a polypeptide. A large polypeptide is called a protein, although there is no sharp distinction between these two terms.

Proteinoids Long chains of polypeptides formed by the linking together of amino acids.

Protoplasm A complex substance in the cell that exhibits those processes generally regarded as living.

Pulsating Universe Pertaining to the hypothesis that the Universe eternally oscillates between expansion (starting with a Big Bang) and contraction (resulting in a Big Crunch). Also called oscillating Universe.

Punctuated equilibrium A recent theory of stair-step evolutionary change which holds that life forms remain basically stable (in equilibrium) for long periods of time and that major changes evolve in relatively brief periods of time.

Pyrimidine Any of several single-ringed nitrogenous bases important in nucleotides; cytosine, thymine and uracil are examples.

Quantum theory A mathematical theory employed in physics to express the relationship between waves and particles of the same underlying entity. The particle associated with a given wave is its quantum.

Quarks In current thinking, quarks are considered one of two (leptons are the other) classes of indivisible particles that comprise the ultimate building blocks of matter. The proton and the neutron are comprised of quarks.

Racemization The curious process by which the optically left-handed amino acid molecules of living organism convert into optically right-handed molecules following death.

Radioactive heating Heating produced by the decay of radioactive isotopes.

Radioactive (radiometric) dating Determining age by measuring the proportions of parent and daughter isotopes of a radioactive element present in materials, based on knowing the decay rate of the isotopes.

Radiocarbon dating The use of changes which occur naturally in carbon to determine the age of a fossil or other material; generally useful in estimating ages less than 50,000 years.

Ramapithecus (Rama ape) An apelike creature that lived in Europe, Asia, and Africa more than eight million years ago.

Red beds Red-tinted sedimentary rocks, usually sandstones and shales. The red color is usually due to compounds of iron oxides.

Reproductive strategies A term used by evolutionists to refer to different methods of insuring offspring survival. Some animals produce numerous offspring and give them little or no care. Other animals produce only one offspring at a time and give it a great deal of care to insure its survival. These are obviously very different reproductive strategies.

Rift A valley or trough formed where two blocks or plates of the Earth's crust move apart.

Scientific creationist See Young Earth creationist.

Scientific method The process and principles regarded as necessary for scientific investigation. Involves proposing a hypothesis or conceptual model and its testing by observations and experiments to determine if it can be substantiated or falsified. The important distinction between the scientific method and other systems of arriving at truth (i.e., philosophy and religion) is that the scientific method requires measured observations and experiments that can be repeated with virtually identical results.

Sea-floor spreading The process wherein new ocean-floor, basaltic rock material rises from the Earth's mantle at the midocean ridges to fill the rift created as the oceanic plates move away from each other.

Sedimentary rock Consolidated generally layered deposits from the waters of streams, lakes or seas or from wind or ice.

Shields Large regions of stable, ancient basement rocks within a continent; generally applied to the exposed portion of continental cratons.

Singularity Something so unique or remarkable that there is little or no rational explanation for its cause. The finite instant of the origin of the Universe, wherein all energy and matter, and even space and time, came into existence as manifested in the Big Bang explosion is considered to be a singularity.

Solar winds The flow or bursts of ionized gases (plasmas) from the Sun toward the Earth and which interact with the Earth's magnetic field.

Spontaneous prebiotic chemical synthesis The belief that original life came into existence as a result of chemical reactions which occurred in accordance with natural laws of statistical probability.

Stromatolites Laminated deposits of fossil material built up by various simple organisms, primarily blue-green algae. The layers are formed mostly of carbonated minerals, but clay or even fine sand may be bound into the structure. Mound and finger-like forms are characteristic.

Static equilibrium A concept in the theory of punctuated equilibrium that holds that life forms remain stable for long periods of time. In essence, the organisms are in equilibrium (in balance) with their habitat and with each other.

Steady state theory An older theory of the origin of the Universe which held that it had always existed in essentially the same state it is in today. Opposite of the Big Bang theory.

Strong force The force or interaction that binds the protons and neutrons into the atomic nucleus, thus holding the nucleus together. Also known as the nuclear force.

Supernova A violently exploding star in which all but the inner core is blown off into interstellar space. Produces extreme and vast amounts of energy.

Subatomic elementary particles A term generally applied to protons, neutrons, electrons, positrons, neutrinos, and photons. These are thought to be in turn composed of the fundamental particles (quarks and leptons).

Therapsids Members of the extinct reptilian order *Therapsida* that existed over 200 million years ago. The various species had many mammal-like characteristics and were of varied size.

Theropods A group of early dinosaurs who were flesh-eating and preyed on their plant-eating relatives.

Trilobites Extinct marine animals of the phylum *Anthropoda* that had a flattened oval body with numerous appendages. Common as fossil forms from 570 to 240 million years ago.

Varves Sedimentary bed or lamination that is deposited within one year's time. Each varve represents one year's deposit, and ordinarily the portion deposited in summer can be distinguished from that deposited in winter.

Verbetrate An animal with a backbone.

Young-Earth creationist One who believes the Earth to have been created within the last 6,000 to 10,000 years. Generally speaking, the term "scientific creationists" is applied to "young-Earth creationists" who gather scientific evidence to support their belief.

SOURCES AND SUGGESTED READINGS

Sources for Chapters 1–12:
Cloud, P. 1978. *Cosmos, Earth and Man: A Short History of the Universe.* New Haven, Conn.: Yale University Press.
Eicher, D. L., and A. L. McAlester. 1980. *History of the Earth.* Englewood Cliffs, N.J.: Prentice-Hall, Inc.
Jastrow, R. 1977. *Until the Sun Dies.* New York: Warner Books, Inc.
Rood, R. T. and J. S. Trefil. 1981. *Are We Alone?: The Possibility of Extraterrestrial Civilizations.* New York: Charles Scribner's Sons.
Scientific American, 1978. *Evolution.* San Francisco: W. H. Freeman.
Stokes, W. L. 1982. *Essentials of Earth History,* 4th ed. Englewood Cliffs, N.J.: Prentice-Hall, Inc.

Additional Sources for Chapters 1–3:
Davies, P. 1978. *The Runaway Universe.* New York: Harper and Row, Inc.
Encyclopedia Britannica. 1979. *Energy, the Fuel of Life.* New York: Bantam/Britannica Books.
Fisher, A. 1981. "And There Was Light," "Light: Nature's Mysterious, Essential Gift," *Geo,* vol. 3 (Oct. 1981), pp. 54–78.
Jastrow, R. 1980. *God and the Astronomers.* New York: Warner Books, Inc.
Jastrow, R. 1980. *Red Giants and White Dwarfs,* rev. ed. New York: Warner Books, Inc.
Lightman, A. 1982. "To the Dizzy Edge," *Science 82,* Oct. 82, pp. 24–25.
Motz, L. 1975. *The Universe.* New York: Charles Scribner's Sons.
Trefil, J. 1983. "Closing in on Creation," *Smithsonian,* vol. 14:2 (May 1983), pp. 32–51.
Weinberg, S. 1977. *The First Three Minutes.* New York: Basic Books, Inc.

Additional Sources for Chapters 4–9:
Attenborough, David. 1979. *Life on Earth.* Boston: Little, Brown & Co.
Ballard, Robert D. 1983. *Exploring Our Living Planet.* Washington, D.C.: National Geographic Society.

Botkin, D. A. and E. A. Keller. 1982. *Environmental Studies*. Columbus, Ohio: Charles Merrill.

Boykin, J. 1982. "Enclave of the Castaways: A Stanford Visit to the Galapagos Islands," *Stanford Magazine*, Winter '82, pp. 10–23.

Boykin, J. 1982. "Liquid Life: the Water Beneath Us," *Stanford Magazine*, Spring '82, pp. 10–21.

Brand, P. and P. Yancey. 1980. *Fearfully and Wonderfully Made*. Grand Rapids: Zondervan.

Case, G. R. 1982. *A Pictorial Guide to Fossils*. N.Y.: Van Nostrand Reinhold.

Dobzhansky, T., F. J. Ayala, G. L. Stebbins, and J. W. Valentine. 1977. *Evolution*. San Francisco: W. H. Freeman.

Folsome, C. E. 1979. *The Origin of Life*. San Francisco: W. H. Freeman.

Gliedman, J. 1982. "Miracle Mutations," *Science Digest*, Feb. 1982, pp. 90–96.

Hallett, M. 1982. "Class Struggle, the Rise of the Mammal," *Science Digest*, Nov. 1982, pp. 60–65.

Hardin, G. and C. Bajema. 1978. *Biology, its Principles and Implications*. San Francisco: W. H. Freeman.

Hoffman, P. 1982. "Asteroid on Trial," *Science Digest*, June 1982, pp. 58–63.

Huyghe, P. 1983. "New Recipe for Cosmic Soup," *Science Digest*, May 1983, pp. 42–44.

Kaufmann, W. 1982. "The Seas of Venus," *Science Digest*, Sept. 1982, pp. 60–65.

LaGrow, C. 1982. "Bacteria Help Find Hidden Oil Fields," *The Stanford Earth Scientist*, Section 2, *The Stanford Observer*, Nov. 1982, p. 5.

McPhee, J. A. 1980. *Basin and Range*. New York: Farrar, Straus, Giroux.

Morowitz, H. 1982. "Ice on the Rocks," *Science 82*, Sept. 1982, pp. 26–27.

Overbye, D. 1982. "The Shape of Tomorrow," *Discover*, Nov. 1982, pp. 29–25.

Press, F. and R. Siever. 1978. *Earth*, 2nd. ed. San Francisco: W. H. Freeman.

Revelle, R. 1982. "Carbon dioxide and world climate," *Scientific American*, vol. 247:2 (Aug. 1982), pp. 35–43.

Russell, D. A. 1982. "The Mass Extinctions of the late Mesozoic," *Scientific American*, vol. 246:1 (Jan. 1982), pp. 58–65.

Smith, D. G., ed. 1981. *The Cambridge Encyclopedia of Earth Sciences*. New York: Crown/Cambridge.

Stout, W., B. Press, and W. Service. 1981. *The Dinosaurs*. New York: Bantam Books.

Van Andel, T. 1981. "Serendipity of Science, 10,000 Feet Underwater," *Stanford Observer*, Mar. 1981, p. 3.

Uwe, G., 1980. "An Ocean Is Born," *Geo*, collectors ed., New York: Gruner and Jahr U.S.A., Inc.

Additional Sources for Chapters 10–11:

Bronowski, J. 1973. *The Ascent of Man.* Boston: Little, Brown and Co.

Gribbin, J. and J. Cherfas. 1982. *The Monkey Puzzle.* New York: Pantheon.

Haviland, W. 1978. *Anthropology 2,* 2nd ed., New York: Holt, Rinehart, and Winston.

Hunter, D. E., and P. Whitten. 1975. *Anthropology,* 2nd ed. Boston: Little, Brown & Co.

Johanson, D. C. and M. A. Edey. 1981. *Lucy: The Beginnings of Humankind.* New York: Simon and Schuster.

Leakey, Richard E. 1982. *Human Origins.* New York: E. P. Dutton.

Leakey, Richard E. 1981. *The Making of Mankind.* New York: E. P. Dutton.

Lewin, R. 1983. "Fossil Lucy Grows Younger Again." *Science,* vol. 219, Jan. 7, 1983.

Lewin, R. 1983. "Were Lucy's Feet Made for Walking?" *Science,* vol. 220, May 13, 1983.

Lipson, S. and D. Philbeam. 1982. "Ramapithecus and Hominoid Evolution," *Journal of Human Evolution,* Sept. 1982, pp. 545–548.

Nelson, H. and R. Jurmain. 1982. *Introduction to Physical Anthropology.* St. Paul, Minn.: West Publishing.

Raeburn, P. 1983. "An Uncommon Chimp." *Science 83,* June 1983.

Washburn, S. L. 1978. "The Evolution of Man," *Scientific American,* vol. 239:3.

Additional Sources for Chapters 12–13:

Hayward, A. 1978. *God Is.* Nashville, Tenn.: Thomas Nelson.

Jastrow, R. 1980. *God and the Astronomers.* New York: Warner Books, Inc.

Young, D. A. 1982. *Christianity and the Age of the Earth.* Grand Rapids, Mich.: Zondervan.

Young, E. J. 1960. *An Introduction to the Old Testament.* Grand Rapids, Mich.: Eerdman's Publishing Co.

Youngblood, Ronald. 1980. *How It All Began: A Bible Commentary for Laymen on Genesis 1–11.* Ventura, Calif.: Regal Books.

Additional Sources for Chapter 14:

Rood, R. T. and J. S. Trefil. 1981. *Are We Alone?: The Possibility of Extraterrestrial Civilizations.* New York: Charles Scribner's Sons.

Schaeffer, F. 1976. *How Should We Then Live?: The Rise and Decline of Western Thought and Culture.* Old Tappan, N.J.: Fleming H. Revell Co.

For Further Reading

Campolo, Anthony. *A Reasonable Faith.* Waco, Texas: Word, 1983. Impressive evidence gathered from the fields of anthropology, sociology, psychology, and philosophy that supports the biblical view of human nature.

Cloud, Preston. *Cosmos, Earth and Man.* New Haven: Yale University Press, 1978.
Basic presentation of scientific evidence.

Hayward, Alan. *God Is.* Nashville: Thomas Nelson, 1978.
Clearly shows the major shortcomings of evolutionary theory as causation for the origin of man and other life.

Jastrow, Robert. *God and the Astronomers.* New York: Warner, 1980.
Especially valuable for the chapter entitled "Science as Religion."

Keller, Werner. *The Bible as History.* New York: William Morrow, 1956.
Presents the Bible as an accurate account of history.

Rifkin, Jeremy. *Algeny.* New York: Viking, 1983.
Explores the possibility that Darwinian theory is primarily a creation myth reflecting the cultural, economic, and political practices of Victorian England.

Rood, R. T. and J. S. Trefil. *Are We Alone?: The Possibility of Extraterrestrial Civilizations.* New York: Charles Scribner's Sons, 1981.
An examination of the Universe which points up the uniqueness of life within it.

Schaeffer, Francis. *How Should We Then Live?* Old Tappan, N.J.: Revell, 1976.
An excellent analysis of the root source of conflict between creation and evolution.

Stokes, W. L. *Essentials of Earth History,* 4th ed. Englewood Cliffs, New Jersey: Prentice-Hall, 1982.
Basic earth science data.

Thurman, L. D. *How to Think About Evolution and Other Bible-Science Controversies.* Downers Grove, Ill.: InterVarsity Press, 1978.
Offers guidance for clear thinking about the creation-evolution controversy.

Youngblood, Ronald. *How It All Began.* Ventura, California: Regal, 1980.
An outstanding biblical commentary on Genesis 1–11.

PICTURE CREDITS

Chapter 1.
Figure 1.3. This picture is reproduced by permission of the Huntington Library, San Marino, California. *Figure 1.4.* Wide World Photo. *Figure 1.5* © Barrett Gallaher DO5, 19 January 1965. *Figure 1.6.* Courtesy of Bell Laboratories. *Figure 1.7.* Courtesy Palomar Observatory, California Institute of Technology.

Chapter 2.
Figure 2.1. W. Lee Stokes, *Essentials of Earth History,* 4th ed., © 1982, p. 140. Reprinted by permission of Prentice-Hall, Inc., Englewood Cliffs, N.J. *Figure 2.4.* Courtesy NASA. *Figure 2.5.* Courtesy Palomar Observatory, California Institute of Technology.

Chapter 3.
Figure 3.2. Wide World Photo. *Figure 3.3.* Don L. Eicher, A. Lee McAlester, *History of the Earth,* © 1980, p. 11. Reprinted by permission of Prentice-Hall, Inc., Englewood Cliffs, N.J. *Figure 3.5.* W. Lee Stokes, *Essentials of Earth History,* 4th ed., © 1982, p. 146. Reprinted by permission of Prentice-Hall, Inc., Englewood Cliffs, N.J. *Figure 3.6.* D. A. Botkin, and E. A. Keller, *Environmental Studies,* © 1982, p. 62. Reprinted by permission of Charles E. Merrill Publishing Co. *Figure 3.7.* Wide World Photo.

Chapter 4
Figure 4.1. D. A. Botkin and E. A. Keller, *Environmental Studies,* © 1982, p. 54. Reprinted by permission of Charles E. Merrill Publishing Co. *Figure 4.2.* Courtesy NASA. *Figure 4.4* Courtesy NASA. *Figure 4.6.* Photo by Austin Post, courtesy U.S. Geological Survey. *Figure 4.9.* Courtesy NASA. *Figure 4.10.* Courtesy U.S. Geological Survey. *Figure 4.13.* Photo by H. Palmer, courtesy U.S. Geological Survey.

Chapter 5.
Figure 5.2. W. Hamilton. *Figure 5.4.* Courtesy U.S. Geological Survey, Professional Paper 1078. *Figure 5.6.* From "The Breakup of Pangaea," by Robert S. Dietz and John C. Holden. Copyright © 1970 by Scientific American, Inc. All rights reserved. *Figure 5.7.* Courtesy of Aluminum Company of America. *Figure 5.8.* Courtesy U.S. Geological Survey. *Figure 5.10.* Courtesy NASA. *Figure 5.12.* Courtesy photoswissair. *Figure 5.14.* Courtesy U.S. Geological Survey. Bulletin

THE GENESIS CONNECTION

324.1907. *Figure 5.16.* W. Lee Stokes, *Essentials of Earth History,* 4th ed., © 1982, p. 217. Reprinted by permission of Prentice-Hall, Inc., Englewood Cliffs, N.J. *Figure 5.17.* Courtesy George Housner, California Institute of Technology.

Chapter 6.
Figure 6.1. Courtesy T. R. Mason, Durban, Natal. *Figure 6.2.* Courtesy J. W. Schopf, University of California, Los Angeles. *Figure 6.3.* From *Earth,* 3rd ed., by F. Press and R. Siever. Copyright © 1982 by W. H. Freeman and Company. All rights reserved. *Figure 6.4.* From *Biology: Its Principles and Implications,* by G. Hardin and C. Bajema. Copyright © 1978 by W. H. Freeman and Company. All rights reserved. *Figure 6.5.* Don L. Eicher, A. Lee McAlester, *History of the Earth,* © 1980, p. 118. Reprinted by permission of Prentice-Hall, Inc., Englewood Cliffs, N.J. *Figure 6.6.* From *Earth,* 3rd ed., by F. Press and R. Siever. Copyright © 1982 by W. H. Freeman and Company. All rights reserved. *Figure 6.7.* Courtesy Field Museum of Natural History, Chicago. *Figure 6.11.* From *Biology: Its Principles and Implications,* by G. Hardin and C. Bajema. Copyright © 1978 by W. H. Freeman and Company. All rights reserved.

Chapter 7.
Figure 7.6. Courtesy U.S. Geological Survey, Professional paper 570. *Figure 7.7.* Courtesy Utah State Historical Society. *Figures 7.9 and 7.11.* From *Earth,* 3rd ed., by F. Press and R. Siever. Copyright © 1982 by W. H. Freeman and Company. All rights reserved. *Figure 7.13.* Don L. Eicher and A. Lee McAlester, *History of the Earth,* © 1980, p. 107. Reprinted by permission of Prentice-Hall, Inc., Englewood Cliffs, N.J. *Figure 7.14.* Photo by Dr. Thierry Juteau, Universitie Louis Pasteur, Strasbourg, France. Courtesy Stephen Miller, Rise Expedition photo archive, University of California at Santa Barbara.

Chapter 9.
Figures 9.2, 9.10, and 9.11. Courtesy Field Museum of Natural History, Chicago. *Figure 9.12.* Smithsonian Institution Photo no. 26449. *Figure 9.15.* W. Lee Stokes, *Essentials of Earth History,* 4th ed., © 1982, p. 392. Reprinted by permission of Prentice-Hall, Inc., Englewood Cliffs, N.J. *Figure 9.16.* Smithsonian Institution Photo no. 30855-B.

Chapter 10.
Figure 10.1. © Zoological Society of San Diego. *Figure 10.3.* Neg. no. 109-353. Courtesy of American Museum of Natural History. *Figure 10.4.* Courtesy of Elwyn L. Simons, Duke University. *Figure 10.5.* Meave Epps Leakey, © National Geographic Society, *Figure 10.6A* and *10.6B.* Neg. nos. 120980 and 313484, Courtesy of American Museum of Natural History. *Figure 10.8, 10.9,* and *10.12.* The Cleveland Museum of Natural History. *Figure 10.13.* From *In the Shadow of Man* by Jane Van Lawick-Goodall. Copyright © 1971 by Hugo and Jane Van Lawick-Goodall. Reprinted by permission of Houghton Mifflin Company.

Chapter 11.
Figure 11.1. From Anthropology, 2nd ed., by William A. Haviland. Copyright © 1978 by Holt, Rinehart and Winston. Reprinted by permission of Holt, Rinehart and Winston, CBS College Publishing. *Figure 11.3.* From "Ice-Age Hunters of the Ukraine," by Richard G. Klein. Copyright © 1974 by Scientific American, Inc. All

rights reserved. *Figure 11.4.* M. E. Challinor for *Science 82. Figure 11.5.* Neg. nos. 150-38 (Reindeer) and 317-637 (Bison). Courtesy American Museum of Natural History.

Chapter 14.
Figure 14.1. Courtesy U.S. Geological Survey.

Appendix.
Figures A1.1, A1.2, and *A1.5.* Don L. Eicher, A. Lee McAlester, *History of the Earth,* © 1980, pp. 6,7,56. Reprinted by permission of Prentice-Hall, Inc. Englewood Cliffs, N.J.

I N D E X

Adam and Eve
  creation of, 187–190
  Genesis account, 177
Amphibians, age of, 137–140
Apes and monkeys
  australopithecine links, 162–164
  biologic relationship to man, 159
  disappearance of fossil record on, 158–159
  distinctive characteristics, 159–161
  early specimens, 158–159
  Ramapithecus, 162, 168–169
Atoms
  composition and properties of, 30
  electromagnetic force, 31
  nuclear force, 30–31

Banded iron formations (BIFs), 102–104
Big Bang theory *See* Universe, creation of
Big Bloom *See* Life, vegetable
Big Crunch theory *See* Universe, creation of
Birds, 121–125
Bondi, Hermann, 20
Bronowski, J., 185, 187

Carbon dioxide
  as pollutant, 107–108
  decrease in since primordial times, 109–110
  removal from atmosphere, 110–112
  in life cycle, 100–101
  role in greenhouse effect, 107–108
Cave, A. J. E., 180
Cells *See also* Life (generic term)
  basic raw materials of, 83
  clumping: microspheres and coacervates, 90–91
  composition of, 92

energy source and proper enviornment for, 83–85
  eukaryotes, 79
  first appearance of multicellular life, 118 ff.
  formation, seven stages of, 83–96
  monomers, 85–88
  polymers, 88–90
  prokaryotes, 79
  proteins, enzymes, and nucleic acid in, 91 ff.
Cherfas, Jeremy, 169, 170
Clark, J. Desmond, 166
Cloud, Preston, 102–103
Continents *See also* Earth (planet)
  biblical version of creation of, 61, 75–76
  composition of, 61, 75
  continental plates, 64–75
  formation of, 63–64, 69
  movement of, 69–75
  Pangaea (prehistoric supercontinent), 69

Dahl, Jeremy, 172
Dart, Raymond, 163
Darwin, Charles, 126–128, 159
Davies, Paul, 24, 28–29
Dinosaurs, age of, 144–149

Earth (planet)
  age of, 41, 54, 227
  atmosphere and water supply, 48, 52–53
  climatic changes, 145, 146, 150, 184
  condition of at creation, 49–50, 53
  cosmic bombardment of, 56–57, 61, 147–148
  floating continents, 63
  great melting of, 54–57
  Ice Age, 152, 181
  key differences of from other planets, 41–44, 47

magnetic core of, 49, 54
outgassing of, 52–53
ozone screen, 98
plate tectonics, 64–71, 75
position in solar system, 41, 42, 44
primordial atmosphere, 86
rebirth of, 54–57
size of, 47, 48
Earthquakes and volcanoes
causes and effects of, 71 ff., 147
role in extinction of dinosaurs, 147
Einstein, Albert, 20
Eldridge, Niles, 132
Evolution
absence of fossil records as proof of, 130–132
central tenets, 212–213
major transformations in life forms, 153–154
macro-evolution, 127–128
theories of, 125–127

Fishes, age of, 118–120, 130–134, 197
Fox, Sidney, 90–91
Friedmann, Alexander, 20

Galaxies
age of, 191
formation of stars in, 40
movements of, 19
number of, 18
Garden of Eden, 185–187
Geologic ages, 193, 195 See also specific Ages
God, 94–96, 134, 157, 159, 211–217
Gold, Thomas, 21
Gould, S. J., 132
Gribbin, John, 169, 170

Haviland, Williams, 162, 164
Hayward, Alan, 201
Hoyle, Fred, 21
Hubble, Edwin, 19
Humason, Milton, 19

Iron Age, 102–105

Jastrow, Robert, 17, 24, 44, 93, 94, 201
Johanson, Donald, 162, 165, 167, 171

Leakey, Louis B., 164
Leakey, Mary, 166
Leakey, Richard, 157, 164, 167–168, 175, 180, 184
Levine, Joel, 86
Lewin, R., 231n
Life (generic term) See also Cells
characteristics of, 87
critical components of, 91 ff.
hypothetical origins of, 83–96, 113–115
metabolism, 87
multicellular plants and animals, classification of, 119
origin on Earth, 94–96
probability of by random chance, 95
reproductive capacity, 87
Life, animal
adaptive radiations, 132
amphibians, types of, 137–140
Cambrian explosion, 117–120, 125 ff., 130–134
classification of multicellular animals, 119
communication methods, 178
creation of: scriptural vs. evolution, 153–156
dinosaurs, extinction of, 144–149
first airborne life, 120–125
first appearance on land, 135
interdependence with vegetable life, 100–101
marine vertebrates, appearance of, 120
multicellular sea life, appearance of, 118–120
Phanerozoic eon, 117
primates See Man; Apes and monkeys
reptiles, prehistoric, 140–144
reptilian development, 121–125, 140–149
role of oxygen supply in, 105 ff.
thecodonts, 151
transition of from water to land, 135–140
Life, vegetable
Big Bloom, 79–80
blue-green algae, 77–79, 99, 101–102, 104
classification of multicellular plants, 119
eukaryotes, 79
first appearance of, 77, 135
land-dwelling plants, 79
photosynthesis, 99–100, 110
Precambrian era, 117
prokaryotes, 79
role in creating oxygen, 101–102

role in creating ozone screen, 99
source of first vegetation, 80–81
stromatolites, 77, 103
Light
  composition of, 37
  conservation of energy, 37 ff.
  necessity of to life, 37
  role in beginning of universe, 44–45
Lightman, Alan, 32
Lipson, Susan, 168

Mammals
  age of, 152, 158
  creation of: scriptural vs. evolution, 153–156
  defined and described, 149–150
  endotherms as differing from ectotherms, 149 ff.
  origin of, 150–152
  therapsids as ancestor of, 150–151
Man
  australopithecine links, 162–164
  Australopithecus afarensis (Lucy), 165–168, 172–173
  biologic relationship to apes, 159
  cave paintings, 183
  civilized man, first, 184–185
  Cro-Magnon man, 182–184
  distinctive characteristics of, 159–161, 177–179, 189
  hominid, defined, 162–163
  hominid hoax, 174–175
  homo erectus, 165, 173
  homo habilis, 164, 173
  Jordan Valley (as cradle of civilization), 185
  molecular genetic studies vs. fossil evidence, 169, 172
  Neanderthal man, 179–182
  Piltdown man hoax, 160
  theoretical specimens of early, 162–169
Matter dominant era, 39–40
Miller, Stanley, 85
Missing links, 159, 169–173

Oceans
  biblical version of creation of, 61, 76
  Cambrian explosion in, 117–120
  composition of basins, 61
  formation of present oceans and seas, 69–71
  Panthalassa (prehistoric world ocean), 61, 69

sea-floor spreading, 67, 71
  Mid-Atlantic Ridge, 67
Oparin, Alexander, 90
Oxygen *See also* Life, animal; Life, vegetable; Ozone
  screen; Water
  as first poison, 101–102
  first produced, 109
  increase in atmosphere, 110–112
Ozone screen, 98, 99, 104–105 *See also* Life, animal;
  Earth; Life, vegetable

Philbeam, David, 157, 162, 168, 169, 170, 173
Planets (other than Earth), 29, 42, 44
Punctuated equilibrium, theory of, 132–133
Public school education
  closed system, teaching of, 216–217
  Creation-Evolution controversy, 211–217
  nonscriptural approach, 45, 81, 96

Radiation-dominant era, 39–40
Reptiles, age of, 140–149, 197
Rocks, granite type
  as core of continents, 61-63
Rocks, sedimentary *See also* Iron Age
  as fossil evidence depository, 77, 158–159, 162–163
  as indication of ancient supply of world's oxygen, 105
  as source for prehistoric carbon, 112
  as scientific research tool, 117, 119
  Cambrian explosion, as evidence for, 125
  how formed, 110
  role in creation of fossil fuels, 110–112
  role of water in forming, 113

Sandage, Alan, 23
Sarich, Vincent, 169, 170
Schaeffer, Francis, 215
Scientific dating methods, 194
  criticism of, 197
  racemization (amino-acid) dating, 194, 226–227
  "radioactive clock," 194–195, 221–224
  radiocarbon dating, 194, 224–226
  "red shift" effect, 219–220
Simons, Elwyn, 162
Slipher, Vesto, 19
Solar system

explosion of stars into supernovas, 41
location of, 18
Milky Way galaxy, 18
Sun as center of, 41
Solecki, Ralph, 181
Stokes, W. L., 59
Strauss, Williams, 180
Sun
   as power plant of Solar System, 97–98
   role in creating life on Earth, 97–101, 114–115

Time, perspective on
   Genesis 1 "days" equal to ages of creation, 197
   time frame (reduced for comprehension), 14,
      191–193
Trefil, James, 213

Universe, creation of
   biblical version of, 17, 27, 37
   Big Bang theory, 23–24, 27, 32, 34, 37, 44
   Big Crunch theory, 27–28, 32
   continuous creation theory, 17–18
   cosmic (microwave) radiation discovery, 21–23
   cosmological conditions of, 31–32
   expansion of, 19–20, 23

length of creation time, 44, 193
proof of a beginning, 20–26
pulsating or oscillating universe, theory of, 27–28
role of light in, 37, 39
steady state theory, 17–18
unique properties of, 28–32, 34–36
Urey, Harold, 85

van Andel, Tjeerd, 154
Venus, 113

Water
   as source of oxygen, 98
   extent of on Earth, 50–52, 57–60
   groundwater and aquifers, 50–51
   how created on Earth, 57–59
   physical and chemical properties of, 51–52
   role in creation of life, 85
   three basic forms of, 51
White, Timothy, 166
Wilson, Alan, 169, 170

Youngblood, Ronald, 59, 198

Zihlman, Adrienne, 172